Michaelina Jakala • Durukan Kuzu
Matt Qvortrup
Editors

Consociationalism and Power-Sharing in Europe

Arend Lijphart's Theory of Political Accommodation

palgrave
macmillan

Editors
Michaelina Jakala
Coventry University
Coventry, United Kingdom

Durukan Kuzu
Coventry University
Coventry, United Kingdom

Matt Qvortrup
Coventry University
Coventry, United Kingdom

International Political Theory
ISBN 978-3-319-88377-9   ISBN 978-3-319-67098-0   (eBook)
https://doi.org/10.1007/978-3-319-67098-0

Cover illustration: Tom Corban / Alamy Stock Photo

Printed on acid-free paper

This Palgrave Macmillan imprint is published by Springer Nature
The registered company is Springer International Publishing AG
The registered company address is: Gewerbestrasse 11, 6330 Cham, Switzerland

Contents

LIST OF CONTRIBUTORS

EDITORS

Michaelina Jakala is a research fellow at the Centre for Trust, Peace and Social Relations, Coventry University. She was awarded a PhD in Peace Studies from the University of Bradford in 2011. Her thesis explored post-war lived experiences of female survivors of wartime sexual violence in Bosnia-Herzegovina (BiH). Prior to joining Coventry, she worked at Newcastle University on an Economic and Social Research Council (ESRC)-funded project exploring individual attitudes towards outreach activities and the implications of these activities and initiatives on community engagement and the practices of the Court of BiH. She has published in journals such as *Political Geography* and the *Annals of the Association of American Geographers*. Dr Jakala is the Co-Director of the Erasmsus+ BUILDPEACE project. Her current research interests focus on the lived experiences of transitional justice and peacebuilding.

Durukan Kuzu is the author of *Multiculturalism in Turkey: The Kurds and the State*. He holds a PhD in Government Politics and an MSc in Comparative Politics from the London School of Economics and Political Science. Dr Kuzu currently works as a Research Fellow/Senior Lecturer at Coventry University and his research interests are centred on contemporary political theory, multiculturalism, human rights, ethnic conflict, diversity, refugees, referendums, Corsican nationalism and the Kurdish question. He was also the co-chair of the Association for the Study of Ethnicity and Nationalism, UK. He has published in peer-reviewed journals such as *Nations and Nationalism*, *Comparative European Politics*, and the *Journal on Ethno-politics and Minority Issues in Europe*.

Matt Qvortrup is Professor of Applied Political Science and International Relations at Coventry University. An expert on comparative constitutional engineering and European Politics, Professor Qvortrup's book *Angela Merkel: Europe's Most Influential Leader* (2017) was described by Kirkus Reviews as "necessary reading for anyone who wants to broaden his or her perspective on the world today." Awarded the *PSA Prize* in 2013 for his research on 'Terrorism and Political Science', he served as a Specialist Advisor to the *House of Commons Public Administration and Constitutional Affairs Committee*. He has previously worked as a member of *President Obama's Special Envoy Team* in Africa (2009–2010). Before his career as an academic Dr Qvortrup served as *Head of the Gun Crime Section* in the *British Home Office* (2002–2004) and before that as a Special Advisor to the Home Secretary (Minister for the Interior). Professor Qvortrup earned his doctorate in Politics at Brasenose College, University of Oxford in 2000. Also a qualified lawyer, he holds a Diploma from the College of Law, London. A frequent commentator for the *BBC*, Professor Qvortrup writes regularly for *Bloomberg*.

CONTRIBUTORS

Andrew Blick (Kings College London) is a lecturer in Politics and Contemporary History at King's College London. Dr Andrew Blick is the author of numerous articles, pamphlets and books on UK constitutional history. He is Director of History and Policy, an organization that brings together historians and policy makers.

Paul Dixon is Honorary Research Fellow at Birkbeck College, University of London. He is the author of *Northern Ireland: The Politics of War and Peace* (Palgrave, 2008, 2nd edition), and the editor of *The British Approach to Counterinsurgency* (Palgrave 2012) and *Performing the Northern Ireland Peace Process: In Defence of Politics*, which will be published in 2018.

Renske Doorenspleet (University of Warwick) is an associate professor in Comparative Politics at the University of Warwick. Her research has focused on democracy in divided countries, building political institutions and how people view democracy. Her articles have been published in *World Politics*, *Democratization*, *Acta Politica*, the *International Political*

Science Review, Ethnopolitics, Government and Opposition and the *European Journal of Political Research*. She is the author of one monograph on transitions to democracy (2005) and the editor of two books on party systems in Africa (2013, 2014).

Henry Jarrett (University of Exeter) is an Associate Lecturer at the University of Exeter, where he completed his PhD in January 2016. His research interests include ethnic politics and electoral systems in divided societies, and he has a particular interest in the cases of Northern Ireland, Belgium, Malaysia and South Africa.

Arend Lijphart is Professor Emeritus of Political Science at University of California San Diego. Lijphart's field of specialization is comparative politics, and his current research is focused on the comparative study of democratic institutions. He is the author or editor of more than a dozen books, including *Democracy in Plural Societies: A Comparative Exploration* (1977), *Democracies: Patterns of Majoritarian and Consensus Government in Twenty-One Countries* (1984), *Power-Sharing in South Africa* (1985), *Electoral Laws and Their Political Consequences* (1986), *Parliamentary Versus Presidential Government* (1992), *Electoral Systems and Party Systems: A Study of Twenty-Seven Democracies* (1994), and *Patterns of Democracy: Government Forms and Performance in Thirty-Six Countries* (1999; 2nd ed., 2012). Lijphart has received numerous awards throughout his prestigious career in recognition of his groundbreaking research. In 1989, he was elected to the National Academy of Arts and Sciences, from 1995 to 1996 he served as President of the American Political Science Association, and in 2010 he received the Constantine Panunzio Distinguished Emeritus Award.

Neophytos Loizides (University of Kent) is a professor in International Conflict Analysis School of Politics & International Relations, Rutherford College University of Kent and the associate editor of Nationalism and Ethnic Politics. His most recent books are *Designing Peace: Cyprus and Institutional Innovations in Divided Societies* (2015) and *The Politics of Majority Nationalism: Framing Peace, Stalemates and Crises* (2015).

Ammar Maleki (Tilburg University) is an assistant professor in Comparative Politics at the Tilburg School of Politics and Public Administration, Tilburg University. His comparative research focuses on the relation between models of democracy, patterns of societal culture, and cultural compatibility. His work has been published in *Cross-Cultural*

Research, Democratization, Acta Politica and *Journal of Comparative Policy Analysis.*

Charis Rice (Coventry University) is a research associate at Coventry University's Centre for Trust, Peace and Social Relations (CTPSR). Her research interests include governmental and political communication, trust, power, and Ministerial Special Advisers.

Ian Somerville (University of Leicester) is Reader in Media and Communication at the University of Leicester. His current research interests include public relations in conflict and post-conflict societies, government public relations, political lobbying and human rights activism.

Timothy J. White (Xavier University) is a professor of Political Science at Xavier University Cincinnati, Ohio, USA. His previous research includes work on civil society and peace in Northern Ireland. He has edited *Lessons from the Northern Ireland Peace Process* (2013) and *Theories of International Relations and Northern Ireland* (2017).

List of Figures

LIST OF TABLES

List of Tables

Introduction to Consociationalism and Power-Sharing in Europe: Arend Lijphart's Theory of Political Accommodation

Consociationalism is an approach to power-sharing in deeply divided societies and it is proposed to achieve conflict management and democratization in such societies by recognizing and accommodating different ethnic or religious communities within governmental and societal structures on a proportional basis (Jarret 2017; Lijphart 1977; McGarry and O'Leary 2009). Since the publication of the *Politics of Accommodation* (1968) and *Democracy in Plural Societies* (1977) Professor Lijphart's theories and recommendations have played a key role in establishing enduring peace settlements in Northern Ireland, Bosnia and currently in Colombia. In his more recent work *Patterns of Democracy* (2nd edition 2012) Professor Lijphart showed how consensus institutions can be conducive to creating a "kinder, gentler democracy."

Scholars such as McGarry and O'Leary often refer to Northern Ireland as an exemplary case. The reason for this might be that, as Jarret (2017) suggests, after 30 years of violent ethno-national conflict, the region is now comparatively stable and it is arguably the inclusiveness of consociationalism that is responsible for this stability.

Although consociationalism finds support in scholarly discussions and practice, critiques continue to challenge its relevance as a political tool in managing conflicts and promoting democracy in divided societies. From a critical point of view, there are outstanding problems in power-sharing systems where deep divisions and hostility between empowered ethno-religious groups remain intact and even escalate. Critiques argue on these grounds that prescribing political significance to ethno-religious differences between groups in such systems might subdue violent conflicts at the expense of deepening divisions between such groups who thereby get more and more essentialized and isolated from each other.

Consociationalism, albeit having contained violent conflict in some divided societies such as the one in Northern Ireland, is still criticized to have whipped up the divisions and differences between ethno-cultural groups. Differences that supposedly contributed to the emergence of violent conflicts in the first place, it is argued, are only made by consociationalism more susceptible to erupting in the future (Dixon 2017).

The success of consociationalism has also been dependent on the willingness of former adversaries to participate in arrangements and engage with each other. It is widely accepted that only under such circumstances can consociationalism prove to be a highly successful method of managing conflict. Consociationalism also keeps to be perceived as deeply reliant on and vulnerable to further exogenous factors that guaranteed its relative success in the first place. Increasing secularization in Europe throughout the nineteenth and the twentieth centuries, for example, helped to make religious identities less politically significant in religiously divided societies as was seen in the Netherlands. Jarret (2017) argues that it might be this secularization process in the Netherlands that was, in fact, more responsible for resolving the conflict than consociationalism. A potential return to a religious mode of governance could have easily seen the deterioration of peace and democracy achieved in the country (Jarret 2017). Similarly, third-party guarantees such as the European Union (EU) guarantees for minority rights and local governments had already been strong incentives in assuring the sides to the conflict in Northern Ireland that they would have equal representation when the power-sharing model was first introduced in 1997 with the Good Friday Agreement. Both Ireland and the UK being committed members of the EU at the time had strengthened this conviction. Now the planned Brexit following the 2016 referendum raises questions about what will happen to the power-sharing arrangements and guarantees in Northern Ireland once all powers that are currently controlled by Brussels are transferred back to Westminster when the UK leaves the EU (Blick 2017).

As can be clearly seen in practical politics, endeavours at accommodating differences between different groups in multi-ethnic and multi-faith societies are still a pressing concern, and in this edited volume scholars and Professor Lijphart himself critically discuss the continued relevance and the practical use and shortcomings of the consociationalist model of democracy.

The discussion in the book has three aspects.

The first aspect of the discussion sheds light on the fundamental principles of the consociationalism theory, their evolution (Lijphart 2017) and how these have manifested themselves throughout history; for example, in the contexts such as Northern Ireland (White 2017) and Switzerland (Qvortrup 2017). Doorenspleet and Maleki (2017) clarify the key differences between the consociational models on the one hand and the consensus models on the other and then explore where and when they can work best by conducting a cross-national comparative analysis. Loizides (2017) also analyses the development of the consociational theory and its implications for the case of Cyprus in the twenty-first century. These cases offer an explanation as to how consociational solutions in different forms, and to a varying extent, can help to overcome deep-seated religious, cultural, economic and political divisions in different cases.

The second aspect focuses on the elements of consociational arrangements that can be interpreted as inherently deficient from a critical point of view. These include the kinds of issues and contradictions, which still exist in post-conflict consociational democracies. For example, Rice and Somerville (2017) discuss that consociational arrangements and communication strategies in Northern Ireland are elitist and do not offer long-term plans for genuine social integration. Jarret (2017) and Dixon (2017) similarly show that a genuinely shared identity is showing few signs of emerging in consociational cases such as Northern Ireland. White (2017) suggests that consociationalism offers no use in cases where it is highly elite driven and when parties to the conflict no longer believe that the power-sharing arrangements associated with consociationalism are in their interest.

The final aspect of the discussion offers important insights into the fundamental mechanisms, institutions, and methods that are necessary to overcome the problems summarized above. For example, introducing referendums to overcome problems around the party interest and elite-driven nature of consociationalism (Qvortrup 2017), developing government communication spheres to facilitate genuine social integration and a common shared identity across adverse groups (Rice and Somerville 2017), and incorporating liberal approaches into the theory to prevent essentialism and isolation (Jarret) will be presented as evidenced-based recommendations to improve consociationalism in practice. Furthermore, Blick (2017) will suggest that additional steps and reforms in a consociational direction might be necessary to deal with the possible tensions between devolved institutions and central administrations when there is no supranational organization such as the EU to take responsibility for regulating the power relations between them.

Each individual chapter in this book mostly presents a balanced account of all three aspects as mentioned above but some of the chapters are more focused on one of them than others. For this reason we believe it is useful for the reader to see separately the main arguments and rationale presented in each chapter as follows.

Coventry, UK   Durukan Kuzu
                                                              Michaelina Jakala

Bibliography

Blick, A. (2017). The 2016 European Union Referendum, Consociationalism and the Territorial Constitution of the United Kingdom. In M. Jakala, D. Kuzu, & M. Qvortrup (Eds.), *Consociationalism and Power-Sharing in Europe—Arend Lijphart's Theory of Political Accommodation*. London: Palgrave Macmillan.

Dixon, P. (2017). What Politicians Can Teach Academics: 'Real' Politics, Consociationalism and the Northern Ireland Conflict. In M. Jakala, D. Kuzu, & M. Qvortrup (Eds.), *Consociationalism and Power-Sharing in Europe—Arend Lijphart's Theory of Political Accommodation*. London: Palgrave Macmillan.

Doorenspleet, R., & Maleki, A. (2017). Understanding Patterns of Democracy: Reconsidering Societal Divisions and Bringing Societal Culture Back in. In M. Jakala, D. Kuzu, & M. Qvortrup (Eds.), *Consociationalism and Power-Sharing in Europe—Arend Lijphart's Theory of Political Accommodation*. London: Palgrave Macmillan.

Jarret, H. (2017). The Limits of Consociational Power Sharing. In M. Jakala, D. Kuzu, & M. Qvortrup (Eds.), *Consociationalism and Power-Sharing in Europe—Arend Lijphart's Theory of Political Accommodation*. London: Palgrave Macmillan.

Lijphart, A. (1968). *The Politics of Accommodation: Pluralism and Democracy in the Netherlands*. Berkeley: University of California Press.

Lijphart, A. (1977). *Democracy in Plural Societies: A Comparative Exploration*. New Haven: Yale University Press.

Lijphart, A. (2017). Consociationalism After Half a Century. In M. Jakala, D. Kuzu, & M. Qvortrup (Eds.), *Consociationalism and Power-Sharing in Europe—Arend Lijphart's Theory of Political Accommodation.* London: Palgrave Macmillan.

Loizides, N. (2017). Arend Lijphart and Consociationalism in Cyprus. In M. Jakala, D. Kuzu, & M. Qvortrup (Eds.), *Consociationalism and Power-Sharing in Europe—Arend Lijphart's Theory of Political Accommodation.* London: Palgrave Macmillan.

McGarry, J., & O'Leary, B. (2009). Power Shared After the Deaths of Thousands. In R. Taylor (Ed.), *Consociational Theory: McGarry and O'Leary and the Northern Ireland Conflict* (pp. 15–85). London: Routledge.

Qvortrup, M. (2017). The Paradox of Direct Democracy and Elite Accommodation: The Case of Switzerland. In M. Jakala, D. Kuzu, & M. Qvortrup (Eds.), *Consociationalism and Power-Sharing in Europe—Arend Lijphart's Theory of Political Accommodation.* London: Palgrave Macmillan.

Rice, C., & Somerville, I. (2017). Dialogue and Government Communication: Consociationalism in Northern Ireland. In M. Jakala, D. Kuzu, & M. Qvortrup (Eds.), *Consociationalism and Power-Sharing in Europe—Arend Lijphart's Theory of Political Accommodation.* London: Palgrave Macmillan.

White, T. (2017). Consociation, Conditionality, and Commitment: Making Peace in Northern Ireland. In M. Jakala, D. Kuzu, & M. Qvortrup (Eds.), *Consociationalism and Power-Sharing in Europe—Arend Lijphart's Theory of Political Accommodation.* London: Palgrave Macmillan.

CHAPTER 1

Consociationalism After Half a Century

Arend Lijphart

It is obviously an honor for me that you are still discussing my contribution to political science now fifty years after I came up with the term consociationalism in my 1969 article (Lijphart 1969). After that time there have—admittedly—been changes in terminology: accommodation—consociation—power-sharing—consensus are some of the other terms I have used. But the basic characteristics have, I think, only been subject to insignificant change. Basically, my contention was—and still is—that an element of consociation and willingness to compromise with other groups can make democracy work even in divided societies if a number of conditions are met. I have divided these conditions in four characteristics, which again can be sub-divided into two categories: (a) cultural autonomy and (b) the other three (grand coalition, proportionality, minority veto). But before I go any further, it is, perhaps, useful to give you a bit of personal background and to outline the personal journey that led me to the

This paper is based on a lecture I delivered when I became an Honorary Research Fellow at the Centre for Trust, Peace and Social Relations at Coventry University in May 2016. It borrows liberally from my 2013 article in the *Taiwan Journal of Democracy* (Lijphart 2013).

A. Lijphart (✉)
University of California San Diego, San Diego, CA, USA

1
M. Jakala et al. (eds.), *Consociationalism and Power-Sharing in Europe*, International Political Theory,
https://doi.org/10.1007/978-3-319-67098-0_1

development of my theory, or rather my observation that certain institutional conditions can make democracy work in a peaceful fashion that benefits everyone.

My interest in the topic grew out of my 1963 Yale doctoral dissertation, published as a book by Yale University Press in 1966 under the title *The Trauma of Decolonization* (Lijphart 1966). In the book I analyzed the Dutch government policy toward West New Guinea. This was the last remnant of the Dutch East Indies colonial empire. While the Dutch recognized Indonesia's independence in 1949 they resisted surrendering West New Guinea until 1962. They did this despite the territory's evident lack of economic value—contrary to the prevalent Marxist and non-Marxist theories of imperialism and colonialism that posited economic advantages as the main explanations. West New Guinea presented an especially clear deviant case because Holland's net economic interest in the colony was not just minimal but actually negative: the efforts to maintain possession put Holland's extensive trade with and investments in Indonesia at risk. This was not an abstract or imaginary risk. Indeed, in late 1957, Indonesia retaliated by confiscating all Dutch property and expelling nearly all of the 50,000 Dutch nationals. No other objective advantages were at stake either, and subjective and psychological factors were therefore not just contributing factors but the determining forces behind Dutch colonialist policy.

I need not say more about this first book because it was only indirectly linked, in two ways, to my subsequent work on democratic institutions. But a few more words are warranted. While I was working on the PhD, I was struck by the fact that the case of Dutch policy toward West New Guinea was also a deviant case in terms of the normally unemotional and level-headed pattern of policy-making in the Netherlands. I was thus led to a general analysis of the country's government and politics. Second, I made use of the deviant case-study method again, by analyzing the Dutch case in the framework of Gabriel Almond's and Seymour M. Lipset's theories of democratic stability (Almond and Verba 1989).

Almond and Lipset had argued that subcultural and mutually reinforcing cleavages made stable democracy very difficult, if not impossible. Dutch democracy, however, was far from unstable and dysfunctional, in spite of the deep religious and ideological divisions in Dutch society. My basic argument was that cooperation at the elite level could overcome the conflict potential inherent in such deep cleavages. I used the term "politics of accommodation" for this democratic pattern—synonymous with what I later called "consociational democracy," or "power-sharing democracy"

(Lijphart 1968b). My book entitled *The Politics of Accommodation* was published in 1968 (Lijphart 1968a).

As I am often called the "father" of consociational theory, I should emphasize that several other scholars were also working on this subject in the late 1960s. In fact, two important books preceded my *Politics of Accommodation*: Gerhard Lehmbruch's *Proporzdemokratie* (Lehmbruch 1967), which compared the Swiss and Austrian cases, was published in 1967, and Sir Arthur Lewis's *Politics in West Africa* (Lewis 1965) appeared before. Other significant studies by Hans Daalder, Luc Huyse, Val R. Lorwin, Kenneth D. McRae, Eric A. Nordlinger, G. Bingham Powell, Jr., and Jürg Steiner were published both in the late 1960s and early 1970s. Their contributions have been a major source of inspiration for me.

When *The Politics of Accommodation* was published (Lijphart 1968a), I had already started looking at other cases of consociational democracy, which I described and analyzed in a series of articles and book chapters. This research culminated in my 1977 book *Democracy in Plural Societies*, in which I defined consociational democracy in terms of four basic principles: (a) power-sharing executives in which all important groups are represented; (b) cultural autonomy for these groups; (c) proportionality in political representation, civil service appointments, and government subsidies; and (d) a minority veto power with regard to the most vital issues such as minority rights and autonomy (Lijphart 1977). I also tried to identify the background factors favorable to the establishment and maintenance of consociational democracy. The nine principal cases that I analyzed were the Netherlands, Belgium, Switzerland, Austria, Lebanon, Malaysia, Cyprus, Suriname, and the Netherlands Antilles. My overall conclusion—which was also intended to be an explicit policy recommendation for constitution-writers in plural (deeply divided) societies—was that a consociational system was a necessary (but not sufficient) condition for stable democracy in such countries.

In the years between my 1968 and 1977 books, my approach changed in four respects, all of which also characterized the further evolution in my research and writing from the 1980s on. I included more and more countries: from the single case in 1968 to the nine cases in 1977 mentioned in the previous paragraph, and then to twenty-one, twenty-seven, and thirty-six countries in my 1984 and 1999 books—as indicated in the subtitles of these three books (Lijphart 1984, 1999).

This increase in the number of cases made for a change in my basic research approach: from the case-study method, to the comparative method, to the statistical method. Especially in the last chapters of my 1999 *Patterns of Democracy* the large number of cases allowed me to make effective use of correlation and regression analysis.

Further, I have become more and more explicit about linking my empirical conclusions to policy recommendations. This was mainly implicit in *The Politics of Accommodation*, but quite explicit in *Democracy in Plural Societies*—and in all of my books since then. Political scientists tend to be very cautious about making policy recommendations—much too cautious, in my opinion. Empirical propositions link independent with dependent variables, or causes with effects. Many of these effects can be described as desirable or undesirable. If that is the case, and if the causes, whether behavioral or institutional, can in principle be changed, a clear recommendation about these causes is implied. In much of my own work on governmental institutions, political parties, and electoral systems, I have therefore included discussions of the policy relevance of my findings.

Moreover, I have become increasingly critical of what used to be the conventional wisdom that the power-sharing type of democracy may have advantages in terms of democratic quality and stability, but has the serious drawback of providing less effective government. In the past, I, too, was completely convinced of the validity of this conventional wisdom, and it has taken me many years to liberate myself from it. In my undergraduate and graduate student days in the late 1950s and early 1960s, I regarded the Westminster majoritarian model as the best form of democracy in every respect and multiparty democracy with proportional representation (PR), coalition cabinets, and so on, as clearly inferior. This admiration for the Westminster model represents a long and strong tradition in American political science. In a second phase, from the mid-1960s to the mid-1980s, I became strongly aware of the dangers of majoritarian democracy for religiously and ethnically divided societies, but I still believed that it was the better choice for more homogeneous countries. Only from the mid-1980s on did I become more and more convinced that the consociational and consensus models of democracy were superior to the majoritarian model for all democracies and in almost all respects.

My next step entailed a twofold effort. First, I wanted to use the contrast between consociational and majoritarian democracy as a general framework for the analysis of all democracies, not just democratic government in divided countries. Second, I wanted to define and measure the four basic characteristics of consociational democracy more precisely, and I made a major attempt to operationalize and quantify degrees of executive power power-sharing, degrees of proportionality, and degrees of minority veto power. In my 1984 *Democracies*, I ended up with eight new characteristics that could indeed be expressed in quantitative terms and that were clearly similar to the four traits of consociational democracy—but also clearly not exactly the same as consociational democracy (Lijphart 1984). I called this similar concept "consensus democracy."

Democracies was a systematic comparison of twenty-one democratic systems in the 1945–1980 period (Lijphart 1984). Its most important conclusion was that the characteristics distinguishing majoritarian from consensus democracy cluster along two dimensions: an executives–parties dimension (based on the organization and operation of executives, party systems, electoral systems, and interest group systems) and a federal–unitary dimension (based on the relationships between central and lower level governments, the organization of legislatures, and rules for constitutional amendment). This dichotomous clustering also allowed me to draw a two-dimensional "conceptual map" of democracy on which each of the democracies could be located.

Two other books were also "next steps" after *Democracy in Plural Societies*, but more specialized than *Democracies*. One, my 1985 *Power-Sharing in South Africa*, was entirely devoted to a policy recommendation; it was published in the "Policy Papers in International Affairs" series of the Berkeley Institute of International Studies. In the 1980s, the outlook for peace and democracy in South Africa was grim, and most observers regarded a violent bloodbath as almost inevitable (Lijphart 1985).

I disagreed with this pessimistic view and argued that a positive outcome was still possible if the contending parties could be persuaded to accept a consociational solution. I analyzed the potential for power-sharing in South Africa, and found that the background conditions were far from completely unfavorable. I also tried to outline the type of consociational democracy that would suit the South African situation best, and I recommended inter alia a legislature elected by PR and a proportionally constituted power-sharing executive. The 1994 interim constitution adopted both of these principles by prescribing one of the most proportional election systems used anywhere in the world and mandatory power-sharing in the cabinet.

My 1994 book *Electoral Systems and Party Systems* was inspired both by my earlier finding of the crucial role of election by PR in power-sharing systems and by the fact that the design of electoral systems is one of the most powerful tools that constitution-makers have at their disposal

(Lijphart 1994). I tried to nail down the exact relationships among the different elements of electoral systems (electoral formulas, district magnitudes, electoral thresholds, and so on) as the independent variables and degrees of proportionality in election outcomes and the numbers of parties in the party system as the dependent variables. The book is mainly a technical treatise but with important policy implications. If one wants proportional election outcomes and adequate minority representation, it is not difficult at all to achieve these goals by designing the proper electoral system.

The next step along more general theoretical lines was *Patterns of Democracy*, published in 1999. My original plan was to simply prepare an updated edition of *Democracies*, but when I began to work on the revision, I realized that it offered me a great opportunity for much more drastic improvements. I decided to add not just the more recent data, updated to 1996, but also fifteen new countries, new operationalizations of the institutional variables, two completely new institutional variables, an attempt to gauge the stability of the countries' positions on the conceptual map, and an examination of the performance of the different types of democracy with regard to a large number of public policies. As a result, while *Patterns of Democracy* grew out of *Democracies*, it became an entirely new book rather than a second edition.

As a result of all these changes, it would not have been surprising if my new findings had diverged from my earlier ones; on the contrary, however, they were powerfully reinforced. Probably the most important new finding in *Patterns* was the overall superiority of consensus democracy (along the executives—parties dimension) with regard to government performance. Consensus democracies score a great deal higher with regard to variables measuring democratic quality (such as political equality, women's representation in legislatures and cabinets, and voter participation) than majoritarian democracies, while scoring at least as well as—in fact, slightly better than—majoritarian systems on government effectiveness, as measured by macroeconomic performance indicators and the control of violence. The clear policy recommendation was that, in designing a democratic system, the consensus type is the preferable choice. Moreover, an important corollary to this recommendation was that the most crucial ingredient for creating a consensus democracy was the combination of PR and a parliamentary (rather than presidential) form of government.

Thinking About Democracy, published in 2008, was mainly a collection of my more important articles and chapters published between 1969 and

2004 on power-sharing, election systems, and parliamentary versus presidential government, but with new introductory and concluding chapters. For the purpose of the present chapter, the one reprinted article that is worth mentioning is my 1996 "The Puzzle of Indian Democracy," originally published in the *American Political Science Review* (Lijphart 1996). In this, I demonstrated that India was an almost perfect example of consociational democracy—an important response to the frequently heard criticism that consociationalism can work only in relatively small countries: the case of India, the world's largest democracy, offers a powerful refutation.

The updated edition of *Patterns of Democracy*, published in 2012, adds fourteen more years to the analysis and covers the period from 1945 to 2010. It gave me the welcome opportunity to test whether my main findings and conclusions continued to be valid—and they were amply confirmed. In fact, the evidence with regard to the interrelationships of my ten majoritarian versus consensus characteristics and with regard to the superior performance of consensus democracy (along the executives—parties dimension) had become even clearer and stronger. A major reason for these stronger results was the higher quality of the new data, compared with the data that I had at my disposal in the mid-1990s and their availability for many more countries.

Finally, so as to bring my thinking and collaborations up to date, I should mention the book published in 2014. Like my books on South Africa and electoral systems, it is also a sideways offshoot of the main line of my research efforts. It originated in conversations that I had with Bernard Grofman while I was working on the first edition of *Patterns* in the 1990s. We were struck by the fact that, of the thirty-six countries in the analysis, the United States was the most difficult case to classify. We moved from this first impression to a more systematic examination of American political institutions and procedures compared with those of other democracies. We found that, across the board, when there are differences in democratic institutions and practices, the United States is almost always in the minority, usually a small minority, and frequently a minority of one—indeed a "different democracy," to cite the book's title. The book that we decided to write on this subject was long delayed by other commitments, but with the help of two co-authors—Matthew S. Shugart and Steven L. Taylor—it was finally completed (Taylor et al. 2014). We cover thirty-one countries in our book, which breaks the trend of including more and more countries in my studies; the reason is that, for comparisons with the large American democracy, we decided that the smallest countries (with fewer than five million inhabitants) should be excluded. In addition to institutional variations, we look at a host of indicators of government performance, on which the United States generally does not score well. We forego explicit policy recommendations, but our implicit conclusion is that Americans should be more self-critical, more willing to consider political and constitutional reforms, and less eager to advocate American-style democracy for other countries.

So, to sum up, while there have been changes my thinking has been rather consistent. Before 1985 I proposed varying number of conditions for consociationalism, from which I was adding and subtracting conditions in different writings. Then from 1985 on, I made no further changes in my list of nine conditions. But my focus shifted. There was a gradual move to thinking of consociationalism as necessary but not optimally democratic to arguing that there is nothing undemocratic about consociationalism. And, more importantly for practical purposes, I began to argue for consociationalism as policy recommendation. This was, admittedly implicit in my earlier writings but it became more and more explicit in my later writings. The latter was important. The more practical framing of the argument led to acceptance by policy-makers. It became recognized that FPTP (first past the post) was ill-suited for divided societies—and even for homogeneous societies. And it was recognized that PR and power-sharing are more conducive to peaceful co-existence and probably also more fair and legitimate (as was recognized in Iraq and the former Yugoslavia).

Bibliography

Almond, G. A., & Verba, S. (1989). *The Civic Culture: Political Attitudes and Democracy in Five Nations*. New York: Sage.

Lehmbruch, G. (1967). *Proporzdemokratie: Politisches System und politische Kultur in der Schweiz und in Österreich*. Tübingen: Mohr.

Lewis, A. (1965). *Politics in West Africa*. London: Allen and Unwin.

Lijphart, A. (1966). *The Trauma of Decolonization*. New Haven: Yale University Press.

Lijphart, A. (1968a). *The Politics of Accommodation: Pluralism and Democracy in the Netherlands*. Berkeley: University of California Press.

Lijphart, A. (1968b). Typologies of Democratic Systems. *Comparative Political Studies, 1*(1), 3–44.

Lijphart, A. (1969). Consociational Democracy. *World Politics, 21*(02), 207–225.

Lijphart, A. (1977). *Democracy in Plural Societies: A Comparative Exploration.* New Haven: Yale University Press.

Lijphart, A. (1984). *Democracies: Patterns of Majoritarian and Consensus Government in Twenty-One Countries.* New Haven: Yale University Press.

Lijphart, A. (1985). *Power-Sharing in South Africa.* Berkeley: University of California Press.

Lijphart, A. (1994). *Electoral Systems and Party Systems: A Study of Twenty-Seven Democracies, 1945–1990.* Oxford: Oxford University Press.

Lijphart, A. (1996). The Puzzle of Indian Democracy: A Consociational Interpretation. *American Political Science Review, 90*(02), 258–268.

Lijphart, A. (1999). *Patterns of Democracy. Government Forms and Performance in Thirty-Six Countries.* New Haven: Yale University Press.

Lijphart, A. (2006). *Thinking About Democracy: Power Sharing and Majority Rule in Theory and Practice.* London: Routledge.

Lijphart, A. (2012). *Patterns of Democracy, Government Forms and Performance in Thirty-Six Countries* (2nd ed.). New Haven: Yale University Press.

Lijphart, A. (2013). Steps in My Research and Thinking About Power Sharing and Democratic Institutions. *Taiwan Journal of Democracy,* Special issue, 1–7.

Taylor, S. L., Shugart, M. S., Lijphart, A., & Grofman, B. (2014). *A Different Democracy: American Government in a 31-Country Perspective.* New Haven: Yale University Press.

CHAPTER 2

Understanding Patterns of Democracy: Reconsidering Societal Divisions and Bringing Societal Culture Back In

Renske Doorenspleet and Ammar Maleki

INTRODUCTION

Deep societal divisions can easily obstruct political efforts to build and maintain a stable democracy in a country. Democratic government is easier in homogeneous countries, but more challenging in countries with divided societies (see e.g. Lijphart 2004: 96–97; Reynolds 2002). How to ensure a stable democratic system in a country with deep divisions? Which types of political institutions are best to be adopted in divided societies? These questions have been at the core of the field of comparative politics, and our chapter builds upon Arend Lijphart's typologies of democracies, as they have played an important role in the academic debates so far. Since the late 1960s, Arend Lijphart has clearly been the leading expert on consociationalism and consensus democracies, which are specific political systems designed to ensure political stability in countries with deeply divided societies.

R. Doorenspleet (✉)
University of Warwick, Coventry, UK

A. Maleki
Tilburg University, Tilburg, Netherlands

© The Author(s) 2018   11
M. Jakala et al. (eds.), *Consociationalism and Power-Sharing in Europe*, International Political Theory,
https://doi.org/10.1007/978-3-319-67098-0_2

We will first give a short overview of Lijphart's work in order to clarify the key differences between the consociational models on the one hand, and the consensus models on the other hand. We will highlight important assumptions in Lijphart's work which have not been tested yet, despite the impressive accumulation of knowledge around Lijphart's ideas and typologies. The first assumption is that divided societies tend to adopt consensus political systems in order to have stable democracies (see also Bogaards 2000: 412–3). The second assumption is that there is a link between culture and politics: a country with a consensual culture is more likely to have a consensus political system (Lijphart 1998). While Lijphart's earlier 1960s work emphasized the importance of culture, we believe the cultural factor needs to be reintroduced in studies on building democratic political institutions in divided societies.

In this chapter, we will test the two assumptions in cross-national comparative research. Conceptually, our chapter presents and defines the new idea of a country's 'societal culture'. Empirically, we will examine the general pattern, and investigate whether there is a link between societal culture (which is a country's cultural orientation, which can be harmonious and cooperative on the one hand, and a competitive and mastery culture on the other hand) and the type of democracy (whether the political system is consensus or not). Our analyses support the second assumption. We will also demonstrate if there is a link between societal structure (whether a country is divided or not) and the type of democracy (the political structure, so whether a country's political system is consensus or not). This supports the first assumption as well, but only partly, as the link is not strong at all. There are many crucial exceptions: for example, many countries are divided but have a majoritarian political system while they still can be classified as stable democracies (e.g. Denmark and Finland). We will also show that a country's societal culture is a more important explanation for types of political systems. In our view, this cultural factor deserves more attention in future studies of political institutions.

Consociationalism and Consensus Democracy: Theory, Critique and Untested Assumptions

Deep societal divisions are generally seen as problematic for democracy. Most experts agree that it is generally more difficult to establish and maintain democratic government in countries with divided societies than in homogeneous countries (see e.g. Lijphart 2004: 96–97; Reynolds 2002; Horowitz 1991; Reilly 2001; Norris 2004, 2008). An influential group of scholars have therefore analysed why some democracies are still stable despite deep divisions in their societies.[1] Since the late 1960s, Arend Lijphart clearly is the leading expert on consociationalism, arguing that segmented societies need consociational democracy to ensure political stability (see e.g. Lijphart 1975, 1977. Consociational democracy combines a fragmented societal structure[2] with coalescent elite behaviour (Lijphart 1968: 38).[3]

Since the 1980s, Lijphart has developed a broader classification of different types of democracy, which distinguishes majoritarian democracies from consensus democracies. This classification dropped the focus on differences in political culture and elite behaviour. Instead, Lijphart created an empirical typology of democracies, which is a 'two-dimensional conceptual map of democracy' (see Table 14.2 in Lijphart 1999: 246). While majoritarian democracies are characterized by a high concentration of political power, consensus systems emphasize the importance of power-sharing. The extent to which a country is a consensus democracy is measured by ten indicators. It appeared that the United Kingdom was almost purely majoritarian on most of the ten indicators (from 1945 to 1996). As a consequence, Lijphart describes this country more in depth, as the archetypical majoritarian democracy. Moreover, New Zealand was also very majoritarian, at least until the country changed its electoral system into a proportional one (see Lijphart 1999, Chap. 2.) A country such as Switzerland fits nicely into the model of consensus democracy, and Lijphart also adds Belgium and the European Union as typical cases of this second type of democracy (see Lijphart 1999, Chap. 3.)

Lijphart's own factor analyses in 36 stable democracies showed that there are actually two dimensions. The first dimension (the executive–parties dimension) includes indicators around power-sharing, like the number of parties in parliament, the degree of electoral proportionality, the frequency of multi-party government and so on. The second dimension (federal–unitary dimension) includes indicators around power-dividing, like the degree of federalism, bicameralism and constitutional rigidity (see Lijphart 1999, 2012).

While consociational democracy was defined by both a country's social structure (whether a country's society is divided or not) and by the type of democracy (whether the political institution is consensual or not), consensus democracy is now distinguished from majoritarian democracies just based on types of political institutions (see Bogaards 2000: 410). Moreover, the typologies of democratic systems have shifted over time: Lijphart changed his focus on normative analyses of ideal types that can achieve and maintain stable democracy (in earlier work on consociational democracy) to empirical analyses of which type of democratic system performs best (in later work on consensus democracy).[4] Finally, Lijphart's work on consensus democracies is more general and includes a wider range of countries, actually all stable democracies. While Lijphart recommended consociationalist systems mainly for deeply divided societies (Lijphart 1968, 1975, 1977), since the 1980s his work has tried to convince us that consensus democracy is the best political system for *any* society (Lijphart 1984, 1999, 2004, 2012).[5]

With the introduction of his work on consensus democracies (see e.g. Lijphart 1984), a new school focusing on democracy and political institutions in divided societies was born. Lijphart's influence has not only been strong in the academic world with many scholars building on his work (see e.g. Sisk and Reynolds 1998; Crepaz et al. 2000; Reynolds 2002; Norris 2004, 2008; Bernauer et al. 2016); his work has also been influential in the world of policy-making, as advisor during the peace processes and constitution making processes of Northern Ireland and South Africa (see e.g. Crepaz et al. 2000; Lijphart 1985; Dixon 1997). Lijphart is not only one of the most quoted contemporary political scientists, his work on different types of democracies[6] has also been acknowledged as the standard for work to come (see e.g. Taagepera 2003) and as the most influential typology of democracies (see e.g. Mainwaring 2001).

However, although Lijphart's work on 'patterns of democracy' (i.e. his typology of consensus versus majoritarian political systems) has been applied and improved extensively, at the same time it has been criticized to a great extent. We distinguish roughly six types of criticism. The first type of critique has focused on conceptualization of the key terms, particularly the types of democracies and the chosen indicators for both types (see e.g. Dahl 1989: 156; Blondel 1995: 22–23; Keman and Pennings 1995; Bogaards 2000: 410; Taagepera 2003). The second group of critique concerns the measurements of the types of democracies and the issue of multidimensionality (see e.g. Vatter 2009; Vatter and Bernauer 2009; Doorenspleet and Pellikaan 2013; Bernauer et al. 2016). Lijphart's typology includes two dimensions, which means that there are not just two types of democracies (majoritarian versus consensus) but actually four types: consensus-federalist (e.g. Switzerland), consensus-unitary (e.g. Sweden), majoritarian-federalist (e.g. USA), and majoritarian-unitary (e.g. United Kingdom) democracies (cf Bormann 2010). However, Lijphart's empirical work focuses on just one dimension (the first dimension), while neglecting the second dimension of federalism (see Doorenspleet and Pellikaan 2013); some scholars argue there is even a third dimension (Bernauer et al. 2016; Maleki and Hendriks 2016). The third group emphasized the normative flaws of Lijphart's work, and particularly the uneasy link between his empirical work and his normative, prescriptive recommendations (see e.g. Bogaards 2000). The fourth group of critical comments refers to the selection of countries (Armingeon 2002). The fifth stream of criticism comes from qualitative country experts who have in-depth knowledge of a particular case, and show that the studied country does not fit into this typology (see e.g. Lustick 1997 on India; Van Cranenburgh 2006 on Namibia; Studlar and Christensen 2006 on Canada). The sixth group of criticism has focused on the empirical flaws in Lijphart's work. Lijphart's analyses have consistently shown that consensus democracies are better than majoritarian systems, but they have been seriously challenged by replications of his work, leading to different conclusions (see e.g. Keman and Pennings 1995 with reply by Crepaz and Lijphart 1995; Anderson 2001; Armingeon 2002; Doorenspleet and Pellikaan 2013; Giuliani 2016).

In other words, Lijphart's ideas have been improved based on ongoing constructive critical comments, particularly in the field of comparative politics; as a consequence, there has been an impressive accumulation of knowledge around Lijphart's ideas and typologies. Nonetheless, in our view there are still some important assumptions in Lijphart's work which need to be investigated more in depth.

The first assumption is that there is a link between divided societies and the choice for a consensus political system. According to Lijphart, consensus democracy should be recommended as 'they entail a set of basic choices that have to be made by constitutional engineers in countries that attempt to introduce or strengthen a democratic regime' (Lijphart 1984: 209). This is particularly important in countries with deep differences between groups in society. In order to ensure a stable democracy, 'consensus democracy is clearly needed by all countries that have deep divisions of any kind', as Lijphart repeatedly emphasized in his work (Lijphart 1990: 73; see also Lijphart 1984: 209). It is important to point out that Lijphart also suggests that there is a causal relationship, meaning that political elites prefer and deliberately choose consensual political institutions when they have to rule a country with a deeply divided society; the general pattern is, according to Lijphart, that 'countries with significant societal divisions tend to adopt forms of democratic government that can accommodate these divisions' and therefore they decide to implement 'rules and institutions of consensus democracy' (Lijphart 1990: 73; see also Bogaards 2000: 412–3).

However, is there a link between the extent of societal divisions in a country on the one hand, and types of democratic systems on the other hand?

The second untested assumption is that there is a link between culture and politics; to be more specific, Lijphart has mentioned that a consensual culture in a country is associated with a consensus type of political system in the same country (see e.g. Lijphart 1998), but this idea has not been investigated yet. He writes that the type of democracy determines a country's culture, or the other way around:

> the structure of consensus democracy may either be based on a consensual culture, or that it may operate in an insufficiently consensual culture in such a way as to first produce the minimum of consensus required for a democracy and then, in the long run, make the country's political culture more consensual. That is, the structure of consensus democracy may be the product of a consensual culture or its causal agent (Lijphart 1998: 107).

But what is the empirical evidence that there is a link between consensus political systems and consensual culture?

It is precisely those two crucial assumptions we would like to examine in the rest of this chapter. Is there a link between social structure (divided society or not) and political institutions (the type of democracy)? And is there a link between a country's cultural orientation (societal culture) and political institutions (the type of democracy)?

Concepts and Measurements

Before we can answer those questions, we need to define and measure the key concepts. The first concept is 'stable democracy'; although the debate around defining and measuring 'democracy' is huge (Munck and Verkuilen 2002; Coppedge et al. 2008, 2011; Doorenspleet 2015), we will follow a very pragmatical approach in this chapter, by simply relying on Lijphart's choice. He used the Freedom House index to select the democracies that are central in his more recent work (Lijphart 1984, 1999, 2012).[7] As an additional step, his selected democracies need to be 'stable', and therefore Lijphart only selected democracies that have been continuously democratic for a long time, namely since the late 1980s or earlier (Lijphart 2012: 50). In addition, Lijphart (2012: 51) defended this choice by stating that his selection of countries contains more than 85 per cent of the population of all democracies; moreover, these democracies have different levels of societal divisions, and the selection includes democracies from each of the three waves of democratization, as was identified by Huntington (1991). Aiming to examine Lijphart's assertions, we will use the same set of Lijphart's 36 stable democracies in our study.

The second concept is 'type of democratic system'. Again, we rely on Lijphart's definitions and measurements. Lijphart (2012: 2) conceptualized and operationalized two types of democracies: majoritarian versus consensus. He started some fundamental questions around the practice of democracy: who will govern and to whose interests should the government be responsive when the people have divergent preferences? The two types of answers to these questions form the basis of two (ideal) types of democracy: if the answer is that 'the majority of the people' is most important in a democracy, then it refers to a majoritarian type of democracy, while the answer is that 'as many people as possible' matter, then it refers to a consensus democracy. As Lijphart (2012: 2) explained further, consensus democracy 'does not differ from the majoritarian model in accepting that majority rule is better than minority rule, but it accepts majority rule only as a minimum requirement: instead of being satisfied with narrow decision-making majorities, it seeks to maximize the size of these majorities'.

Lijphart relied on ten institutional variables and performed factor analysis to extract two dimensions of democracy for the 36 countries: not just the dimension of 'executive–parties' but also the dimension of 'federal–unitary'. Lijphart's first dimension, executive–parties, is widely used as a measure for distinguishing between majoritarian and consensus democracy. Over recent decades, many scholars have tried to replicate, revise or extent Lijphart's conceptualization and operationalization of democratic models (see e.g. Fortin 2008; Vatter 2009; Hendriks 2010; Kriesi and Bochsler 2012; Maleki and Hendriks 2016; Bernauer et al. 2016). We use the scores of this dimension, averaged for the range of 1981–2010, as the measure of types of democracy (Lijphart 2012).

The third concept, 'divided societies', is more challenging to conceptualize and operationalize. Lijphart (2012: 55–57) mentioned and referred to this concept as 'the degree of societal divisions' but his conceptualization and operationalizations have been very vague in his study (see also Andeweg 2000: 519; Doorenspleet 2005: 372). While taking the critical points around his conceptualization seriously, Lijphart proposes different criteria, which enable us to identify the divisions between different segments in society, and to determine the size of each segment[8] (Lijphart 1981: 356). Still, the actual operationalization and measurement of the concept has been vague, and it is unclear how Lijphart has classified the countries into deeply divided (or 'plural') and not divided (or 'non-plural'), let alone the category in the middle (semi-plural). Lijphart himself has admitted that the actual classification is 'subjective' and 'rough' (see e.g. Lijphart 1999: 58).

So how can we measure 'divided societies'? Three dimensions of societal divisions have received most attention, and appeared to be politically relevant: *ethnicity, language and religion* (cf. Selway 2011; Stoll 2008). The most commonly used measure of aggregate is called fractionalization which measures the probability that two randomly selected individuals from the entire population will belong to different [ethno/linguistic/religious] groups (Alesina et al. 2003: 158–9). Among other measures, three operationalizations of fractionalization have widely been used in political science studies, namely the measures by Roeder (2001), Fearon (2003) and Alesina et al. (2003). In Roeder's dataset, ethnic and linguistic differences are lumped together and called ethnolinguistic fractionalization (known as ELF). Fearon's measures discriminate between ethnic and linguistic[9] fractionalization. The work by Alesina et al. (2003) distinguishes between ethnic, linguistic and religious fractionalization and measures these types separately. Despite the different conceptualization, databases and time periods, the three measures of ethnic fractionalization have high, significant correlations (see Alesina et al. 2003: 162 and Fearon 2003: 210).

Lijphart (2012: 56) criticized such measures of ethnic fractionalization. His first comment was that ethnicity is not the only relevant division and other types of fractionalization—like language or religion—might be more important and relevant in some societies. Second, Lijphart argued that measures of fractionalization have ignored crucial divisions within social groups, such as the difference between faithfully practicing and non-practicing people within religious groups. Third, measures of fractionalization do not measure the saliency of divisions in societies. These measures cannot take the depth of division into account and equate the divisions which are important in one society and unimportant in another. Finally, the measures do not show which ethno/linguistic/religious groups differentiate themselves organizationally. Taking these challenges into account, Lijphart has therefore used a subjective measure, and he categorized his set of 36 countries into three categories of plural, semi-plural and non-plural societies (see Fig. 2.1).

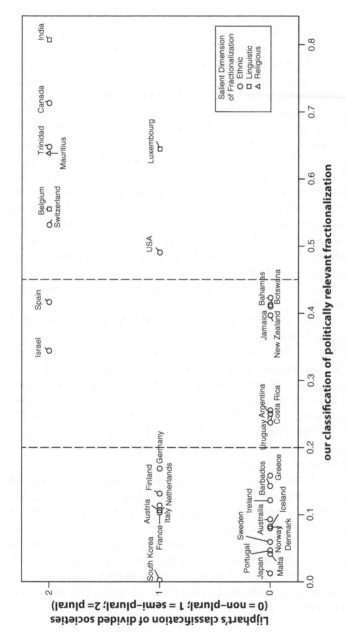

Fig. 2.1 Measures of Divided Societies: Lijphart's subjective classification (y-axis) compared with our classification of politically relevant fractionalization (x-axis)

Although Lijphart's critical comments on measures of fractionalization are certainly important, his own alternative measure is very subjective, unsystematic and unreliable. As a consequence, we follow a more systematic approach, which takes into account the core of the critical points while still building on existing measures of fractionalization. The first step is to find and recognize the most relevant and important dimension of fractionalization in each country. In order to do so, we first rely on a very recent and innovative version of the Ethnic Power Relations (EPR) data set, which provides annual data on politically relevant ethnic, language and religious groups (Vogt et al. 2015). The EPR data enables us to recognize which dimensions of fractionalization are most relevant for each country under study. Then, knowing the politically relevant dimensions of fractionalization in each country, as a second step we will focus our attention to the most fractionalized dimension and measure it. We use the measurement of fractionalization developed by Alesina et al. (2003), because it not only includes all three dimensions of fractionalization but also covers all 36 countries under study. With this procedure, we can alleviate some main challenges arisen by Lijphart, while still using existing reliable measures in a systematic way.

Relying on the EPR data set during our first step, we discovered that ethnic fractionalization is the most politically relevant dimension for 32 democracies. In four countries the situation is slightly different. In three countries (India, Belgium and Luxembourg) the linguistic fractionalization is most salient, while in one country (Mauritius) the religious fractionalization seems to be the most politically relevant dimension. During our second step, we measure the extent of fractionalization (how deeply divided a society actually is), based on Alesina et al. (2003). Figure 2.1 shows our classification of countries versus Lijphart's classification.

The figure shows that Lijphart's classification is quite inconsistent with the empirical studies of societal divisions. For example, Lijphart categorizes Italy, Germany, South Korea, Austria and Finland as semi-plural societies, while these countries have a low score of ethnic fractionalization (<0.2) and while their other dimensions of fractionalization are politically irrelevant (Vogt et al. 2015). On the other hand, Lijphart categorizes New Zealand, Jamaica, Botswana and Bahamas as non-plural societies whereas these countries have scores of ethnic fractionalization which are higher than 0.4, showing that they are (semi-) plural societies. It is also ambiguous why Lijphart has classified the USA and Luxembourg as semi-plural instead of plural societies, considering the high scores for ethnic and linguistic fractionalization in these countries. We believe our classification, which is based on both the EPR data (step 1) and Alesina's fractionalization scores (step 2), is a more valid and reliable operationalization of societal division. In our analyses below, we will compare the results of our classification with Lijphart's classification.

Last but not least, we need to define and measure the concept of 'societal culture'. Culture has been central in Lijphart's work but he has never defined it, let alone measured. Societal culture is a set of 'shared values, beliefs and interpretations', which 'guide the way social actors select actions, evaluate people and events, and explain their actions and evaluations' (House et al. 2002: 5; Schwartz 1999: 24). Societal culture is empirically operationalized by a set of cultural dimensions which in turn are extracted from public surveys at the national level. Among different theories and measurements of national culture,[10] we use Schwartz's cultural theory and operationalizations. Schwartz (2006) acknowledged that cultural values will change only gradually and slowly over decades; hence, we can assume that cultural values are relatively stable. Cultural values are different from 'situational attitudes' which change and fluctuate fast (Maleki and Hendriks 2015b). Schwartz developed his framework in a theoretical way, and empirically he examined the frameworks using large-scale multi-country samples. He found larger cultural differences between countries than within countries, suggesting the framework could be used to compare countries (Ng et al. 2007).

Schwartz developed his own survey (Schwartz Value Survey, SVS) which included 56 value items to operationalize the values priorities of individuals. In the SVS questionnaires, respondents are asked to rate the importance of each abstract items (e.g. social justice, humility, creativity, social order, pleasure, ambition) 'as a guiding principle in MY life' (Schwartz 2006). Aggregating individual responses to the national level, Schwartz identified seven 'cultural orientations' which form three bipolar dimensions of culture: embeddedness versus autonomy, harmony versus mastery and egalitarianism versus hierarchy.

The harmony versus mastery dimension represents to what extent the majority of a society values consensus and compromise on the one hand, versus competitiveness and achievement on the other hand. While harmony orientation is more sympathetic towards the weak, mastery orientation has more sympathy for the strong. The significance of harmony versus mastery dimension on societal preference for different democratic models has been corroborated in recent research (Maleki and Hendriks 2015a; Maleki and Doorenspleet forthcoming).

Schwartz measured the mastery and harmony orientations at the cross-national level for 80 countries; the data was gathered by surveys between 1988 and 2007 (Schwartz 2008). The cultural scores of 26 countries under study (out of 36 democracies) are available in Schwartz data set. Using the scores of mastery and harmony orientation, we calculate the bipolar dimension of harmony versus mastery, based on Schwartz's procedure to subtract the scores of mastery from harmony (Schwartz 2004). Scandinavian countries, Belgium, Austria and Italy are examples of countries with a high consensual (harmony) culture, while the USA, South Korea, India, Israel and the United Kingdom are countries with a high competitive (mastery) culture.

DIVIDED SOCIETIES AND SOCIETAL CULTURE: THE EMPIRICAL LINK WITH TYPES OF DEMOCRACIES

The aim now is to test the two hypotheses:

(a) Among stable democracies, countries with divided societies are more likely to have a consensus type of democracy.
(b) Among stable democracies, countries with a consensual societal culture are more likely to have a consensus type of democracy.

What are the findings of testing the first hypothesis? Our analyses show there is only weak and not significant empirical support for the idea that countries with a divided society have a consensus type of democracy, while countries without a divided society have a majoritarian type of democracy (see Fig. 2.2 below). The countries which confirm Lijphart's idea can be found in the right upper corner of Fig. 2.2: six stable democracies have not only a divided society, but also a consensus type of democracy. Switzerland and Belgium fit into this expected pattern, and—unsurprisingly—those countries have been mentioned by Lijphart often, as ideal types of his work on consensus democracies. Israel, Mauritius, India and Luxembourg also fit into Lijphart's expected patterns, as those divided countries have consensus political systems. Moreover, there are quite a few stable democracies which are majoritarian but they also fit into Lijphart's pattern as they are not divided; those countries can be found in the left

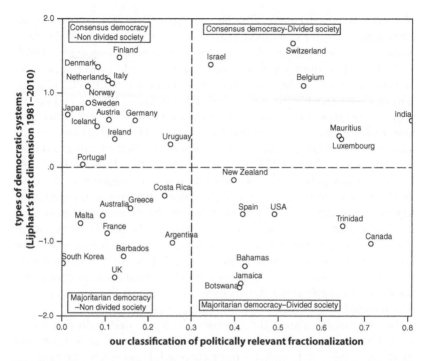

Fig. 2.2 The relationship between politically relevant fractionalization (x-axis) and types of democratic systems (y-axis)

lower corner of Fig. 2.2. Again, here we can find some 'typical' countries, which have been described by Lijphart into depth (see e.g. 1984, 1999, 2012) as the ideal types of majoritarian democracies (e.g. the United Kingdom).

Still, it is important to acknowledge that there are also many stable democracies which do not fit into this idea. As can be seen in the left upper corner of Fig. 2.1, there are 13 countries which do not have deeply divided societies and still have consensus democracies, despite the fact that they do not really 'need' such a political system and can adopt a more majoritarian system. Countries such as Finland and Denmark are very homogeneous but have adopted consensual political systems. But also the Netherlands does not fit Lijphart's own expectations, which is remarkable as this country formed the foundation of Lijphart's entire work on consociationalism and consensus democracy. In one of his first books, Lijphart presents the

Netherlands as a paradox: 'On the one hand, it is characterized by an extraordinary degree of social cleavage (while) on the other hand, Holland is also one of the most notable examples of a successful democracy' (1968: 1–2). In such a country with deep divisions we would expect 'dissension and antagonism (…) ideological tension and extremism' (1968: 1–2), but 'Dutch democracy is eminently stable and effective!' (1968: 15). Lijphart wanted to explain this paradox, which led to the development of his ideas how to build democracies in divided societies. However, many scholars have questioned Lijphart's characterization of the Netherlands as a deeply divided society (Barry 1975; Van Schendelen 1985; Daalder 1985). As Daalder clearly argued 'the Netherlands was not characterized by clear blocks around 1910, at least not of the nature and severity as depicted by Lijphart' (Daalder 1985: 57). Lijphart's own classification also shows that the Netherlands is not a clear plural country, and he classifies it as a semi-plural country (see Fig. 2.1, y-axis), while our own classification shows the country is not deeply divided at all (see Fig. 2.1, x-axis). In other words, while it is true that the Netherlands has a consensual political system, the society is not deeply divided, which does not support the general pattern which would be expected based on Lijphart's ideas.

In addition, there are eight countries which have deeply divided societies and have majoritarian political systems. Based on Lijphart's theory and model, instability and conflict is to be expected. However, to the contrary, those countries can also be classified as stable democracies. As can be seen in the right lower corner of Fig. 2.2, examples of these countries are not only the USA but also Canada and Trinidad. Of course, it depends on where to draw the line; when is a country divided, and when is it not, and do we put the threshold at 0.3, at 0.4 or at 0.5? It matters for the individual cases, which are classified in a different way, depending on the choice of the cut-off point. In general, however, the pattern is the same: there also many stable democracies which have a consensus political system while they do not have divided societies. More importantly, there also many countries which have divided societies, but a majoritarian system, and still they are very stable democracies. As can be seen in Table 2.1, the correlation between the two variables, that is, the 'type of democracy' and 'divided societies' is quite weak and not statistically significant. Only if Lijphart's classification of divided societies is used, then we can see a weak correlation between the two variables (see Table 2.1), but we have already argued why Lijphart's classification is unreliable and would be misleading.

Table 2.1   Bivariate correlational results

	1	2	3	4
1. Type of democracy (Lijphart's first dimension)	1			
2. Societal culture (harmony vs. mastery)	0.51***(25)[a]	1		
3. Divided societies (our classification of politically relevant fractionalization)	−0.09(36)	−0.25(26)	1	
4. Divided societies (Lijphart's classification)[b]	0.30*(36)	0.05(26)	0.55***(36)	1

Note: Pearson correlations [except as otherwise noted]. $^*p < 0.1$ $^{**}p < 0.05$ $^{***}p < 0.01$. Number of countries in parentheses
[a]This is the correlation when excluding Israel as an outlier. Including Israel, the correlation will be 0.36*
[b]Spearman's rho correlations

What about the other assumption? Is there evidence that among stable democracies, the more consensual the societal culture, the more likely it is that a country has a consensus type of democracy? What are the findings when testing the second hypothesis? Our analyses show there is strong support. The correlations in Table 2.1 show that the link between the two variables is the strongest of all links (with 0.51) and statistically significant (if $p < 0.01$) when excluding an extreme outlier of Israel. Figure 2.3 also shows that there is a positive relationship between societal culture and types of democratic systems. Among stable democracies, the more consensual the societal culture, the more likely a country has a consensus type of democracy. Of course there are some notable exceptions to this general pattern. For example, there are some countries which have a competitive societal culture, but have still adopted the consensual political system; India and Ireland are such exceptions, while Israel is the extreme outlier (see Hazan 1996; Lis 2014).[11]

In the other corner with exceptions (the right lower corner), France and Spain can be found, but in general the pattern is quite strong, and the overall number of exceptions is relatively low. Moreover, another important conclusion is that the type of societal culture in a country seems to be more important than its societal structure in order to get a stable democratic model. This finding, which is based on analyses of stable democracies by using Lijphart's operationalization of democratic models, is in line with the results of another empirical study for a broader range of democracies. Operationalizing democratic models for

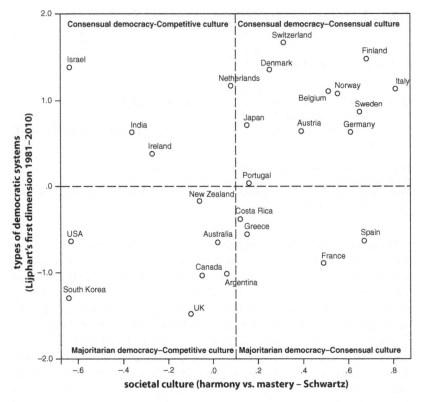

Fig. 2.3 The relationship between societal culture (x-axis) and types of democratic systems (y-axis)

80 electoral democracies, Maleki and Hendriks (2015a) also found a significant correlation between Schwartz's mastery dimension and majoritarianism for 44 democracies.[12] The role of societal culture is not only important when adopting different democratic models, but it also seems important for the stability and workability of the specific type of adopted models. The latter should be examined more by empirical research in the future.

We have to emphasize that we do not assume that culture determines politics. It can easily be the other way around, and we need both more theoretical work (on link between culture and politics) and empirical work (i.e. on the mechanisms) in the near future in order to expand our knowledge around the direction of the relationship, its causes and effects. As we all know, correlation is not causation. Lijphart also acknowledges he cannot say anything about causality (see e.g. 1998). Still, he argues that when the type of political system has an impact on a country's culture, then 'the country in question can also afford to move from a consensus system of democracy to a more majoritarian one'. So if a consensus political system influences the country and leads to a more consensual culture, then the country might be ready for a majoritarian system. This shows how important Lijphart believes the power of culture actually is.

Setting aside any ideas around causality and the link between culture and politics, Lijphart eventually does not recommend a change from a consensus to majoritarian political system, because 'why give up consensus democracy and its "kinder, gentler" qualities if one does not have to?' (Lijphart 1998: 107). Hence, Lijphart keeps repeating the message that consensus democracies are always best (Lijphart 1998, 1999, 2012), but we do not really know as there is still a lack of studies. Recent studies suggest it is not necessarily the case that consensus democracies are best (see e.g. Selway and Templeman 2012; Doorenspleet and Pellikaan 2013; Bernauer et al. 2016). Moreover, if there is a 'mismatch' between societal culture and type of political system, then this might lead to poor democratic performance. In a recent study, we found that the compatibility between the type of democracy and societal culture significantly affects the level of satisfaction with democracy among established democracies (Maleki and Doorenspleet forthcoming).

The 'cultural compatibility thesis' of democracy suggests that the compatibility of cultural orientations with institutional choices does matter (Maleki 2015). The theory asserts that countries in which culture is incompatible with their type of political institutions will have problems with the functioning of their model of democracy. Accordingly, it is expected that countries with incompatible institutional arrangements are likely to reform their political institutions. For example, the electoral systems in New Zealand and Japan were reformed, and changed from a majority to a mixed system. These changes transformed the democratic models into a more consensual democracy. These are examples of institutional reforms into the direction of closing the incompatibility gap between institutional arrangement and societal culture.

Conclusion

Among stable democracies, the more the divided a society, the more likely the country has a consensus type of democracy. This is one of the assumptions based on Lijphart's work but our analyses showed that the support for the hypothesis is weak, and not significant. There are many notable exceptions of countries with a divided society which have a majoritarian type of democracy, while other countries are quite homogeneous but at the same time have a consensus democracy. We did find support for the other assumption, though, that there is a link between culture and politics: stable democracies with a mastery cultural orientation are more likely to have majoritarian systems, while the countries with a harmony cultural orientation generally have consensus democracies.

Our first contribution is that we explored the link between types of democracies (consensus versus majoritarian systems), societal culture (whether a country's cultural orientation is mastery or harmony) and societal structure (whether a society is divided or homogeneous). Although the factor of societal structure should be taken into account when designing democratic models, we think there is an overemphasis on its importance. At the same time, another key factor, that is, societal culture, has been underestimated or even ignored. This is the very factor that Lijphart had incorporated in his theory in his early work, but later it disappeared again and has been ignored in the field of building political institutions in divided societies. The findings of this chapter show the necessity for bringing societal culture back in.

Our second contribution is that we presented a new operationalization for the concept of 'divided societies'. We first detected the most relevant and important dimension of fractionalization in each country, using the EPR data set (Vogt et al. 2015). Then, we focused on the politically relevant dimensions of fractionalization in each country, and measure the extent of fractionalization cross-nationally, using the fractionalization data (from Alesina et al. 2003). This new operationalization takes into account the saliency of societal divisions; moreover, it is more systematic than Lijphart's classification which distinguished non-plural, semi-plural and plural societies.

Moreover, we brought culture back in, and we added a measurement of societal culture in the analyses. Measuring culture is a hard and controversial endeavour in social science. However, there is a well-established field in which scholars measure cultural differences (see e.g. Schwartz 2004).

Using these measures we could not only examine our hypothesis empirically, but also introduced a different measure of culture in the field of comparative politics in which Inglehart's cultural dimension of postmaterialism has been dominant so far (among others Inglehart and Baker 2000; Inglehart and Welzel 2005).

Future research needs to add more control variables, and investigate to what extent socio-economic development, legacy of violent conflict and other relevant factors influence the pattern between the three variables which have been central in our chapter. Moreover, we need to improve the measurements, although our attempts can be seen as a foundation for further work. Most importantly, future research should focus not just on stable democracies, but also on countries which are in transition or democratizing.

As a relevant example, we would like to mention the case of Iraq, which clearly has a deeply divided society. Based on theory, constitutional engineers would recommend a consensual type of democracy (Lijphart 2004), and actually this model was also brought to Iraq in practice (McGarry and O'Leary 2007). The institutional setting in Iraq has been designed to create an inclusive political structure; however, a large number of parties with a low harmony/consensual culture leads to a very fragile, weak and highly competitive political system. Iraqi's constitutional/institutional design is a recent example of building a specific type of political system, which is solely based on a country's societal structure without acknowledging its societal culture.

The key issue is whether this consensual democratic model is the most compatible model within Iraq's context; and if this is not the case, the challenge is to develop a democratic model which would be a more compatible one. This is not just relevant for Iraq, but also for other transitional countries. When developing institutional scenarios for countries which are still in the middle of a civil war and have deeply divided societies, we do not just need to consider the societal structure, but also the cultural context (see e.g. whether a country is competitive and has a mastery culture). This brings us to a new paradigm in institutional design of democracy: we need to take different contextual factors seriously, and particularly different cultural orientations of societies. Instead of looking for the *best model of democracy*, we should seek for the *most compatible model of democracy (Maleki 2015)*. Studying patterns of democracy remains important in our turbulent times, but in our view societal structure needs to be reconsidered, while societal culture needs to be brought back in.

NOTES

1. See Andeweg (2000) for an excellent overview; see also the bibliographies in all the books by Arend Lijphart (i.e. 1999, 2012).
2. See also Van Schendelen (1985: 149). Lijphart has used the term 'fragmented political culture' in this context as well. To avoid confusion, however, we make a clear distinction between societal culture (or 'a country's cultural orientation') and societal structure ('divided societies') in our chapter.
3. Another form of democratic government is a majoritarian system, which is characterized by a homogeneous societal structure with competitive elite behaviour (see also Bogaards 2000: 401).
4. This shift is well described by Bogaards (2000).
5. Although Lijphart still keeps focusing on stable democracies, so in this sense the range of countries is certainly not all-encompassing (see e.g. Lijphart 1999, 2012).
6. Since Lijphart's 1984 book.
7. To be more precise, Lijphart only selected countries which are classified as 'free' by the Freedom House; in this way, he has extracted the democracies which have been central in his work since 1984.
8. The two other criteria are that (a) the boundaries between the segments and between political, social, and economic organizations must coincide; (b) the segmental parties must receive stable electoral support from the respective segments.
9. Or 'cultural', as Fearon (2003) calls it in his work.
10. For a review see Maleki and de Jong (2014).
11. Israel, like the Netherlands, has had a very low electoral threshold of 1 per cent resulting in a high effective number of parties in parliament which in turn leads to a challenging process of coalition making and unstable governments. In recent decades, some changes have been adopted to transform Israeli's democratic model to a less consensual democracy by introducing a direct election for the prime minister between 1992 and 2003 (Hazan 1996), and recently by increasing the electoral threshold to 3.25 per cent (Lis 2014).
12. Moreover, in their regression analysis, they added a control variable for societal division and found no significant impact of fractionalization on the relation between democratic models and societal culture.

REFERENCES

Alesina, A., Devleeschauwer, A., Easterly, W., Kurlat, S., & Wacziarg, R. (2003). Fractionalization. *Journal of Economic growth, 8*(2), 155–194.

Anderson, L. (2001). The Implications of Institutional Design for Macroeconomic Performance. *Comparative Political Studies, 34*(4), 429–452.

Andeweg, R. B. (2000). Consociational Democracy. *Annual Review of Political Science, 3*(1), 509–536.

Armingeon, K. (2002). The Effects of Negotiation Democracy: A Comparative Analysis. *European Journal of Political Research, 41*(1), 81–105.

Barry, B. (1975). Political Accommodation and Consociational Democracy. *British Journal of Political Science, 5*(4), 477–505.

Bernauer, J., Bühlmann, M., Vatter, A., & Germann, M. (2016). Taking the Multidimensionality of Democracy Seriously: Institutional Patterns and the Quality of Democracy. *European Political Science Review, 8*(3), 473–494.

Blondel, J. (1995). Consensual Politics and Multiparty Systems. *Australian Journal of Political Science, 30,* 7–26.

Bogaards, M. (2000). The Uneasy Relationship Between Empirical and Normative Types in Consociational Theory. *Journal of Theoretical Politics, 12*(4), 395–423.

Bormann, N. C. (2010). Patterns of democracy and its critics. *Living Reviews in Democracy, 2.*

Coppedge, M., Alvarez, A., & Maldonado, C. (2008). Two Persistent Dimensions of Democracy: Contestation and Inclusiveness. *Journal of Politics, 70,* 632–647.

Coppedge, M., Gerring, J., Altman, D., Bernhard, M., Fish, S., Hicken, A., ... & Semetko, H. A. (2011). Conceptualizing and measuring democracy: A new approach. *Perspectives on Politics, 9*(2), 247–267.

Crepaz, M. M. L., & Lijphart, A. (1995). Linking and Integrating Corporatism and Consensus Democracy: Theory, Concepts and Evidence. *British Journal of Political Science, 25*(2), 281–288.

Crepaz, M. L., Koelble, T., & Wilsford, D. (2000). *Democracy and Institutions— The Life Work of Arend Lijphart.* Ann Arbor: University of Michigan Press.

Daalder, H. (1985). Politicologen, sociologen, historici en de verzuiling. *BMGN- Low Countries Historical Review, 100*(1), 52–64.

Dahl, R. A. (1989). *Democracy and Its Critics.* New Haven: Yale University Press.

Dixon, P. (1997). Consociationalism and the Northern Ireland Peace Process: The Glass Half Full or Half Empty? *Nationalism and Ethnic Politics, 3*(3), 20–36.

Doorenspleet, R. (2005). Electoral Systems and Good Governance in Divided Countries. *Ethnopolitics, 4*(4), 365–380.

Doorenspleet, R. (2015). Where Are the People? A Call for People-Centred Concepts and Measurements of Democracy. *Government and Opposition, 50*(3), 69–494.

Doorenspleet, R., & Pellikaan, H. (2013). Which Type of Democracy Performs Best? *Acta Politica, 48*(3), 237–267.

Fearon, J. D. (2003). Ethnic and Cultural Diversity by Country. *Journal of Economic Growth, 8*(2), 195–222.

Fortin, J. (2008). Patterns of Democracy? Counterevidence from Nineteen Post-communist Countries. *Zeitschrift für Vergleichende Politikwissenschaft, 2*(2), 198–220.

Giuliani, M. (2016). Patterns of Democracy Reconsidered: The Ambiguous Relationship Between Corporatism and Consensualism. *European Journal of Political Research, 55*(1), 22–42.

Hazan, R. Y. (1996). Presidential Parliamentarism: Direct Popular Election of the Prime Minister, Israel's New Electoral and Political System. *Electoral Studies, 15*(1), 21–37.

Hendriks, F. (2010). *Vital Democracy: A Theory of Democracy in Action.* Oxford: Oxford University Press.

Horowitz, D. L. (1991). *A Democratic South Africa?: Constitutional Engineering in a Divided Society.* California: University of California Press.

House, R., Javidan, M., Hanges, P., & Dorfman, P. (2002). Understanding Cultures and Implicit Leadership Theories Across the Globe: An Introduction to Project GLOBE. *Journal of World Business, 37*(1), 3–10.

Huntington, S. P. (1991). *The Third Wave, Democratization in the Late Twentieth Century.* Norman: University of Oklahoma Press.

Inglehart, R., & Baker, W. E. (2000). Modernization, cultural change, and the persistence of traditional values. *American Sociological Review, 65*(1), 19–51.

Inglehart, R., & Welzel, C. (2005). *Modernization, cultural change, and democracy: The human development sequence.* New York: Cambridge University Press.

Keman, H., & Pennings, P. (1995). Managing Political and Societal Conflict in Democracies: Do Consensus and Corporatism Matter? *British Journal of Political Science, 25*(2), 271–281.

Kriesi, H., & Bochsler, D. (2012). *Varieties of Democracy.* [Online] Available at: http://www.democracybarometer.org/Papers/Bochsler_Kriesi_2012.pdf. Accessed July 2012.

Lijphart, A. (1968). Typologies of Democratic Systems. *Comparative Political Studies, 1*(1), 3–44.

Lijphart, A. (1975). *The Politics of Accommodation: Pluralism and Democracy in the Netherlands.* Berkeley: University of California Press.

Lijphart, A. (1977). Majority Rule Versus Democracy in Deeply Divided Societies. *Politikon: South African Journal of Political Studies, 4*(2), 113–126.

Lijphart, A. (1981). Consociational Theory: Problems and Prospects. A Reply. *Comparative Politics, 13*(3), 355–360.

Lijphart, A. (1984). *Democracies: Patterns of Majoritarian and Consensus Government in Twenty-One Countries.* New Haven: Yale University Press.

Lijphart, A. (1985). *Power-sharing in South Africa.* Berkeley: University of California, Institute of International Studies.

Lijphart, A. (1990). The Southern European Examples of Democratization: Six Lessons for Latin America. *Government and Opposition, 25*(1), 68–84.

Lijphart, A. (1998). Consensus and Consensus Democracy: Cultural, Structural, Functional, and Rational-Choice Explanations. *Scandinavian Political Studies, 21*(2), 99–108.

Lijphart, A. (1999). *Patterns of Democracy: Government Forms and Performance in Thirty Six Countries.* New Haven: Yale University Press.

Lijphart, A. (2004). Constitutional Design for Divided Societies. *Journal of Democracy, 15*(2), 96–109.

Lijphart, A. (2012). *Patterns of Democracy: Government Forms and Performance in Thirty Six Countries*. New Haven: Yale University Press.

Lis, J. (2014). *Israel Raises Electoral Threshold to 3.25 Percent*. [Online] Available at: http://www.haaretz.com/news/national/1.579289. Accessed Aug 2014.

Lustick, I. S. (1997). Lijphart, Lakatos, and Consociationalism. *World Politics, 50*(1), 88–117.

Mainwaring, S. (2001). Two Models of Democracy. *Journal of Democracy, 12*(3), 170–175.

Maleki, A. (2015). *Patterns of Culture and Models of Democracy: Towards the Cultural Compatibility Thesis of Democracy*. PhD thesis, Tilburg University.

Maleki, A., & de Jong, M. (2014). A Proposal for Clustering the Dimensions of National Culture. *Cross-Cultural Research, 48*(2), 107–143.

Maleki, A., & Doorenspleet, R. (forthcoming). Cultural Compatibility and Satisfaction with Democracy: A Cross-National Comparative Study.

Maleki, A., & Hendriks, F. (2015a). The Relation Between Cultural Values and Models of Democracy: A Cross-National Study. *Democratization, 22*(6), 981–1010.

Maleki, A., & Hendriks, F. (2015b). Grid, Group, and Grade: Challenges in Operationalizing Cultural Theory for Cross-National Research. *Cross-Cultural Research, 49*(3), 250–280.

Maleki, A., & Hendriks, F. (2016). Contestation and Participation: Operationalizing and Mapping Democratic Models for 80 Electoral Democracies, 1990–2009. *Acta Politica, 51*(2), 237–272.

McGarry, J., & O'Leary, B. (2007). Iraq's Constitution of 2005: Liberal Consociation as Political Prescription. *International Journal of Constitutional Law, 5*(4), 670–698.

Munck, G. L., & Verkuilen, J. (2002). Conceptualizing and Measuring Democracy: Evaluating Alternative Indices. *Comparative Political Studies, 35*, 5–34.

Ng, S. I., Lee, J. A., & Soutar, G. N. (2007). Are Hofstede's and Schwartz's Value Frameworks Congruent? *International Marketing Review, 24*(2), 164–180.

Norris, P. (2004). *Electoral Engineering: Voting Rules and Political Behavior*. Cambridge: Cambridge University Press.

Norris, P. (2008). *Driving Democracy: Do Power-Sharing Institutions Work?* New York: Cambridge University Press.

Reilly, B. (2001). *Democracy in Divided Societies: Electoral Engineering for Conflict Management*. Cambridge: Cambridge University Press.

Reynolds, A. (Ed.). (2002). *The Architecture of Democracy: Constitutional Design, Conflict Management, and Democracy*. Oxford: Oxford University Press.

Roeder, P. G. (2001). *Ethnolinguistic Fractionalization (ELF) Indices, 1961 and 1985*. [Online] Available at: http://pages.ucsd.edu/~proeder/elf.htm. Accessed 20 Apr 2017.

Schwartz, S. H. (1999). A Theory of Cultural Values and Some Implications for Work. *Applied Psychology: An International Review, 48*(1), 23–47.

Schwartz, S. H. (2004). Mapping and Interpreting Cultural Differences Around the World. In H. Vinken, J. Soeters, & P. Ester (Eds.), *Comparing Cultures, Dimensions of Culture in a Comparative Perspective* (pp. 43–73). Leiden: Brill.

Schwartz, S. H. (2006). A Theory of Cultural Value Orientations: Explication and Applications. *Comparative Sociology, 5*(2/3), 137–182.

Schwartz, S. H. (2008). The 7 Schwartz cultural value orientation scores for 80 countries. [Online] https://www.researchgate.net/publication/304715744_The_7_Schwartz_cultural_value_orientation_scores_for_80_countries

Selway, J. S. (2011). The Measurement of Cross-Cutting Cleavages and Other Multidimensional Cleavage Structures. *Political Analysis, 19*(1), 48–65.

Selway, J., & Templeman, K. (2012). The Myth of Consociationalism? Conflict Reduction in Divided Societies. *Comparative Political Studies, 45*(12), 1542–1571.

Sisk, T. D., & Reynolds, A. (Eds.). (1998). *Elections and Conflict Management in Africa.* Washington, DC: US Institute of Peace Press.

Stoll, H. (2008). Social Cleavages and the Number of Parties: How the Measures You Choose Affect the Answers You Get. *Comparative Political Studies, 41*(11), 1439–1465.

Studlar, D. T., & Christensen, K. (2006). Is Canada a Westminster or Consensus Democracy? A Brief Analysis. *PS: Political Science & Politics, 39*(4), 837–841.

Taagepera, R. (2003). Arend Lijphart's Dimensions of Democracy: Logical Connections and Institutional Design. *Political Studies, 51*, 1–19.

Van Cranenburgh, O. (2006). Namibia: Consensus Institutions and Majoritarian Politics. *Democratization, 13*(4), 584–604.

Van Schendelen, M. P. C. M. (1985). Consociational Democracy: The Views of Arend Lijphart and Collected Criticisms. *Political Science Reviewer, 15*(1), 143–183.

Vatter, A. (2009). Lijphart Expanded: Three Dimensions of Democracy in Advanced OECD Countries? *European Political Science Review, 1*(1), 125–154.

Vatter, A., & Bernauer, J. (2009). The Missing Dimension of Democracy: Institutional Patterns in 25 EU Member States Between 1997 and 2006. *European Union Politics, 10*(3), 335–359.

Vogt, M., et al. (2015). Integrating Data on Ethnicity, Geography, and Conflict: The Ethnic Power Relations Data Set Family. *Journal of Conflict Resolution, 59*(7), 1327–1342.

CHAPTER 3

The Limits of Consociational Power Sharing

Henry Jarrett

INTRODUCTION

The primary aim of consociational power sharing is to achieve conflict management in divided societies by accommodating and recognising different groups or communities within governmental and societal structures on a proportional basis (Lijphart 1977; McGarry and O'Leary 2009a). If conditions are conducive, such as the willingness of former adversaries to participate in arrangements and engage with each other, consociationalism can prove to be a highly successful method of managing conflict. Northern Ireland is heralded by many as an example of such a case. After 30 years of violent ethno-national conflict, the region is now comparatively stable and it is arguably the inclusiveness of consociationalism that is responsible for this stability.

As is the case with any form of conflict management, however, consociational power sharing is not without its limitations. One of the most common criticisms of the approach relates to its accommodative nature, which some argue fails to mitigate the significance of different groups in a divided society and ultimately leaves the root cause of conflict intact (Taylor 2009a; Dixon 1997). Despite this, McGarry and O'Leary (2009a, p. 83) argue that consociationalism may have the ability to break down

H. Jarrett (✉)
University of Exeter, Exeter, UK

© The Author(s) 2018
M. Jakala et al. (eds.), *Consociationalism and Power-Sharing in Europe*, International Political Theory,
https://doi.org/10.1007/978-3-319-67098-0_3

group ideologies in a divided society, with a majority of the population assuming a common identity that is genuinely shared. It is important to emphasise that they provide no guarantee that this will happen and argue that if it is achievable, it will take place gradually, with a minimum time-frame of 20 years, and apply their prognosis to the case of Northern Ireland. It is assumed that McGarry and O'Leary consider consociational-ism to have the ability to achieve such an identity as its arrangements facili-tate, and ultimately require, cross-communal cooperation between political elites and this may have a trickle-down effect on wider society, which may in turn weaken the salience of traditional identities. A genu-inely shared, common identity is one that the majority of the population considers to supersede the identity of their background group.

This chapter will test the likelihood of such an identity being achieved as a result of consociational power sharing. Whilst it will focus on the cases of Northern Ireland and Brussels, evidence from Malaysia and the Netherlands will also be utilised in order to support the analysis. Political parties are a useful gauge of opinion within wider society, as most parties seek to maximise their electoral support by being in tune with their con-stituents. This chapter will argue that if a genuinely shared common iden-tity is being realised in a divided society, this will be reflected in the political arena, with parties that previously expressed a largely exclusive appeal to one particular group being forced to moderate towards inclusivity or face being superseded by cross-communal parties that seek to represent all communities within a society. If this is taking place, it is expected that the election campaign literature of parties would be showing increasing signs of moderation towards socio-economic issues of a non-sectarian nature and that these parties would be demonstrating a willingness to campaign beyond their traditional support base. If the campaign literature and strat-egy of ethno-national parties does not indicate that this is taking place, it is expected that cross-communal parties would be attracting increasingly significant levels of electoral support if a shared identity is showing strong signs of emerging.

In analysing the potential of consociational power sharing to achieve such an identity, this chapter will examine a combination of political party election literature (primarily manifestos) and electoral results data to gauge how divisions have—or have not—changed over time. The chapter will firstly engage with the debate around different forms of conflict manage-ment, before considering evidence from the aforementioned case studies and will conclude with a discussion designed to analyse the results. Whilst supporting the assertion that consociational power sharing is the most effective means of managing violent conflict in divided societies, the chapter will conclude that the argument that it may have the potential to break down divisions and bring about a genuinely shared identity is ultimately not supported by evidence. This finding establishes the limits to what consociationalism is capable of achieving.

Sharing Power to Manage Conflict

Plural societies are those that are divided into two or more segmental cleavages, which may be ethnic, racial, linguistic, cultural, religious, regional, ideological or other (Eckstein 1966, p. 34; Lijphart 1977, pp. 3–4). Divisions are not necessarily mutually exclusive and may, for example, be based on a combination of ethnicity *and* nationality or ethnicity *and* language. Due to the choice of the case studies of Northern Ireland and Brussels, it is these that this chapter will focus on. Plural societies become deeply divided when 'a large number of conflict group members attach overwhelming importance to the issues at stake, or manifest strongly held antagonistic beliefs and emotions towards the opposing segment, or both' (Nordlinger 1972, p. 9). It is at this time that the need for conflict management often arises.

Yakinthou and Wolff (2012, p. 1) define conflict management as 'a process that aims at channelling the violent manifestation of an incompatibility of goals between two or more parties into a political process where their disputes can be addressed by non-violent means'. Whilst recognising that conflict management may eventually lead to conflict resolution, for example when the dispute becomes less politically salient, they argue that the main objective 'is to find and sustain an institutional arrangement in which conflict parties have greater incentives to abide by political rules of dealing with their dispute than to use, or revert to, violence in pursuit of their incompatible objectives'. McGarry and O'Leary (2009a, pp. 16–18) identify two options for conflict management in plural societies. The first is integration, the proponents of which consider identities to be malleable and transformable, and oppose political mobilisation around ethnic, national, cultural or religious divisions. It is often preferred by majority communities within states but also by small minority groups, such as immigrants.

A second option is accommodation. Accommodationists consider identities to be largely fixed and inflexible, and strive to encompass 'dual or multiple public identities in many-roomed political mansions'. In deeply divided societies, McGarry and O'Leary (2009a, pp. 17–18, 83) consider an integrationist approach to be unsuitable as a means of conflict management, as accommodation and the clearly designated representation that it offers is usually the preferred choice of minorities. Similarly, Lijphart (1977, quoted in Taylor 2009b, p. 4) argues that accommodation offers 'a far more realistic democratic option for deeply divided societies' than integration or majoritarian rule. The two major arms of the accommodation approach are consociational and centripetal power sharing, which are usually considered to be opposing methods.

Centripetalism

Centripetalists, like consociationalists, are largely supportive of the need for accommodative power sharing to manage conflict in divided societies (McGarry and O'Leary 2009a, pp. 16–17). Where the two approaches differ, however, is in the centripetalist argument that power sharing should not be solely accommodative and should also include some integrationist principles, as accommodation and integration are not mutually exclusive (Horowitz 2003; O'Flynn 2009). This disagreement is rooted in the belief that inter-group divisions in plural societies are not as fixed and entrenched as consociationalists claim (Nagle and Clancy 2012, p. 83). Reilly (2012, p. 57) asserts that centripetalists consider the most effective means of conflict management not 'to replicate existing ethnic divisions in the legislature and other representative organs, but rather to put in place institutional incentives for cross-ethnic behaviour in order to encourage accommodation between rival groups'. The approach is, therefore, critical of elite-driven methods such as consociationalism, which centripetalists believe entrenches divisions. Both Horowitz (2003) and O'Flynn (2009) argue that executives would better serve democracy and conflict management if they were to be comprised of a voluntary inter-group coalition of moderates, as opposed to the mandatory coalition prescribed by consociationalists.

Reilly (2012, p. 62) argues that centripetalism is of most benefit to societies in which demographics favour inter-party and inter-communal vote-pooling, such as those where communities are numerous and small in size, and where they are regionally spread and intermixed. To facilitate this, centripetalists reject proportional representation (PR) for divided societies as they argue that it encourages smaller parties that are more likely to base their appeal around narrow ethno-national issues. Instead, they recommend non-proportional electoral systems such as the Alternative Vote (AV), as under this system parties and their candidates are required to garner a higher percentage of votes in order to be elected, which incentivises a broader appeal and vote-pooling (Horowitz 2003). Reilly (2012, p. 57) suggests that this is 'perhaps the clearest distinction between centripetalism and other approaches' to conflict management, as he considers PR to be a cause of, rather than a solution to, ethno-national politics. Fiji is an important example of a divided society in which a centripetal approach to power sharing has been implemented, with elections contested using AV (McGarry and O'Leary 2009a, pp. 62–63).

The main critique of centripetalism as a means of conflict management in divided societies is that it is majoritarian in character (Reilly 2012, p. 63). In support of this, Bingham Powell (2000, p. 26, quoted in Reilly 2012, p. 63) argues that the approach is focused on the aggregation of votes, parties and opinions, whilst other methods stress the importance of the PR of all points of view in legislative arrangements. Although he acknowledges that centripetalism is a majoritarian model, Reilly (2012, p. 63) asserts that its majoritarianism is focused on broad-based parties and inclusive coalitions, rather than majorities and minorities formed around ethno-national divisions. As such, he does not consider the majoritarian nature of centripetalism to impact upon its ability to deliver successful conflict management. McGarry and O'Leary (2009a, pp. 62–64) nevertheless argue that the approach does not have the moderating effect that centripetalists claim it does, as the AV electoral system encourages hard-line appeals in small, single member constituencies that are likely to have a majority from one community, and results in the under-representation of minorities. They cite Fiji as an example of where this has occurred.

Consociationalism

Consociationalism is defined as an accommodative arrangement for power sharing that includes all significant groups in legislative and executive institutions, and one which promotes proportionality within public administration, with a preference for proportional electoral systems (McGarry and O'Leary 2009a, pp. 16–17). It is an elite-orientated, 'top–down' model (Dixon 1997, p. 1). The origins of consociationalism are to be found primarily in the work of Lijphart (1968, 1969, 1977). Although a system for managing divided societies based on this theory had been in place in the Netherlands since 1917—and a number of other states thereafter—Lijphart is largely credited with having formulated its characteristics into an approach for fragmented, but stable, states (Lijphart 1969). Lijphart (1969) refers to this theory as 'consociational democracy' and first applied it to cases such as Austria, Switzerland, Belgium and the Netherlands. Lorwin (1971) also applies the concept of consociationalism to states featuring 'segmented pluralism', and, similarly to Lijphart at the time, focuses exclusively on democratic states and nations, therefore neglecting deeply divided societies (Lorwin 1971, p. 144).

Lijphart (1977, pp. 25–44) identifies four defining characteristics of consociational democracy. Firstly, 'government by a grand coalition', which includes the political elites of all significant segments within a society, is necessary to ensure inclusiveness and representation, and is argued to be the most important element of consociationalism. Secondly, a 'mutual veto' is required in order to provide political protection for minority segments and facilitate their continued participation in a grand coalition. Thirdly, 'proportionality', in which segments are represented in government and society based upon their population size, is necessary. Whilst opinion differs over which electoral system is most conducive to consociational societies, such as party list PR or Proportional Representation—Single Transferable Vote (PR-STV) (Mitchell 2014), most consociationalists agree that some form of PR is necessary (Wolff 2012, pp. 24–25). Finally, 'segmental autonomy' is needed to allow segments to exercise decision-making power over areas concerning only their members.

Lijphart (1969, pp. 217–19) identifies three factors that are conducive to the successful implementation and operation of consociationalism. Firstly, the existence of an external threat is necessary in order to encourage cooperation between elites from different segments. Secondly, a multiple balance of power is needed, as this reduces the probability that a particular segment will aim to dominate, as is likely in societies with two segments of a similar size or in those where one segment has a majority. Finally, it is argued that it is important that the decision-making apparatus is not overloaded, as burdens on this may hinder the successful maintenance of consociational power sharing. Over time, however, these favourable factors for the establishment of consociational settlements have been amended, with some removed and others included.

In the mid-1980s, Lijphart (1985, pp. 119–28, quoted in Bogaards 1998, p. 478) amended the requirement of a multiple balance of power to the need for there to be no majority segments and for groups to be of a similar size. He removed the necessity for the decision-making apparatus to not be overloaded but the requirement of an external threat remained. Lijphart (1985, pp. 119–28, quoted in Bogaards 1998, p. 478) additionally added several other factors that he considered necessary for consociationalism to be sustained. These included a geographical concentration of segments, a small population size, the existence of overarching loyalties, a tradition of elite accommodation, socio-economic equality and a small number of segments. These amendments reflect the change over time in Lijphart's application of consociational democracy to include situations requiring conflict management, rather than only European democracies (Lijphart 1985, 1996).

Rather than focusing on the presence of an external 'threat', for example one which recommends partition, McGarry and O'Leary (2009a, pp. 37–38, 42) argue that benign external intervention can facilitate the implementation of a consociational agreement in divided societies, despite early work on the approach neglecting this possibility. They highlight that methods such as mediation and the use of pressures or incentives can play a crucial role in encouraging parties to reach agreement. McGarry and O'Leary (2009a, pp. 38–42) cite Northern Ireland as an example of where external input has been vital in achieving a settlement, not only from the British and Irish governments but also the United States and the European Union. This demonstrates that conflict management is not always solely internal, as outsiders can play a positive role in its implementation and operation. Consociational agreements, or at least settlements with significant consociational elements, have been credited with managing violent conflict in societies such as Lebanon, Bosnia-Herzegovina, Macedonia and Northern Ireland (Taylor 2009b, p. 6).

Consociationalism is not, however, without its critics. The main criticism is that it entrenches ethno-national divisions at the expense of the rights and identities of individuals, and does not offer a stable, lasting settlement (Wolff 2012, p. 40). Wolff (2012, p. 40) argues that this criticism is unsubstantiated as it refers to corporate, rather than liberal, consociationalism, which accommodates communities based on an ascriptive criterion (McGarry 2007, p. 172). He cites the works of Lijphart (1995) and McGarry and O'Leary (2008a, b) in demonstrating that contemporary consociationalism 'favours self-determined over predetermined groups in its institutional prescriptions and arrangements'. Wolff (2012, p. 40) supports this assertion with recent evidence by arguing that whilst the 1995 Dayton Agreement in Bosnia-Herzegovina is corporate to some extent, most other consociational settlements (for example, the 1998 Good Friday (Belfast) Agreement and the 2005 Iraq constitution) are inherently liberal, as defined by McGarry and O'Leary (2008a, b).

The form of consociational arrangements differs on a case by case basis. The primary way in which they do so is based on the corporate/liberal distinction (McCulloch 2012), which McGarry and O'Leary (2007, p. 675) argue is determined by whether identities should be predetermined by the settlement or self-determined by democratic elections. In corporate consociations groups are accommodated according to an ascriptive criterion on the assumption that 'group identities are fixed and that groups are both internally homogeneous and externally bounded' (McGarry and O'Leary 2007, p. 675). This privileges these identities over those that are not accommodated, including any existing intra-group and inter-group identities. Conversely, in liberal consociations political identities that emerge in democratic elections are rewarded, regardless of whether they are based on ethno-national groups, or on intra-group or inter-group identities (McGarry and O'Leary 2007, p. 675).

Summary

Whilst consociationalism is not without limitations, its record of successfully managing violent conflict between groups in many divided societies is too strong to ignore. Although the result has been less fruitful in certain cases, such as Iraq, evidence from Northern Ireland, Bosnia-Herzegovina, Macedonia and others supports its success. Consociationalism has not, however, only been useful in providing a solution to intense violence. In several cases, such as Belgium, the Netherlands and Switzerland, it has offered a democratic form of government that provides relative stability. Compared to majoritarian centripetal power sharing, consociationalism is a tried and tested method that has the potential for success if conditions, such as those identified by Lijphart, are conducive. As it has been claimed, however, that consociational power sharing may have the ability to change the entire nature of identity in divided societies where it has been implemented, the focus of the remainder of this chapter will be on assessing whether the approach is able to achieve such a transformation.

Northern Ireland

At the 2011 census, Northern Ireland had a majority/minority ratio of 48 per cent Protestant, who are primarily unionist/loyalist and identify as British, and 45 per cent Catholic, most of whom are nationalist/republican and have an Irish identity (Devenport 2012). The need for conflict management is due to deep divisions between these groups, beginning with the plantation of Ulster from the early seventeenth century and culminating in the outbreak of violent ethno-national conflict in the late 1960s. This resulted in the deployment of the British Army in Northern Ireland in 1969, and the suspension of Stormont (the Parliament of Northern Ireland) and implementation of direct rule in 1972. The formation of republican and loyalist paramilitary organisations, the presence of the British Army and the role of other groups led to 3500 deaths from the late 1960s to 1998 in what is commonly referred to as the 'Troubles'. A first attempt to manage conflict through power sharing was made in 1973 with the Sunningdale Agreement but it was short-lived, primarily due to its exclusion of hardliners and those involved in violence.

The Good Friday Agreement has had considerably greater success in regulating conflict in Northern Ireland. The talks culminating in the Agreement included the British and Irish governments and all significant political parties in the region, with the exception of the Democratic Unionist Party (DUP). Crucial to the success of these talks was the inclusion of parties with links to paramilitary organisations, principally Sinn Féin, the Progressive Unionist Party and the Ulster Democratic Party. The Agreement is consociational in character and established a 108-member legislature (reduced to 90 members for elections after 2016), the Northern Ireland Assembly, which is elected using PR-STV in 18 multimember constituencies, allowing voters to rank candidates in order of preference and transcend party and communal lines, should they choose to do so. The Agreement is considered to be primarily liberal, with Assembly members required to designate as 'unionist', 'nationalist' or 'other' and no pre-election designation of seats, meaning that the legislature is flexible to any population changes or identity shifts (McGarry and O'Leary 2009a, p. 71). After elections, a mandatory executive is formed using the d'Hondt model on a proportional basis of the numerical strength of parties in the legislature, with the First Minister from the largest party and the deputy First Minister from the second largest party, whilst both cannot represent the same community (McGarry and O'Leary 2009a, pp. 61–62). Parties are, nevertheless, able to decline their proportional allocation of ministerial positions if they wish (McGarry and O'Leary 2009b, p. 354). This occurred after the 2016 Assembly election, with the Ulster Unionist Party (UUP), the Social Democratic and Labour Party (SDLP) and the Alliance Party of Northern Ireland forming an official opposition to the DUP and Sinn Féin government (BBC 2016a).

It has, however, been argued that the method of executive formation and the mutual veto is evidence that Northern Ireland's consociational arrangements are not liberal and are instead corporate. It is claimed by some that executives in divided societies more effectively serve democracy and conflict management if they are comprised of a voluntary inter-group coalition, with an opposition, as this is more likely to promote moderate politics (Horowitz 2003; O'Flynn 2009). Consociationalists, however, dispute this claim and argue that voluntary coalition formation could lead to the exclusion of major political parties against their will, which would fail to provide adequate representation of all groups in society (McGarry and O'Leary 2009b, p. 379). Certain aspects of the Good Friday Agreement, such as the North-South Ministerial Council and the British-Irish Council, which are cross-border bodies, are not consociational, leading O'Leary (1999) to refer to the Agreement as 'power sharing plus'. Despite several suspensions, most notably between 2002 and 2007, the arrangements have been largely successful in managing violent ethno-national conflict in Northern Ireland, with the number of shootings and assaults falling from 310 in 2003–04 to 53 in 2007–08 (Stationery Office 2008, pp. 17–18, quoted in McGarry and O'Leary 2009b, p. 370).

Whilst most unionists identify as British and most nationalists identify as Irish (NILT 2009), a Northern Irish identity does exist (Nagle and Clancy 2012, p. 88; Tonge and Gomez 2015). The number of people claiming this identity has nevertheless remained below 30 per cent of the overall population of Northern Ireland and there has been little or no increase since the implementation of consociational power sharing (Tonge and Gomez 2015, p. 283). A Northern Irish identity may also mean different things to different people. It may, for example, be perceived by some Catholics as a regional identity on the island of Ireland and by some Protestants as a regional identity within the United Kingdom (Nagle and Clancy 2012, p. 89). It is, therefore, impossible to determine whether those identifying as Northern Irish subscribe to a genuinely shared identity that supersedes their respective traditional unionist or nationalist ideology.

It could nevertheless be argued that these results suggest that Northern Ireland is showing signs of moving towards a shared identity and this is coming about as a result of consociationalism. If this is the case, however, it would be expected that the survey data would demonstrate an increase in the number of people identifying as Northern Irish as the consociational institutions have become more embedded. This is not so, as there has been little increase in numbers since the re-establishment of power sharing in 2007, and a significant decrease was recorded between 2010 and 2012 (Tonge and Gomez 2015, p. 283), which is likely to be due to the decision of Belfast City Council to limit the days on which the union flag is flown at City Hall, resulting in unionist protests. It is therefore evident that a Northern Irish identity is failing to significantly impact upon the salience of British and Irish identities (Tonge and Gomez 2015, p. 284).

The party political environment in Northern Ireland can be characterised as an ethnic party system (Michell 1999, p. 101), with the vast majority of parties representing either the unionist or nationalist community. Of the five major parties, two are affiliated with unionism (the DUP and UUP), two with nationalism (Sinn Féin and the SDLP) and one, the Alliance Party, is cross-communal. Electoral results data from the 2016 Northern Ireland Assembly election supports the continued salience of British unionist and Irish nationalist identities (BBC 2016b). A total of 78 per cent of first preference votes were received by the four major ethno-national parties, with the DUP winning 38 seats, Sinn Féin 28 seats, the UUP 16 seats and the SDLP 12 seats. The cross-communal Alliance Party received seven per cent of first preferences and eight seats. This represents only a 0.5 per cent increase on the party's electoral performance at the first Assembly election after the implementation of consociational arrangements in 1998 (Tonge and Gomez 2015, p. 283), which suggests that consociationalism has had little impact in facilitating an increase in support for cross-communal parties. This evidence in turn discredits the argument that the arrangements may lead to a shared identity in Northern Ireland, as if this was taking place it would be expected that such parties would be reaping the electoral benefits.

The manifestos of the two largest ethno-national parties in Northern Ireland—the DUP and Sinn Féin—for the 2017 Assembly election also reflect the continued significance of British unionist and Irish nationalist identities. The DUP's (2017) manifesto makes frequent reference to the party as an upholder of unionism and includes, for example, a commitment to 'not compromise on fundamental unionist principles in order to retain power'. It also emphasises that the party is not prepared to submit to 'radical republican demands' and opposes a border poll on Irish unity unless it is within the terms of the Good Friday Agreement. This focus suggests that the party has little interest in appealing for votes from outside of the unionist community and believes that it will find very limited support beyond this cohort of voters.

Similarly in its ethno-national focus, Sinn Féin's (2017) manifesto is strongly geared towards the nationalist/republican community. It includes frequent references to the party's support for 'a new, united and agreed Ireland' and dedicates a section to 'building the momentum towards Irish unity'. This section refers to how partition has been a 'disaster' for Ireland and calls for an all-Ireland referendum on Irish unity. With just two per cent of Protestants supporting the unification of Ireland (BBC 2013), it is highly unlikely that Sinn Féin is attempting to win support from beyond the nationalist/republican community. As the two largest parties in Northern Ireland, the DUP and Sinn Féin received a collective 53 per cent of first preference votes at the 2016 Assembly election (BBC 2016b). Given these levels of support, it is clear that their largely exclusive election campaigns continue to resonate with voters in Northern Ireland, which indicates that moves towards a shared identity are showing few signs of being realised.

It could, however, be argued that consociational arrangements have not been in place long enough to facilitate such a transformation, as despite the signing of the Good Friday Agreement in 1998, its institutions have been subjected to several significant suspensions. It is nevertheless expected that Northern Ireland would be showing much greater signs of moving towards a shared identity if this is achievable and whilst there has been some slight moderation of the election campaigns of ethno-national parties, most notably the DUP, it is negligible, which is corroborated by there being little increase in electoral support for cross-communal parties. Ultimately, an ethnic party system remains in place in Northern Ireland, with the two largest parties utilising an exclusive focus to appeal to their respective communities, as this approach continues to resonate with the electorate.

Brussels

Consociationalism in Belgium has been in place since 1918 and was first based on the ideologies of Catholicism, socialism and liberalism (Deschouwer 2009, p. 7). However, the intensification of primarily non-violent divisions between French speakers and Flemish speakers throughout the twentieth century led to the federalisation of the state along linguistic lines in 1970 (Deschouwer 2009, p. 40). This divided Belgium into Flemish-speaking Flanders and French-speaking Wallonia (including a small German-speaking community), which are both monolingual, and bilingual Brussels, as despite its geographical location within the traditional boundaries of Flanders, French is today the most spoken language in the city. Due to the status as Brussels as the only bilingual region of Belgium, and the only significant area where members of the francophone and Flemish ethno-linguistic communities are in close contact with one another, this chapter will analyse consociational arrangements in the city. Of languages spoken at home in 2013, 38 per cent of inhabitants spoke French, 23 per cent French and another language (excluding Flemish), 17 per cent French and Flemish, 17 per cent neither French nor Flemish, and five per cent Flemish (BRIO 2013).

The contemporary state of Belgium features several regional parliaments based on linguistic territorial divisions, with the number of seats in each based on the population size of the respective Flemish-, francophone- and German-speaking communities. In contrast to those in Northern Ireland, Brussels's consociational arrangements are inherently corporate. The Parliament of the Brussels Capital Region was established in 1989 and, since 2004, elects 89 members: 72 from the francophone community and 17 from the Flemish community (Deschouwer 2009, pp. 51–53). Executive formation in Brussels is also corporate in character, with power sharing in place in the Parliament. Government formation in the Brussels Capital Region is by voluntary coalition and is loosely proportional, with the French-speaking community allocated two ministers, two secretaries of state and the Minister-President, and the Flemish-speaking community allocated two ministers and a secretary of state. Although consociational arrangements in Brussels are primarily corporate, the formation of coalitions on a voluntary basis is evidence of some liberal components being included within them.

Elections to all levels of government in Belgium are contested using semi-open party list PR, with legislative seats allocated using the d'Hondt formula (Deschouwer 2009, p. 112). All elections in Brussels are contested by parties representing both the francophone and Flemish language groups and are obliged to designate their linguistic affiliation, with a separate list for each designation on ballot papers. Unlike in the Northern Ireland Assembly, there is no alternative designation (Pilet 2005, p. 403).

This creates a difficulty for national parties in that they are obliged to select one, or both, language designations. Voters in Brussels are not, however, required to select a linguistic identity for electoral purposes and may, therefore, choose to vote for a party from either the francophone or Flemish list, regardless of their own ethno-linguistic background (Pilet 2005, p. 403).

Similarly to some in Northern Ireland subscribing to a Northern Irish identity, a Brussels identity does exist (Cartrite 2002, p. 64). There are several factors influencing this identity, including the city's constitutional distinctiveness within Belgium, its capital city status, the presence of European institutions and a significant level of immigration (Govaert 1998, pp. 236–38, quoted in Cartrite 2002, p. 64). As is the case in Northern Ireland, however, it is difficult to gauge how genuine this identity is and the extent to which it overlaps with the more traditional Flemish and francophone (including Walloon) identities, and whether it is showing any signs of genuinely transcending them.

It is clear from recent election results that ethno-linguistic parties are the mainstay of politics in Brussels and, in common with Northern Ireland, the city can be characterised as having an ethnic party system. In the Brussels Capital district at the 2014 Belgian federal, European Parliament and Brussels regional elections, parties representing one of the two ethno-linguistic communities collectively secured more than 90 per cent of the popular vote (Elections 2014). The only genuinely cross-communal party, *Pro Bruxsel*, submits candidates to both the francophone and Flemish language lists due to corporate consociational requirements that do not allow for an alternative designation, such as 'Other', as in the Northern Ireland Assembly. The party has very limited electoral support. At the 2014 election to the Parliament of the Brussels Capital Region, *Pro Bruxsel*'s Flemish language list received 1.24 per cent and its French-language list received 0.72 per cent of the respective electoral language bloc votes (Elections 2014). This electoral results data indicates that there is very little support for cross-communal parties in Brussels, which in turn suggests that a shared, common identity is showing few signs of being realised.

The inability of consociationalism to achieve a common, shared identity in Brussels can be demonstrated by analysing recent election manifestos of the largest francophone party in the city, *Parti Socialiste*, and the largest Flemish party, *Open Vlaamse Liberalen en Democraten* (Open VLD). In its manifesto for the 2014 Brussels regional election, *Parti Socialiste* (2014) does, however, focus significantly on areas such as health, education and the economy. There is also some, albeit limited, discussion of integration initiatives, such as encouraging citizens of Brussels to learn Flemish and English. The manifesto, nevertheless, makes significant reference to promoting the French-speaking community and its language by, for example, referring to the need for non-Belgian citizens of Brussels to speak French as a prerequisite for employment and social integration, and calls for the abolition of fees imposed on Belgian booksellers to stock French-language texts published in France. It also promotes a position of 'otherness' towards the Flemish-speaking community by, for example, emphasising the link between Brussels and Wallonia, and by making significant reference to the Belgian francophone population.

There are many commonalities between the approach of francophone *Parti Socialiste* and that of Flemish Open VLD (2014). The latter's manifesto for the 2014 Brussels regional election is very policy specific and focuses on many of the socio-economic issues emphasised by *Parti Socialiste*. It also makes some limited reference to integrative policies, including the need for Flemish-speaking children to learn French and vice versa, and the establishment of a 'culture dome' to bring together cultural organisations representing all communities in Brussels. Elsewhere, however, the manifesto makes significant reference to the needs of the Flemish-speaking community in Brussels by, for example, emphasising the necessity of Flemish language schools, libraries and community centres. It also promotes the need for Flemish to be spoken in hospitals. Unlike *Parti Socialiste*, though, Open VLD publishes campaign literature in languages other than Flemish (French and English) and therefore demonstrates some intention of appealing to francophone and other non-Flemish-speaking communities. Whilst the manifestos of ethno-linguistic parties operating in Brussels are less strident and more inclusive than those of many ethno-national parties in Northern Ireland, there is little doubt that the primary aim of these parties is to maximise the share of the vote from their respective francophone or Flemish community. This indicates that ethno-linguistic policies and rhetoric resonates with voters, which in turn suggests that whilst a Brussels identity does exist, it is not shared by the majority of its inhabitants. This is despite Brussels having a long history and experience of consociationalism compared to Northern Ireland.

Although ethno-linguistic parties in Brussels undoubtedly make more inclusive appeals than ethno-national parties in Northern Ireland, this finding can be explained by factors other than the possible moderating effect of consociational power sharing (Jarrett 2016a). The most significant influence is the ratio of the communities in Brussels, with francophones making up a large proportion of the population and Flemish speakers a comparatively small minority. This divergent population ratio explains why Flemish Open VLD also publishes campaign literature in French and English, as it recognises the potential of appealing beyond its own community to maximise its electoral support, whilst there is little incentive for francophone *Parti Socialiste* to adopt such a strategy. If this was in response to the existence of a genuinely common identity that is shared by a majority of the population, it would be expected that all parties in Brussels, whether francophone or Flemish, would demonstrate a willingness to engage with and appeal to voters from all communities. Other factors that explain the less strident approach of parties in Brussels compared to Northern Ireland include an absence of violent ethnic conflict and considerable levels of immigration affecting demographics. If a significant shared identity did exist, it could also be expected that moves would be underway to reform Brussels's corporate consociational arrangements by adopting more liberal practices, such as the establishment of an 'Other' linguistic designation category designed to accommodate this identity.

CONCLUSION

During his paper at the *Arend Lijphart Symposium* at Coventry University in May 2016, Lijphart (2016) referred to the Netherlands as a case where consociationalism had worked to break down divisions and achieve a shared identity, which rendered its consociational arrangements obsolete and resulted in their replacement in 1967. Divisions in the Netherlands were between Catholics and secular socialists (Lijphart 1977, p. 104). During the twentieth century, many states in Western Europe went through a process of secularisation, with religion no longer as significant as it once was. It is this, not any impact of consociationalism, that is responsible for the formation of a shared identity in the Netherlands. Ethnicity, however, remains salient in many divided societies and it is for this reason that such an identity transformation has not taken place in Northern Ireland and Brussels. This conclusion is corroborated by evidence from beyond Europe. In Malaysia, an informal consociation was imposed by the United Kingdom at the time of independence in 1957, with the Malay, Chinese and Indian ethnic groups recognised within a coalition government (Brown 2005, pp. 430–31). Despite a significant history and experience of consociationalism, Malaysia nevertheless remains a divided society, with ethnic parties reigning supreme and little evidence of genuinely cross-communal politics (Jarrett 2016b).

The purpose of this chapter has not been to dispute the role played by consociational power sharing in providing effective conflict management in many divided societies. It is instead to argue that some consociational-ists are unrealistic in what they consider may be the parameters of the approach. Consociationalism does what it is designed to do: manage conflict through recognising and accommodating different groups in a divided society. It has been shown that it does not have the potential to bring about a genuinely shared, common identity as some claim it may. This conclusion establishes the limits of consociational theory.

Acknowledgements Please note that some parts of this chapter have been previously published in two publications: Jarrett, H. (2016). Beyond Consociational Theory: Identity in Northern Ireland and Brussels. *Nationalism and Ethnic Politics, 22*(4), 412–432; and Jarrett, H. (2018). *Peace and Ethnic Identity in Northern Ireland: Consociational Power Sharing and Conflict Management.* Abingdon: Routledge.

References

BBC. (2013). *Spotlight Survey.* http://downloads.bbc.co.uk/tv/spotlight/survey.pdf. Accessed 23 Feb 2017.

BBC. (2016a). *NI Assembly: SDLP to Go into Opposition.* http://www.bbc.co.uk/news/uk-36337431. Accessed 1 Mar 2017.

BBC. (2016b). *NI Election 2016: Results.* http://www.bbc.co.uk/news/election/2016/northern_ireland/results. Accessed 23 Feb 2017.

Bingham Powell, G. (2000). *Elections as Instruments of Democracy: Majoritarian and Proportional Divisions.* New Haven/London: Yale University Press.

Bogaards, M. (1998). The Favourable Factors for Consociational Democracy: A Review. *European Journal of Political Research, 33,* 475–496.

BRIO. (2013). *BRIO-taalbarometer 3: diversiteit als norm.* Brussels: BRIO. http://www.briobrussel.be/assets/onderzoeksprojecten/brio_taalbarometer_3_brussel_2013.pdf. Accessed 23 Sept 2015.

Brown, G. K. (2005). Playing the (Non)Ethnic Card: The Electoral System and Ethnic Voting Patterns in Malaysia. *Ethnopolitics, 4*(4), 429–445.

Cartrite, B. (2002). Contemporary Ethnopolitical Identity and the Future of the Belgian State. *Nationalism and Ethnic Politics, 8*(3), 43–71.

Democratic Unionist Party (DUP). (2017). *Our Plan for Northern Ireland: The DUP Manifesto for the 2017 Northern Ireland Assembly Election.* Belfast: DUP.

Deschouwer, K. (2009). *The Politics of Belgium: Governing a Divided Society.* Basingstoke: Palgrave Macmillan.

Devenport, M. (2012, December 11). Census Figures: NI Protestant Population Continuing to Decline. *BBC*. http://www.bbc.co.uk/news/uk-northern-ireland-20673534. Accessed 21 Apr 2015.

Dixon, P. (1997). Paths to Peace in Northern Ireland (I): Civil Society and Consociational Approaches. *Democratization, 4*(2), 1–27.

Eckstein, H. (1966). *Division and Cohesion in Democracy: A Study of Norway*. Princeton: Princeton University Press.

Elections. (2014). *Resultats Officieux*. http://bru2014.irisnet.be/web5Site/fr/bru/results/results_graph_BRR21004.html. Accessed 24 Sept 2015.

Govaert, S. (1998). A Brussels Identity? A Speculative Interpretation. In K. Deprez & L. Vos (Eds.), *Nationalism in Belgium: Shifting Identities, 1780–1995* (pp. 229–239). New York: St. Martin's Press.

Horowitz, D. L. (2003). The Northern Ireland Agreement: Clear, Consociational and Risky. In J. McGarry (Ed.), *Northern Ireland and the Divided World: Post-agreement Northern Ireland in Comparative Perspective* (pp. 89–105). Oxford: Oxford Scholarship Online.

Jarrett, H. (2016a). Beyond Consociational Theory: Identity in Northern Ireland and Brussels. *Nationalism and Ethnic Politics, 22*(4), 412–432.

Jarrett, H. (2016b). Consociationalism and Identity in Ethnically Divided Societies: Northern Ireland and Malaysia. *Studies in Ethnicity and Nationalism, 16*(3), 401–415.

Lijphart, A. (1968). *The Politics of Accommodation: Pluralism and Democracy in the Netherlands*. Berkeley: University of California Press.

Lijphart, A. (1969). Consociational Democracy. *World Politics, 21*(2), 207–225.

Lijphart, A. (1977). *Democracy in Plural Societies: A Comparative Exploration*. New Haven/London: Yale University Press.

Lijphart, A. (1985). *Power-Sharing in South Africa*. Berkeley: Institute of International Studies, University of California.

Lijphart, A. (1995). Self-Determination Versus Pre-Determination of Ethnic Minorities in Power Sharing Systems. In W. Kymlicka (Ed.), *The Rights of Minority Cultures* (pp. 275–287). Oxford: Oxford University Press.

Lijphart, A. (1996). The Framework Document on Northern Ireland and the Theory of Power-Sharing. *Government and Opposition, 31*(3), 267–274.

Lijphart, A. (2016, May 10). *Reflections on Half a Century of Consociationalism*. Paper Presented at the *Arend Lijphart Symposium*, Coventry University.

Lorwin, V. (1971). Segmental Pluralism: Ideological Cleavages and Political Cohesion in the Smaller European Democracies. *Comparative Politics, 3*(2), 141–175.

McCulloch, A. (2012). Consociational Settlements in Deeply Divided Societies: The Liberal-Corporate Distinction. *Democratization, 21*(3), 501–518.

McGarry, J. (2007). Iraq: Liberal Consociation and Conflict Management. In B. Roswell, D. Malone, & M. Bouillon (Eds.), *Iraq: Preventing Another Generation of Conflict* (pp. 169–188). Boulder: Lynne Rienner Press.

McGarry, J., & O'Leary, B. (2007). Iraq's Constitution of 2005: Liberal Consociation as Political Prescription. *International Journal of Constitutional Law, 5*(4), 670–698.

McGarry, J., & O'Leary, B. (2008a). Consociation and Its Critics: Northern Ireland After the Belfast Agreement. In S. Choudhry (Ed.), *Constitutional Design for Divided Societies: Integration or Accommodation?* (pp. 369–408). Oxford: Oxford University Press.

McGarry, J., & O'Leary, B. (2008b). Iraq's Constitution of 2005: Liberal Consociation as Political Prescription. In S. Choudhry (Ed.), *Constitutional Design for Divided Societies: Integration or Accommodation?* (pp. 342–368). Oxford: Oxford University Press.

McGarry, J., & O'Leary, B. (2009a). Argument: Power Shared After the Deaths of Thousands. In R. Taylor (Ed.), *Consociational Theory: McGarry and O'Leary and the Northern Ireland Conflict* (pp. 15–84). Abingdon: Routledge.

McGarry, J., & O'Leary, B. (2009b). Under Friendly and Less-Friendly Fire. In R. Taylor (Ed.), *Consociational Theory: McGarry and O'Leary and the Northern Ireland Conflict* (pp. 333–388). Abingdon: Routledge.

Mitchell, P. (1999). The Party System and Party Competition. In P. Mitchell & R. Wilford (Eds.), *Politics in Northern Ireland* (pp. 91–116). Boulder: Westview Press.

Mitchell, P. (2014). The Single Transferable Vote and Ethnic Conflict: The Evidence from Northern Ireland. *Electoral Studies, 33*(1), 246–257.

Nagle, J., & Clancy, M.-A. (2012). Constructing a Shared Public Identity in Ethno Nationally Divided Societies: Comparing Consociational and Transformationist Approaches. *Nations and Nationalism, 18*(1), 78–97.

Nordlinger, E. (1972). *Conflict Regulation in Divided Societies.* Cambridge, MA: Center for International Affairs, Harvard University.

Northern Ireland Life and Times Survey (NILT). (2009). Which of These Best Describes the Way You Think of Yourself? *ARK.* http://www.ark.ac.uk/nilt/2009/Community_Relations/NINATID.html. Accessed 21 Apr 2015.

O'Flynn, I. (2009). Progressive Integration (and Accommodation, Too). In R. Taylor (Ed.), *Consociational Theory: McGarry and O'Leary and the Northern Ireland Conflict* (pp. 264–278). Abingdon: Routledge.

O'Leary, B. (1999). The 1998 British-Irish Agreement: Power-Sharing Plus. *Scottish Affairs, 26,* 15–37.

Open Vlaamse Liberalen en Democraten (Open VLD). (2014). *Verkiezingsprogramma 2014.* Brussel: Open VLD.

Parti Socialiste. (2014). *PS Programme 2014: Elections europeennes, federales et regionales.* Bruxelles: PS.

Pilet, J.-B. (2005). The Adaption of the Electoral System to the Ethno-Linguistic Evolution of Belgian Consociationalism. *Ethnopolitics, 4*(4), 397–411.

Reilly, B. (2012). Centripetalism: Cooperation, Accommodation and Integration. In S. Wolff & C. Yakinthou (Eds.), *Conflict Management in Divided Societies* (pp. 57–66). Abingdon: Routledge.

Sinn Féin. (2017). *Sinn Féin Assembly Manifesto 2017.* Dublin: Sinn Féin.

Stationery Office. (2008). *The Eighteenth Report of the International Monitoring Commission.* London: The Stationery Office.

Taylor, R. (2009a). The Injustice of a Consociational Solution to the Northern Ireland Problem. In R. Taylor (Ed.), *Consociational Theory: McGarry and O'Leary and the Northern Ireland Conflict* (pp. 309–329). Abingdon: Routledge.

Taylor, R. (2009b). Introduction: The Promise of Consociational Theory. In R. Taylor (Ed.), *Consociational Theory: McGarry and O'Leary and the Northern Ireland Conflict* (pp. 1–11). Abingdon: Routledge.

Tonge, J., & Gomez, R. (2015). Shared Identity and the End of Conflict? How Far Has a Common Sense of 'Northern Irishness' Replaced British or Irish Allegiances Since the 1998 Good Friday Agreement? *Irish Political Studies, 30*(2), 276–298.

Wolff, S. (2012). Consociationalism: Power Sharing and Self-Governance. In S. Wolff & C. Yakinthou (Eds.), *Conflict Management in Divided Societies* (pp. 23–56). Abingdon: Routledge.

Yakinthou, C., & Wolff, S. (2012). Introduction. In S. Wolff & C. Yakinthou (Eds.), *Conflict Management in Divided Societies* (pp. 1–20). Abingdon: Routledge.

CHAPTER 4

What Politicians Can Teach Academics: 'Real' Politics, Consociationalism and the Northern Ireland Conflict

Paul Dixon

INTRODUCTION

Consociationalism is a highly influential but controversial theory of conflict management because it is based on a discredited Primordialist view of conflict and as a consequence prescribes segregation, or 'voluntary apartheid' and authoritarian rule by 'elite cartel' (Lijphart 1977). Consociationalists have claimed over 40 favourable case studies (Table 4.2) as diverse as the Soviet Union, Switzerland, the Lebanon, South Africa and Sri Lanka (Lijphart 1985: 84). Consociationalists are positivists who claim that they are neutral observers of the 'facts'. They are 'realists' because they are prepared to see and accept the world 'as it is' and define themselves against more optimistic, integrationist advocates of the idealist 'Civil Society' approach (Dixon 1997a, 2011a, 2017). Consociationalists appear unconcerned that their theory reinforces the arguments of 'chauvinist' nationalists, racists and fascists because their commitment is to the 'truth'

P. Dixon (✉)
Birkbeck College, University of London, London, UK

© The Author(s) 2018
M. Jakala et al. (eds.), *Consociationalism and Power-Sharing in Europe*, International Political Theory,
https://doi.org/10.1007/978-3-319-67098-0_4

55

and 'objectivity'. Consociationalists are powerful within the academy and seek to use this power to influence the policy debate. They have acted as advisers in various conflict situations including South Africa, Northern Ireland and Iraq.

On Northern Ireland, Consociationalists claim the peace process (1994–), the Belfast Agreement (1998) and the St Andrews Agreement (2006). 'Civil Society' critics argue that the peace process is Consociational and, therefore, this is problematic because its institutions reinforce the most antagonistic and 'sectarian' forces in Northern Ireland without providing sufficient support for integration, reconciliation and the erosion of communal divisions. By contrast, a Constructivist Realist approach argues that both the first (1972–74) and second (1994–) peace processes pursued the goal of integrationist 'power sharing' based on the 'moderate' political parties designed to undermine the communalisation and polarisation of politics (Dixon 1997a, b, 2008). The success of the second peace process is the result of a 'pragmatic realist' approach to negotiations that has involved deception and creative 'political skills' in order to give political actors the flexibility or 'wriggle room' to achieve accommodation. The peace process is a triumph of politics and 'pragmatic realism' from which advocates of the 'Civil Society' and Consociational approaches to conflict management might learn (Dixon 2002, 2017).

The peace process is not Consociational because it does not fulfil the definition—both description and prescription—set out in Arend Lijphart's classic *Democracy in Plural Societies* (1977). The definition of Consociationalism has constantly changed as its advocates attempt to capture favourable case studies, distance themselves from unfavourable ones and mitigate the damage from critics to their theory. This pattern is apparent in the evolution of Consociational theory on Northern Ireland. While Lijphart has written about Northern Ireland, his followers, John McGarry and Brendan O'Leary (MOL), have made a more extensive attempt to 'revise' Consociational theory to claim Northern Ireland for Consociationalism and, more recently, Iraq after 2003. Consociationalists rejected Northern Ireland as a supporting case study before the Irish Republican Army (IRA's) ceasefire 1994 and then embraced it afterwards. Consociationalism has shifted from the pessimistic conservative realism of its origins towards a more optimistic liberal idealism. McGarry and O'Leary reinvented 'Revisionist' and 'Complex' Consociationalism to more convincingly claim Northern Ireland and then 'Complex Consociationalism' to justify the invasion of Iraq and its 2005 constitution.

Consociationalism's constant redefinition allows it to be successfully marketed as 'all things to all people'. But this has made the theory incoherent and disguised its normative implications. The success of Consociationalism, it is argued, is the result of the political and rhetorical skills of its powerful academic advocates (Lustick 1997; Dixon 2011a; Dixon 2018).

This chapter:

1. First, argues the 'classic' Consociationalism is a universal, conservative realist and nationalist theory of conflict management that is constructed on a primordial foundation and, therefore, prescribes segregation and rule by 'elite cartel'.
2. Second, it is argued that Consociationalism takes a positivist approach to the social sciences and this emphasis on descriptive theory influences its conservative nationalism and realism. Since 1977, however, Consociationalism has reinvented itself as a liberal idealist and normative theory tending to deny its primordial, segregationist and elitist origins.
3. Third, Consociationalists have tried to capture the Northern Ireland peace process to enhance the credibility of their theory and to pursue a neo-nationalist agenda. Yet there is little or no evidence that the negotiators of the peace process were influenced by Consociationalism and its prescriptions of segregation and elitism were explicitly rejected.

Interpreting Consociationalism: Primordial, Segregationist and Elitist

The Dutch political scientist Arend Lijphart based Consociational theory on his interpretation of how the Netherlands managed 'plural conflict' between 1917 and 1967. In his seminal work, *Democracy in Plural Societies* (1977) he argued that the Dutch experience was a model for the global management of conflict. Consociationalism is a universal, one size fits all, solution to conflict in 'plural societies'. A full definition of Consociational theory logically contains a description or diagnosis of conflict and prescriptions for managing it (unless we know what is wrong with the patient how can we prescribe treatment?). It was originally built on a Primordialist foundation that describes 'ethnic identities' as biological and deeply rooted in human nature. This gives Consociational theory a strong structuralist orientation suggesting that these primordial identities are 'facts' to be accepted and worked around rather than challenged and remade. Consociationalism, therefore, prescribes segregation of ethnic groups into ethnic pillars that will be dominated by their respective ethnic elites. This cartel of ethnic elites is assumed to be benign and to have the power to manage conflict through cooperation over the heads and often against the wishes of their ethnic pillar. Consociationalism's four institutional prescriptions are implemented to achieve segregation and rule by elite cartel. There are three key elements to Consociationalism (Lijphart specified seven 'favourable conditions' which Consociationalists now usually ignore):

1. Description or diagnosis of conflict: Primordial
2. Prescription: Segregation and rule by elite cartel
3. Four institutional prescriptions:

    (a) Grand coalition—the political leaders of all significant elements should share power in a *consensual or cooperative* coalition: 'Elite cooperation is the primary distinguishing feature of consociational democracy' (Lijphart 1977: 1, 21, 5).
    (b) Proportional representation (PR)—in the distribution of government resources and List system of PR in elections since it tends to give elites control over selection of candidates and does not provide incentives for cross-community voting (Lijphart 1977: 25).
    (c) Mutual veto—a minority veto on vital rights and autonomy.
    (d) Autonomy—maximise each pillar's self-government.

'Civil Society' and Constructivist Realist critics of Consociationalism are not necessarily opposed to the four institutional prescriptions but their implementation in order to achieve segregation and rule by elite cartel rather than integration. The tendency of Consociationalists has been to retreat from a full definition towards an emphasis on four institutional prescriptions precisely because this conceals the Primordial foundation and normative implications of the theory. It is the conservative theory behind Consociationalism's segregationist and elitist prescriptions that make the four institutional recommendations Consociational (Dixon 2005).

Defenders of Consociationalism continue to insist that it is not based on Primordialism. Lijphart has admitted that it is, in 1993 he stated: '...

in my earlier writings, I tended to accept the primordialist interpretation of ethnic divisions and ethnic conflict'. He argued that his description of 'ethnic differences' as an 'unalterable fact' was 'rhetorical hyperbole' (Lijphart 1993: 94–5, 2001: 11; Lustick 1997: 110). Primordialists argue that 'ethnic' and national identities are natural and unchangeable aspects of 'human nature' that exert a very powerful, structuralist influence on action. Accordingly people favour their own ethnic group over others and this makes 'plural societies' highly unstable and 'unnatural'. Radical nationalists have used Primordialism to provide intellectual legitimacy for murderous ethnic chauvinism arguing that a state for every nation is the natural and inevitable outcome of primordial attachments (Jenkins 1997: 44). The widespread discrediting of Primordialism has led some Consociationalists to drop Primordialism and embrace an Ethnonationalist perspective that bases its essentialist arguments on 'culture' rather than 'biology' even though the implications are the same. In 2001, Lijphart embraced constructivism even though this position undermines the foundation on which Consociationalism is built (Lijphart 2001). Segregation may not be necessary if identities can be reconstructed into less antagonistic forms and other measures taken to ameliorate conflict.

Consociationalists seek to avoid conflict between primordial actors from different groups by reducing contact between them. This leads to a preference for the segregation of groups or 'voluntary apartheid'.

> Consociational theory differs from other theories of integration not only in its refutation of the thesis that cultural fragmentation necessarily leads to conflict, but also in its insistence that distinct lines of cleavage among subcultures may actually help rather than hinder peaceful relations among them. Because *good social fences may make good political neighbours, a kind of voluntary apartheid policy may be the most appropriate solution for a divided society. Political autonomy for the different subcultures is a crucially important element of a Consociational system, because it reduces contacts, and hence strain and hostility, among the subcultures at the mass level.* (Lijphart 1971: 11; on Consociationalism as voluntary apartheid see also Lijphart 1969: 219 *my emphasis*)

Consociationalists favour the *consolidation* and *reinforcement* of these group identities in order to make them into the stable pillars on which communal elites can build a settlement (Lijphart 1977: 42). The image of pillars suggests strong but completely separate columns: 'Consociational democracy results in the division of society into more homogenous and self-contained elements' (Lijphart 1977: 48). The territorial intermingling of nationalists and unionists in Northern Ireland was seen as a negative condition for Consociationalism (Lijphart 1977: 140–41).

The 'primary instrument' of Consociationalism is an 'elite cartel' involving '…government by a grand coalition of the political leaders of all significant segments of the plural society' (Lijphart 1977: 25). While consensus did not exist at a mass level, it was achieved at the elite level and could be imposed on a deferential population. What matters for Lijphart is the consensual behaviour of elites and rejection of the adversarial style of politics (Bogaards 2000: 404, 405). Consociation, with its prescription of rule by elite consensus and popular deference, is not very democratic. It is applied to and may be more compatible with authoritarian states.

Consociationalists oppose social integration because they claim it is 'unwanted' and likely to antagonise rather than ameliorate a conflict situation (McGarry and O'Leary 1995b: 210). MOL conclude their attack on integrationist initiatives, 'it must always be remembered … at best … [they] will fall short of what is required to resolve the conflict, and at worst they may even deflect attention and energy from the crucial political measures necessary to change the logic of the cruel game in which the participants are presently trapped' (McGarry and O'Leary 1995b: 307).

CRITIQUING CONSOCIATIONALISM

Consociationalism takes a positivist approach to the social sciences and this explains some of the drawbacks of this theory. Positivism applies the methods of the natural sciences to the social sciences to uncover useful objective knowledge, developing general, universal laws from which hypotheses can be made to predict the future. The positivist sees herself standing outside the context in which she pursues research and is, therefore, able to find scientific truth and produce facts that are free from value judgements and personal subjective elements. Positivists, therefore, are 'precise' in their 'scientific' use of concepts. They present themselves as empiricists who see normative work as completely separate.

Post-positivists reject this approach and argue that all descriptive and normative theory contains elements of both types of theorising (Bell 2010: 7). There is no neutral point from which to observe the world so social science cannot be 'objective' and 'value free'. Theory and experiment are not separable; rather theory affects both the facts we focus on and how we interpret them. Ironically Consociationalism's primordialist (or essentialist) assumption suggests that the Consociational analyst herself will be determined or strongly influenced by their 'ethnic background' and this will affect their research. The existence of diverse interpretations of the Northern Ireland conflict and Consociational theory itself lead Consociationalists to try and explain this away by claiming that they are the only 'objective' academics. Post-positivists see the assertion of 'scientific neutrality' and empiricism, therefore, as rhetoric that disguises Consociationalism's normative position: a conservative realist, nationalism (leading to prescriptions of segregation and elitism). Positivism tends to be conservative because of its emphasis on explaining what is rather than what could and should be. The assumption of regularity underpins this conservatism and it makes problematic explaining political change, such as the peace process (Hay 2002).

Conservative Realism and Descriptive Theory

Arend Lijphart, since his classic formulation in 1977, has shifted from Consociationalism as descriptive theory (realism) to Consociationalism as normative theory (idealism). It is no longer necessary, he argues, to have an analysis of conflict in order to prescribe for that conflict (Lijphart in Bogaards 2015: 92). There is an affinity between Positivism and Conservative Realism. They portray themselves as reluctantly concluding that the 'fact' of Primordialism has to be accepted and worked around, whereas 'Civil Society' Idealists 'wish away' these 'facts'. The spectre of barbaric 'ethnic' war is used to justify the implementation of Consociationalism's unpalatable, conservative prescriptions and advocacy of emergency 'triage'. This world-weary 'realism' sees a gap between popular, publicly proclaimed idealism and the reality of private primordialism and antagonism. The choice posed by Consociationalists is between restrictive 'Consociational Democracy' and no democracy at all (Lijphart 1977: 48), and between segregation and elite control on the one hand and primordial slaughter on the other. This rhetorical strategy allows Consociationalists to claim credit where conflict becomes less violent (Northern Ireland after 1994) and to relinquish responsibility when conflict is more violent (Northern Ireland 1975–94). Their problem is that their pessimistic primordialism led them to predict that the conflict was getting worse when it was getting better. In addition, they cannot convincingly account for the success of the peace process, which exceeded Consociationalism's limited institutional prescriptions and was explicitly integrationist.

There is ambiguity over the definition and desirability of Consociationalism. Consociationalists have adopted three normative strategies:

1. *Pessimistic Realism*: Primordial conflict is ubiquitous and although Consociationalism is anti-democratic and reinforces antagonistic communal identities it is the best 'triage' that can be hoped for in such tragic circumstances. Integration and contact will make conflict worse rather than better. Since Consociationalists have a segregationist orientation and say little about how an integrated society will be created, it is difficult to take seriously their hope that the pillars will naturally erode (Lijphart 1977: 228).
2. *Conservative Nationalist Idealism*: Consociationalists may, on the other hand, celebrate the creation of a 'voluntary apartheid' and rule by elite cartel because it is their political ideal (McGarry and O'Leary 1995b: 338). MOL see the triumph of the hard-line parties in Northern Ireland and the continuing degree of segregation and lack of grass roots reconciliation as unproblematic (McGarry and O'Leary 2009a: 26).
3. *Liberal Idealist Interventionism*: According to this perspective Consociationalism is a democratic and normative ideal. 'Revisionist' and 'Complex' Consociation incorporates 'liberalism' and 'integration'. This perspective is idealistic and 'transformationalist', they are optimistic that the invasion of Iraq and the correct constitutional architecture will create a new liberal democracy (O'Leary 2009).

While Consociationalists claim to be Realists they make 'unrealistic' assumptions about politics. There is an important contradiction between Consociationalism's primordialist, or essentialist, assumptions and its elite prescriptions. Primordialism suggests powerful, unstoppable, *structural* forces coming from the people below. This attributes little agency to politics and political actors. To then expect these highly constrained elites to be able to manage conflict is, therefore, contradictory. Consociationalists make heroic or idealist assumptions that political elites:

1. Will be motivated to engage in consensual, conflict management.
2. Will be able to lead their parties and voters to a settlement that may be against their wishes.
3. Will engage in a cooperative, power sharing executive (McGarry and O'Leary 1995b: 339–40).

Presumably, if these conditions of elite dominance do not exist then Consociationalists would favour the engineering of these authoritarian conditions. When Consociation was seen to have failed in Northern Ireland, Consociationalists prescribed authoritarian 'solutions' that had little party or popular consent, such as repartition and joint authority (see below). Consociationalists have an 'unrealistic' and unsophisticated interpretation of politics. In the 'real world' political elites are not necessarily benign, enjoy a complex range of relations with supporters and can rarely be sure of their followers and the intentions of rivals. This crude understanding of politics helps to explain why they have such an uncompromising attitude towards the negotiation of the peace process and have advocated such partisan 'solutions' to the Northern Ireland conflict.

It is important that Consociationalists carefully define their theory because it echoes the assumptions of chauvinist nationalists and racists. Rupert Taylor has argued that Lijphart's statements on apartheid in South Africa appeared to offer a defence of National Party policy by assuming that ethnic differences were 'an unalterable fact' and that the apartheid government's policies had succeeded not in manufacturing differences but in counteracting and softening them (Taylor 1994: 166). The Consociational maxim that 'good fences make good neighbours' finds its echo on the radical right (Lijphart 1977: 140; McGarry and O'Leary 1995b: 210). MOL have also suggested that, '...There may, sadly, be something in the North American folk wisdom that white liberals are those whites who do not live near blacks' (McGarry and O'Leary 1995a: 855). Consociationalists support a 'separate but equal' policy but they have played down the role of materialism in managing conflict. Lijphart did not see as significant inequality between or among Catholics and Protestants in Northern Ireland (Lijphart 1991: 497).

There is ample evidence that the promotion of contact in the right context and of the right quality can have a beneficial effect in reducing prejudice and conflict (Hewstone et al. 2005). There is strong evidence of a desire for integration in Northern Ireland. Certainly political parties do not openly advocate segregation and opinion polls show considerable support for integration, people prefer to work in mixed-religion workplaces, live in mixed-religion areas, do not mind if people marry people from the 'other' religion and send their children to mixed-religion schools.[1] There is some truth in the claim that people tend to conceal some of their true beliefs from pollsters, but even allowing for this the evidence of support for integration is consistent and substantial.

Liberal Idealism and Normative Theory

Consociationalists have combined Conservative Realism with Liberal Idealism. Lijphart had argued that Consociationalism was descriptive theory that described the world as it really is and based on that analysis arrived at its theory of conflict and four prescriptions. Increasingly, he argued that Consociationalism was not descriptive but normative and by the mid-80s he was arguing for its democratic merits (Lustick 1997: 111–12; Bogaards 2000: 402). Bogaards argues that by the early 90s, 'Consociationalism no longer derives its usefulness from the accuracy with which it describes existing political systems in relations to their divided societies, but from its usefulness as a democratic solution for divided societies such as South Africa. The main implication is that Consociationalism as a normative type becomes immune from empirical criticism' (Bogaards 2000: 408). In 2015 Lijphart argued that it is not necessary to diagnose conflict in order to prescribe for it.

> In a way I am more like an 'irrelevantist': we do not try to figure out what the causes of the ethnic conflict are, we just look at the ethnic conflict and see how it can be solved. (Bogaards 2015: 92)

This statement avoids controversy over the diverse possible interpretations of conflicts and correspondingly contrasting prescriptions for 'solving' it. Instead the same prescription is made for every conflict regardless of the context (Bogaards 2015: 92–3).

MOL have 'revised' Consociationalism to changing circumstances in order to capture a key case study, Northern Ireland, and to defend Consociationalism against charges that it promotes a normative conservative, realist and segregationist nationalism. Consociationalists at one point defined themselves against 'liberalism' and 'integrationism' but this limited the theory's appeal so revisions have taken place to incorporate these into 'Revisionist' or 'Complex' Consociationalism. MOL's Liberal Idealism was reinforced by their support for the invasion of Iraq in 2003 and its transformation through Consociation into a liberal democracy or a Western protectorate. Shortly after the invasion O'Leary stated: 'viable consociations that address ethno-national disputes may have to be the de facto or de jure protectorates of external powers'. He points out 'High commissioners appointed by great powers, as in Bosnia and Herzegovina, are indistinguishable from the prefects of protectorates' (O'Leary 2005a, b: xxxi). Another Consociationalist states: 'Consociation has become a tool favoured by the west for intervention in regions where its interests are threatened' (Kerr 2005: 40). O'Leary is an academic advisor to the British Neoconservative organisation the Henry Jackson Society.

MOL's Liberal Idealist and optimistic attitude towards the transformation of Iraq contrasted with their simultaneous advocacy of Consociationalism as 'a form of pragmatic realism' and 'political triage' (O'Leary 2005a, b: xviii). 'Pragmatic realism' and Consociationalism's essentialist and Primordialist assumptions might have suggested that the invasion of Iraq was unwise in removing the authoritarian power that prevented 'ethnoreligious' civil war. This 'pragmatic realism' was not in evidence in the way MOL promoted a partisan and uncompromising interpretation of the Northern Irish and Iraqi peace processes (Dixon 2011b).

All Things to All People? Defining and Redefining Consociationalism

Consociationalism has been constantly defined and redefined in a vague and elastic way that allows it to be marketed as 'all things to all people' (Barry 1975; Halpern 1986; Lustick 1997). Debates around the 'technical' aspects of the institutional prescriptions, for example over types of PR, have obscured the conservative nationalist theoretical framework that informs its prescriptions for conflict management. The elastic and vague definition of Consociationalism (see Table 4.1) allows its champions to claim favourable case studies and reject unfavourable ones, such as Rwanda. The full definition of Consociationalism, set out in *Democracy in Plural Societies* (1977), means that fewer case studies can be claimed and its segregationist and elitist prescriptions are exposed (column 2). This full definition can be reduced to four institutional prescriptions, to two 'primary characteristics', one 'primary instrument' (consensual 'Grand Coalition')

Table 4.1 The elasticity of consociationalism: from the full definition to half a 'primary instrument'

Consociationalism full definition	Full definition	Conditions and prescriptions	Four prescriptions	Two primary characteristics or instruments (grand coalition, autonomy)	One primary instrument (consensual, grand coalition)	Half primary instrument (participation, grand coalition)
Theory	✓	✗	✗	✗	✗	✗
Primordialism	✓	✗	✗	✗	✗	✗
Prescription	✓	✗	✗	✗	✗	✗
Segregation	✓	✗	✗	✗	✗	✗
Elite Cartel	✓	✓	✗	✗	✗	✗
Seven Conditions	✓	✓	✓	✗	✗	✗
Four Institutional Prescriptions	✓	✓	✓	✓	✗	✗
(4) Minority Veto	✓	✓	✓	✗	✗	✗
(3) Proportional	✓	✓	✓	✗	✗	✗
(2) Autonomy	✓	✓	✓	✓	✗	✗
(1) Grand Coalition	✓	✓	✓	✓	✓	✓

or half a 'primary instrument' (merely 'participation in Grand Coalition') (Lijphart 1977: 31). By reducing the definition Consociationalists can stretch their claim to more favourable cases, and they have claimed between 5 and over 40 cases. Table 4.2 illustrates this conceptual elasticity and the disagreements among Consociationalists about their theory. Reducing Consociationalism to four or less institutional prescriptions then means the theory suffers from what Brubaker calls the 'architectonic illusion', that the right constitutional architecture will 'solve' conflicts (Brubaker 2004). Consociationalists have also inaccurately used Consociationalism interchangeably with 'power sharing'. This suggests that any case of power sharing, even one with integrationist intent, can be claimed for Consociationalism.

The attempt to shrink the definition of Consociationalism in order to stretch the theory to incorporate such a wide variety of conflicts has placed a considerable strain on the theory's coherence. MOL invented 'Revisionist' and 'Complex' Consociationalism in order to more convincingly claim the Northern Ireland peace process and promote the theory as a solution to the conflict in Iraq. In Iraq, MOL redefined Consociationalism to reject the primary instrument of 'Grand Coalition', legitimise the exclusion of the 'Sunnis' from the Iraqi Constitution 2005 and promote the secessionist claims of the Kurds (Dixon 2011b). Grand coalition of all the significant segments is at the heart of Consociational theory (Lijphart 2007; McGarry 2001: 15). In 2008, however, MOL declared that Consociation required only 'some element of jointness' and 'does not require every community to be represented in government...' (McGarry et al. 2008: 58). Consociationalism's 'groupist' analysis (Brubaker 2004) led MOL to hold all 'Sunnis' collectively responsible for the crimes perpetrated by the Baathists. By contrast MOL (rightly) do not blame all 'Catholics' or 'nationalists' for the violence of the IRA (O'Leary 2009: 81, 19).

The proliferating definitions of Consociationalism add to the confusion about what Consociationalism is, what it is not and, therefore, whether it has been successful in managing conflict. This allows its advocates to claim success and reject failure. Consociationalism, according to MOL, can be, non-ethnic, democratic, non-democratic, regional, central, weak, ambivalent, complete, pluritarian, traditional, 'revisionist', corporate, liberal, rigid, concurrent, complete, semi, quasi, formal, informal and 'flexible'. 'Complex' consociation allows the combination of Consociationalism with 'one other additional strategy' such as integration or partition

Table 4.2 On countries claimed by leading consociationalists over time

Country	1977	1985	1995	1996	2002	2005	2007
	Lijphart	*Lijphart*	*MOL*	*Lijphart*	*Lijphart*	*O'Leary*	*Lijphart*
Afghanistan	✓					✓	✓
Antilles (NL)							✓
Austria	✓	✓		✓	✓	✓	✓
Belgium	✓	✓		✓	✓	✓	✓
Bosnia					✓	✓	✓
Burundi							✓
Canada	✓	✓	✓	✓	✓	✓	✓
Chile		✓					
Colombia		✓					
Cyprus	✓	✓		✓	✓		✓
Czechoslovakia				✓			✓
European Union				✓			✓
Fiji		✓	✓	✓			✓
Gabon		✓					
Gambia		✓					
Guyana		✓					
India	✓	✓		✓	✓		✓
Indonesia							
Iraq	✓	✓					
Israel	✓	✓		✓	✓		✓
Italy		✓					
Ivory Coast		✓					
Kenya				✓			
Kosovo							✓
Lebanon	✓	✓	✓	✓	✓	✓	✓

(continued)

Table 4.2 (continued)

	13 (or 9)	31	4	21	15	11	25
Liechtenstein							✓
Luxembourg						✓	✓
Malaysia	✓		✓			✓	✓
Macedonia					✓		✓
Netherlands	✓	✓				✓	✓
Nigeria	✓	✓		✓			✓
Northern Ireland							
Portugal		✓		✓	✓		✓
South Africa					✓		
Spain		✓		✓		✓	
Sri Lanka		✓		✓			✓
Sudan		✓		✓	✓		✓
Surinam	✓	✓			✓		
Switzerland	✓	✓					
Tanzania		✓					
Uruguay	✓	✓		✓			
USSR		✓		✓			
Venezuela		✓		✓			
Yugoslavia		✓					
Total 44 cases	13 (or 9)	31	4	21	15	11	25

(Lijphart 1985: 84, 'applied' also to European Community, Manitoba, New Brunswick and Northern Ireland; McGarry and O'Leary 1995b: 338; Lijphart 2002: 40–41; O'Leary 2005a: 3; Lijphart 2007: 5)

(O'Leary 2005a: 34). Consociationalism is defined against the adversarial, British majoritarian system but the 'post-war consensus' and the alternation of Labour and Conservative governments could qualify the UK as a 'diachronic grand coalition' and, therefore, Consociational (Dixon 1997c). This theoretical confusion obscures the primordialist, segregationist and elitist theoretical framework that continues to influence Consociationalist's interpretation of Consociational prescriptions except this normative position is obscured by academic jargon.

Ian Lustick, following the insights of Imre Lakatos, has argued that Consociational theory's academic success does not depend on its value as a coherent theory but is attributable to 'the relative abilities of scientist-protagonists to mobilize economic, reputational and institutional resources, both inside and outside the academy' (Lustick 1997: 89). Rhetorical considerations were apparent in Lijphart's conflation of power sharing with Consociationalism: 'Using "power sharing" instead [of Consociationalism] has greatly facilitated the process of communication beyond the confines of academic political science' (Lijphart 2007: 6). MOL's embrace of integration has similar rhetorical benefits: integrationists 'should not be allowed to monopolize a concept with positive connotations ... ' (McGarry and O'Leary 2009b: 378).

CONSOCIATIONALISM AND NORTHERN IRELAND

Consociationalism has mainly been interpreted to support a nationalist perspective on Northern Ireland. Consociationalism's institutional *prescriptions* may focus on maintaining the unity of a state but its *analysis* of conflict has led Consociationalists to advocate repartition, joint authority and protectorates. These reflect 'classic' Consociationalism's segregationist and elitist theory because the imposition of such policies reinforce communal identities and often go against popular consent. The 'first peace process' 1972–74 resulted in the power sharing experiment which lasted five months in 1974. In 1975 Lijphart prescribed repartition for Northern Ireland—an involuntary apartheid—in spite of the lack of popular or political support for that option (Lijphart 1975: 99). In 1977, he described the prospects for Consociationalism as 'overwhelmingly unfavourable' in 'the basically unfavourable environment of Northern Ireland' (Lijphart 1977: 137, 141). By 1991, Lijphart 'almost agree[d] with Rose' that the problem in Northern Ireland is that there is no solution' (Lijphart 1991: 496).

MOL's twists and turns on Northern Ireland were informed by Consociational theory's pessimistic primordial or essentialist interpretation of conflict and authoritarian prescriptions. In 1989, just four years after the 'failure' of the Anglo-Irish Agreement to 'coerce Consociationalism' MOL argued that 'Repartition is the drastic but logical solution to Consociational failures' (O'Leary 1989: 587–8). The 'essential conditions' for Consociationalism were not present and the Anglo-Irish Agreement (AIA) 1985 had not worked to develop these (McGarry and O'Leary 1990: 295). In 2004 MOL denounced their previous position since the threat of partition can be 'self-fulfilling and encourages pre-emptive ethnic expulsions...' (McGarry and O'Leary 2004: 43–44). By 2005, MOL were advising the Kurdistan National Assembly and they were arguing then that 'complex consociations' enable secession (O'Leary 2005a: 25–26). In January 1993 O'Leary had shifted from advocating partition to supporting joint authority, which involved joint British-Irish rule with little input from the people of Northern Ireland. This proposal had some sympathy among Irish nationalists and republicans but was opposed by the overwhelming majority of unionists. In 1989 MOL had argued that joint authority was unlikely to produce power sharing and more likely to create support for a unilateral declaration of independence by unionists (O'Leary 1989: 586). By 1995 they, again, acknowledged that imposing joint authority would be 'problematic' (McGarry and O'Leary 1995b: 372). In 1993 MOL's pessimistic essentialism led them to predict that the conflict was getting worse, ethnic antagonisms were 'being reforged rather than resolved' (O'Leary and McGarry 1993: 325). By 1995, they were arguing that the problem with Consociationalism was that 'it has not worked' (McGarry and O'Leary 1995b: 338).

Consociationalism's pessimistic essentialism could neither predict nor convincingly explain the peace process. MOL predicted the demise of the hard-line parties just as they were about to rise to dominance. In 1993 they concluded, '... Sinn Féin almost certainly cannot grow much in the foreseeable future, and may be beginning a permanent decline' (O'Leary and McGarry 1993: 324). In 1995, MOL suggested that, 'The party most threatened by long-term peace is therefore the DUP' (McGarry and O'Leary 1995b: 405). By 1998, they were arguing that '... As nationalist support grows through demographic change, hard line unionists will become a minority in the assembly – and that will require them to learn a new politics. ... Irish governments present and future will have to prepare for the possibility of a federal Ireland in which there will be a very significant British minority' (*The Guardian* 7 April 1998).

The IRA's ceasefire announced on 31st August 1994 and the publication of the Framework Documents in February 1995 turned Consociationalism's pessimistic primordialism into optimism. Lijphart and MOL now claimed, unconvincingly, that it was a British *conversion* to the principles of Consociationalism that had resulted in the peace process and the signing of the Good Friday or Belfast Agreement of 1998 (Lijphart 1996; McGarry and O'Leary 1995a; for a critique see Dixon 2001).

Why the Belfast Agreement Is Not Consociational?

The outline of the Belfast Agreement 1998 was widely anticipated and to a considerable extent it was shaped by what was perceived to be 'politically possible'. What was remarkable was that it won the support of the leadership of both Sinn Féin and the UUP, when the deal fell so far short of their previous, publicly stated positions. This was facilitated by 'creative ambiguity' in which the deal was sold to unionists as strengthening the Union and to nationalists as a step down the road to a united Ireland. Nonetheless, deception still had to be used to win sufficient unionist consent during the subsequent referendum campaign (Dixon 2013).

Consociationalists do not provide any evidence that the key actors that negotiated the peace process or the Belfast Agreement were influenced by Consociationalism. The memoirs and diaries of all leading actors do not mention Consociationalism. Dr Martin Mansergh, a former republican Fianna Fail TD and long-standing advisor on Northern Ireland to successive Irish Taoisigh, notably during the peace process, has explicitly rejected the assertion that Consociationalism was influential.

> Though I am familiar with academic research both from personal engagement and for family reasons (my father Nicholas Mansergh was an external examiner here in UCC [University College Cork] in the 1960s), it is nonetheless always a somewhat curious sensation to be faced with academic analysis of discussions and negotiations in which one has been a participant. While I was not deeply involved in Strand 1, the internal governance of Northern Ireland, I can remember a mild sense of shock listening to Professor Brendan O' Leary expound a year or two after the Good Friday Agreement the Consociational model underlying the creation of the Executive. I have my doubts whether Bertie Ahern or Tony Blair had ever

heard of the term either or been able to get their tongues round it, though no doubt some negotiators, particularly from the SDLP and backroom political scientists, were familiar with it. No doubt, there are many other examples where political scientists rationalise the more empirical efforts of pragmatic politicians and make crooked paths straight. (Martin Mansergh, 'Remarks by Dr. Martin Mansergh', University College Cork, 20 May 2014)

Consociationalist theorists claim that when there is no evidence of their theory on policymakers then Consociational agreements are the result of a 'natural' but unconscious creative political response by politicians (O'Leary 2005a, b: 18; Lijphart 2007: 269, 278). The problem is, as we have seen, Consociationalism is so vague and ambiguous that its definition can be manipulated to claim any favourable case study. MOL, however, have argued inconsistently that the BFA is 'unarguably Consociational' and that it was more complex than Consociationalism. If the BFA had been limited to Consociational institutions 'there would have been no settlement' (McGarry and O'Leary 2004: 348). Table 4.3 compares a full definition of Consociational theory (Lijphart 1977) and finds that it certainly does not accurately describe the conflict and its segregationist and elitist prescriptions were explicitly rejected. If we reduce Consociationalism to its four institutional features then it does bear some resemblance to some of the Agreement. Nevertheless, at its heart Consociationalism is supposed to have a consensual or cooperative power sharing Grand Coalition. By contrast the Executive has been more power dividing or splitting and adversarial, with ministers using their veto power to frustrate rivals.

The scope of the peace process extends beyond Consociationalism's 'architectonic illusion'. The most toxic issues were decommissioning, prisoner releases, reform of the police, demilitarisation, 'On the Runs', parading, dealing with the past and the flying of flags. In addition to this Consociationalism has nothing to say about the relationship between Northern Ireland, the UK, the Republic of Ireland, the USA and the international community. The proposals for a Civic Forum, elections and a referendum on the Agreement resembled more the democratic enthusiasm of the 'Civil Society' approach. There are commitments to promoting economic growth and social inclusion, new regional and development strategies, plans for reduction in the armed forces, the removal of security installations and emergency powers, a review of the criminal justice system

Table 4.3 Comparing and contrasting Consociational theory to the Northern Ireland peace process

Consociationalism	Northern Ireland peace process
Description or analysis of conflict	
Pessimistic primordialism	Optimism of peace process and agreement, radical shift in ideologies (SF, DUP)
Favourable conditions	
Not present in Northern Ireland	
Prescription	
Segregation	Explicit integrationism of Agreement. Social inclusion; community relations; equality; education; housing; human rights
Sceptical of democracy	Political process of negotiation
Negotiated by elite cartel, top down	Top down AND bottom up
	Participatory democracy: Civic Forum and referendum 1998
Consensual elite cartel, moderate	Adversarial but 'moderate', then 'hard line'
Power sharing	Power splitting (dividing), some sharing and use of veto against rivals
Four institutional prescriptions	
(1) Grand Coalition	(1) Power sharing, splitting or veto to obstruct ministerial rival
Power sharing	Opposition of SDLP/APNI/UUP 2016_–17
Consensual	Adversarial, very limited cooperation
Voluntary	D'Hondt
(2) Proportional Representation (List PR)	(2) PR STV. No proportionality in state resources, limited recruitment quotas for PSNI
(3) Mutual veto	(3) Partial veto. This leads to deadlock in the Executive because of lack of consensus
	External British veto used to suspend devolution and sovereignty
(4) Autonomy	(4) 'Two traditions' but also integrative bias of BFA
Extra consociational and institutional aspects of the BFA	
Security: Silence	Security: most important issues non-constitutional: decommissioning, prisoners, policing, demilitarisation, 'On the Runs'
	Policing: rejection of federated/segregated police structure

(*continued*)

Table 4.3   (continued)

Consociationalism	Northern Ireland peace process
External Dimension: Silence	External Dimension: British-Irish, All Ireland, US role, international mediation
Politics: Top Down	Politics: lacks a 'realistic' understanding of dynamic politics of peace making, top down and bottom up, 'constructive ambiguity' and pragmatic realism
Materialism and Reformism: Sceptical	Extensive reformist aspirations

and prisoner releases. The section 'Rights, Safeguards and Equality of Opportunity' reflects the explicitly integrationist dimension of the Agreement:

> ... An essential aspect of the reconciliation process is the promotion of a culture of tolerance at every level of society, including initiatives to facilitate and encourage integrated education and mixed housing. (BFA: 18 para 13)

There is support for the promotion of good community relations, reconciliation and mutual understanding including a Victims Commission. While there is discussion of respect for the Irish language and Ulster-Scots the Agreement also includes the languages of ethnic minority communities (BFA: 19 para 3). Consociationalists advocated segregated communal police forces for different areas of Northern Ireland but these were rejected (McGarry and O'Leary 2004: 403). The 50:50 (Catholic/Protestant) recruitment quota to the Police Service of Northern Ireland, to increase Catholic representation, is seen as a short-term necessity and the Policing Board includes representatives of civil society. The joint declaration by the British and Irish governments in 2003 reiterated their integrationist approach. They recognised 'the importance of building trust and improving community relations, tackling sectarianism and addressing segregation, including initiatives to facilitate and encourage integrated education and mixed housing' (Joint Declaration 2003, p. 8, para. 27). This integrationism has even survived SF/DUP power sharing. *Together: Building a United Community* (2013) produced by the First and Deputy First Minister is explicitly integrationist and seeks to address the issues that have perpetuated segregation.

Consociationalism's crude 'top down' analysis and prescriptions for politics combined with an uncompromising, nationalist interpretation of the peace process threatened to undermine rather than support the peace process. Consociationalists again played 'catch up' with events in Northern Ireland. After the 'triumph of extremes' in 2007 did they argue that this outcome was beneficial to the peace process, preventing 'ethnic outbidding' (Mitchell et al. 2009: 416). In 2009, they claimed victory and left Northern Ireland. Consociationalists saw as unproblematic the political dominance of the hard-line parties and continuing communalism and segregation believing these divisions would somehow naturally 'biodegrade' (McGarry and O'Leary 2009a, b: 68). In 1995 MOL argued that ethnic divisions are resilient and, 'rather than rapidly biodegradable', 'must be recognized rather than wished away' (McGarry and O'Leary 1995b: 338). In 'Consociational' Belgium, Lebanon and Bosnia communal divisions do not seem to have biodegraded in the way that Consociationalists predict for Northern Ireland.

Neo-Nationalist Consociationalists and the Demise of the Moderates

Consociationalists claim to be 'objective' political scientists but MOL have also admitted to being partisans of nationalism in Northern Ireland and the PUK/KDP in Iraq (O'Leary 2005b: xvii; Dixon 2011b: 315–17). MOL's support for the Anglo-Irish Agreement 1985 and Joint Authority (1993) were initiatives strongly opposed by unionists (nationalists would also oppose repartition). After 1994, MOL were 'Constitutional Traditionalists', who insisted that they had the only correct interpretation of the Agreement. Their uncompromising, neo-nationalist interpretation of the peace process undermined pro-Agreement unionism and the 'constructive ambiguity' necessary to allow that process to survive (Dixon 2008: 282–84). 'New Constitutionalists' argue that Agreements are necessarily more ambiguous, dynamic and open to interpretation to allow politicians to make peace (Hart 2001; Dixon 2008: 282–4). During the peace process political actors have deployed an array of 'political skills' including 'creative ambiguity' which has allowed political elites the 'wriggle room' to manage their key audiences and bring them to accommodation (Dixon 2002). The BFA, for example, was deliberately designed so that it could be presented as a victory for nationalists and unionists (Mowlam 2002: 231).

MOL's research conclusions were in tension with their normative neo-nationalism. MOL's opinion research suggested that it was pro-Agreement unionism that was most politically vulnerable in the wake of the BFA. They did not, however, connect this realisation with policy proposals to shore up pro-Agreement unionism but quite the opposite (Evans and O'Leary 2000: 98–99). In February 2000 they argued that the BFA prevented the British government from suspending devolution, even though this was likely to result in the end of UUP leader David Trimble's political career and a major, possibly fatal blow to the peace process (*The Guardian* 2 February 2000). The British government, however, suspended devolution and preserved Trimble's position so that he could participate in devolution later that year.

MOL also advocated the *unilateral* release of all paramilitary prisoners *prior* to the negotiations of the BFA. This proposal, again, lacked an understanding of the politics of the peace process because it expected unionists to make a major concession, on a highly sensitive issue and to get nothing in return. Paramilitary prisoner releases were conceded as part of the BFA but it caused so much controversy among unionists that it almost destroyed the deal (Dixon 2013). MOL's lack of criticism of nationalists reinforced the perception of partisanship. The IRA's continuing violence and other activities during the peace process were not deemed to constitute a breach of its ceasefire. The former Taoiseach, John Bruton, took O'Leary to task for calling for fresh elections and being too tolerant of the IRA's failure to disarm. In Summer 2001, O'Leary called for fresh assembly elections even though this threatened the prospects of both moderate unionists and nationalists (*The Guardian* 13 July 2001). Bruton criticised O'Leary's 'unrealistic view' arguing that his proposals would result in the triumph of the hard-line parties and deadlock the peace process (*Irish Times* 8 October 2001). After the triumph of the hard-line parties in 2007, MOL believed Consociationalism had secured the peace and focused their attention on Iraq.

Conclusion: Bringing Politics Back In

Lijphart's full and classic formulation of Consociationalism in *Democracy in Plural Societies* (1977) is an interesting example of a Primordial description of conflict leading logically to segregationist and elitist prescriptions for conflict management. This is why the theory was attractive to the apartheid regime in South Africa, because it echoes the assumptions of chauvinist nationalists and racists. The theory is a useful contrast to the 'Civil Society' approach, which has an instrumentalist description of conflict and integrationist approach to managing it (Dixon 1997a, 2011a, b).

Both approaches are problematic because of their crude understanding of politics. Neither Consociationalism's conservative realism nor '*Civil Society's*' idealism can accurately account for the success of the peace process and the triumph of politics (Dixon 2011a, 2017).

The definition of Consociationalism has become increasingly ambiguous, contradictory and elastic over the years. It can be interpreted to claim any successful case study and distance itself from, or be silent about, any unsuccessful case. Lijphart shifted from Consociationalism as both descriptive and prescriptive theory to a prescriptive theory that, illogically, claimed to require no analysis of conflict. During 1975–94 Consociationalists decided that the conditions for Consociationalism did not exist in Northern Ireland. But their Primordialist analysis of conflict, however, led them logically to segregationist and elitist prescriptions: repartition 1975; coercive Consociationalism 1989; repartition 1989 and Joint Authority 1993.

MOL have invented 'revised, complex' Consociationalism in an attempt to catch up with political practice and capture the Northern Ireland peace process. This 'success' is then used to justify the invasion of Iraq and its 2005 constitution. Consociationalists cannot credibly claim the Northern Ireland case when judged against the full and logical definition of Consociationalism as both diagnosis (Primordialism, essentialism) and prescription (segregation, elite cartel) (Lijphart 1977). This is the (segregationist, elitist) theory that informs the interpretation of Consociationalism's four institutional features. Consociationalism's 'Traditional Constitutionalism' has been used in an uncompromising pursuit of a neo-nationalist political agenda that threatened to undermine the 'pragmatic realism' necessary for political actors to achieve accommodation. In Iraq this intransigence was used in pursuit of a KDP/PUK political agenda that demonised and excluded the 'Sunni' minority (Dixon 2011b: 315–17).

The practice of British and Irish political actors has much to teach Consociational and 'Civil Society' academic theorists (Dixon 2017). Important political actors have taken a 'pragmatic realist' approach to negotiations and their judgement as to what is politically possible has driven the first (1972–74) and second (1994–) peace processes rather than the imposition of partisan agendas or narrow, institutional blueprints. British policy towards Northern Ireland is marked by continuity and 'tactical adjustments' and this explains why the two peace processes bear a considerable resemblance to one another. These two processes are as follows:

1. First promoted power sharing with an Irish dimension based on the 'moderate parties' but, arguably, were prepared to include those with paramilitary links.
2. Second,favoured integration in order to undermine the communalisation and polarisation of politics and consolidate agreement based on these 'moderate' parties.
3. Third, politicians took a 'pragmatic realist' approach to negotiations using 'political skills' (or for some, 'dirty politics') to achieve accommodation. Landmark agreements, such as BFA/StA, and ongoing negotiations reflect what was judged to be politically possible at the time, which often exceeded popular, media and academic expectations (Dixon 2008).

The failure of the 'moderate' parties at the 2003 Assembly Election led the governments to pursue 'Plan B' an accommodation between the DUP and Sinn Féin. This was achieved in 2007 and, although this arrangement is preferable to direct rule, it is, arguably, less ideal than power sharing based on the moderate parties. Nonetheless, given the constraints and opportunities facing political parties the Belfast and St Andrews Agreements were remarkable achievements and may have been, more or less, all that were politically possible in that context. Integrationist critics are right, nonetheless, to point to the problems created by a constitution that reinforces communalism and leads to deadlock and inefficient government. The task is not to be complacent about the governance of Northern Ireland but to seek further reforms—promoting reconciliation, integration and social justice—to consolidate peace process. But this should be addressed in a pragmatic realist way, judging what is 'politically possible', rather than attempting to impose 'ideal' solutions that might destabilise the still ongoing negotiations and renegotiations of the peace process.

NOTES

1. http://www.ark.ac.uk/nilt/results/comrel.html#contact.

BIBLIOGRAPHY

Barry, B. (1975). The Consociational Model and Its Dangers. *European Journal of Political Research, 3*(4), 393–412.
Bell, D. (2010). Ethics and World Politics: Introduction. In D. Bell (Ed.), *Ethics and World Politics*. Oxford: Oxford University Press.

Bogaards, M. (2000). The Uneasy Relationship Between Empirical and Normative Types in Consociational Theory. *Journal of Theoretical Politics, 12*(4), 394–423.

Bogaards, M. (2015). Making a Difference: An Interview with Arend Lijphart. *Comparative Governance and Politics, 9*(1–2), 83–96.

Brubaker, R. (1998). Myths and Misconceptions in the Study of Nationalism. In J. A. Hall (Ed.), *The State of the Nation.* Cambridge: Cambridge University Press.

Brubaker, R. (2004). *Ethnicity Without Groups.* Cambridge: Harvard University Press.

Dixon, P. (1997a). Paths to Peace in Northern Ireland (I): Civil Society and Consociational Approaches. *Democratization, 4*(2, Summer), 1–27.

Dixon, P. (1997b). Paths to Peace in Northern Ireland (II): Peace Process 1973–74, 1994–96. *Democratization, 4*(3, Autumn), 1–25.

Dixon, P. (1997c). Consociationalism and the Northern Ireland Peace Process: The Glass Half Full or Half Empty? *Nationalism and Ethnic Politics, 3*(3, Autumn), 20–36.

Dixon, P. (2001). British Policy Toward Northern Ireland 1969–2000: Continuity, Tactical Adjustment and Consistent 'Inconsistencies'. *British Journal of Politics and International Relations, 3*(3, Autumn), 340–368.

Dixon, P. (2002). Political Skills or Lying and Manipulation? The Choreography of the Northern Ireland Peace Process. *Political Studies, 50*(4), 725–741.

Dixon, P. (2005). Why the Good Friday Agreement in Northern Ireland Is Not Consociational. *Political Quarterly, 76*(3), 357–367.

Dixon, P. (2008). *Northern Ireland: The Politics of War and Peace* (2nd ed.). Basingstoke: Palgrave.

Dixon, P. (2011a). The Politics of Conflict: A Constructivist Critique of Consociational and Civil Society Theories. *Nations and Nationalism, 17*(4), 98–121.

Dixon, P. (2011b). Is Consociational Theory the Answer to Global Conflict? From the Netherlands to Northern Ireland and Iraq. *Political Studies Review, 9*(3, Autumn), 309–322.

Dixon, P. (2013). An Honourable Deception? The Labour Government, the Good Friday Agreement and the Northern Ireland Peace Process. *British Politics, 8*(2), 108–137.

Dixon, P. (2017). The 'Real' and 'Dirty' Politics of the Northern Ireland Peace Process: A Constructivist Realist Critique of Idealism and Conservative Realism. In T. White (Ed.), *Theories of International Relations and Northern Ireland.* Manchester: Manchester University Press.

Dixon, P. (2018). *Performing the Northern Ireland Peace Process.* Basingstoke: Palgrave.

Evans, G., & O'Leary, B. (2000). Northern Irish Voters and the British-Irish Agreement: Foundations of a Stable Consociational Settlement? *Political Quarterly, 71*(1), 78–101.

Halpern, S. (1986). The Disorderly Universe of Consociational Democracy. *West European Politics, 9*(2), 181–197.

Hart, V. (2001). Constitution-Making and the Transformation of Conflict. *Peace and Change, 26*(2), 153–177.

Hay, C. (2002). *Political Analysis.* Basingstoke: Palgrave.

Hewstone, M., et al. (2005). Intergroup Contact in a Divided Society: Challenging Segregation in Northern Ireland. In D. Abrams et al. (Eds.), *The Social Psychology of Inclusion and Exclusion.* Philadelphia: Psychology Press.

Horowitz, D. (2002). Constitutional Design: Proposals Versus Processes. In A. Reynolds (Ed.), *The Architecture of Democracy.* Oxford: Oxford University Press.

Jenkins, R. (1997). *Rethinking Ethnicity.* London: Sage.

Kerr, M. (2005). *Imposing Power Sharing.* Dublin: Irish Academic Press.

Lijphart, A. (1969). Consociational Democracy. *World Politics, 21*(2), 207–225.

Lijphart, A. (1971). Cultural Diversity and Theories of Political Integration. *Canadian Journal of Political Science, 4*(1), 1–14.

Lijphart, A. (1975). Review Article: The Northern Ireland Problem; Cases, Theories, and Solutions. *British Journal of Political Science, 5*(1975), 99.

Lijphart, A. (1977). *Democracy in Plural Societies.* New Haven: Yale.

Lijphart, A. (1985). *Power-Sharing in South Africa.* Berkeley: Institute of Inernational Studies.

Lijphart, A. (1991). The Power-Sharing Approach. In J. V. Montville (Ed.), *Conflict and Peacemaking in Multiethnic Societies* (p. 496). New York: Lexington Books.

Lijphart, A. (1993). Power-Sharing, Ethnic Agnosticisms and Political Pragmatism. *Transformation, 21,* 94–99.

Lijphart, A. (1996). The Framework Documents on Northern Ireland and the Theory of Power Sharing. *Government and Opposition, 31*(3), 267–274.

Lijphart, A. (2001). Constructivism and Consociational Theory. *APSA-CP Newsletter, 12*(1), 11–13.

Lijphart, A. (2002). The Wave of Power-Sharing Democracy. In A. Reynolds (Ed.), *The Architecture of Democracy.* Oxford: Oxford University Press.

Lijphart, A. (2007). *Thinking About Democracy: Power Sharing and Majority Rule in Theory and Practice.* London: Routledge.

Lustick, I. (1997). Lijphart, Lakatos, and Consociationalism. *World Politics, 50,* 88–117.

McGarry, J. (1995). Explaining Ethnonationalism: The Flaws in Western Thinking. *Nationalism and Ethnic Politics, 1*(4), 121–142.

McGarry, J. (Ed.). (2001). *Northern Ireland and the Divided World.* Oxford: Oxford University Press.

McGarry, J., & O'Leary, B. (1990). *The Future of Northern Ireland.* Oxford: Clarendon.

McGarry, J., & O'Leary, B. (Eds.). (1993). *The Politics of Ethnic Conflict Regulation*. London: Routledge.

McGarry, J., & O'Leary, B. (1995a). Five Fallacies: Northern Ireland and the Liabilities of Liberalism. *Ethnic and Racial Studies, 18*(4), 837.

McGarry, J., & O'Leary, B. (1995b). *Explaining Northern Ireland*. Oxford: Blackwell.

McGarry, J., & O'Leary, B. (2004). *Consociational Engagements*. Oxford: Oxford University Press.

McGarry, J., & O'Leary, B. (2006a). Consociational Theory, Northern Ireland's Conflict, and Its Agreement. Part 1: What Consociationalists Can Learn from Northern Ireland. *Government and Opposition, 41*(1), 43–63.

McGarry, J., & O'Leary, B. (2006b). Consociational Theory, Northern Ireland's Conflict, and Its Agreement 2. What Critics of Consociation Can Learn from Northern Ireland. *Government and Opposition, 42*(2), 277.

McGarry, J., & O'Leary, B. (2007). Iraq's Constitution of 2005: Liberal Consociation as Political Prescription. *International Journal of Constitutional Law, 5*(4), 670–698.

McGarry, J., & O'Leary, B. (2009a). Power Shared After the Deaths of Thousands. In R. Taylor (Ed.), *Consociational Theory: McGarry and O'Leary and the Northern Ireland Conflict*. London: Routledge.

McGarry, J., & O'Leary, B. (2009b). Under Friendly and Less Friendly Fire. In R. Taylor (Ed.), *Consociational Theory: McGarry and O'Leary and the Northern Ireland Conflict*. Routledge: London.

McGarry, J., O'Leary, B., & Simeon, R. (2008). Integration or Accommodation? The Enduring Debate in Conflict Regulation. In S. Choudhry (Ed.), *Constitutional Design for Divided Societies: Integration or Accommodation*. Oxford: Oxford University Press.

Mitchell, P., Evans, G., & O'Leary, B. (2009). Extremist Outbidding in Ethnic Party Systems Is Not Inevitable: Tribune Parties in Northern Ireland. *Political Studies, 57*(2), 397–421.

Mowlam, M. (2002). *Momentum*. London: Hodder and Stoughton.

O'Leary, B. (1989). The Limits to Coercive Consociationalism in Northern Ireland. *Political Studies, 37*(4), 562–588.

O'Leary, B. (1995). Introduction: Reflections on a Cold Peace. *Ethnic and Racial Studies, 18*(4), 695–714.

O'Leary, B. (1996). War About Talks About War. *LSE Magazine* (Summer), 4–6.

O'Leary, B. (2005a). Debating Consociational Politics: Normative and Explanatory Arguments. In S. Noel (Ed.), *From Power-Sharing to Democracy*. London: McGill-Queens University Press.

O'Leary, B. (2005b). 'Foreword' to M. Kerr, *Imposing Power Sharing*. Dublin: Irish Academic Press.

O'Leary, B. (2009). *How to Get out of Iraq with Integrity*. Philadelphia: University of Pennsylvania Press.

O'Leary, B., & McGarry, J. (1990). Northern Ireland's Future: What Is to Be Done? *Conflict Quarterly, 10*(2), 42–62.

O'Leary, B., & McGarry, J. (1993). *The Politics of Antagonism: Understanding Northern Ireland.* London: Athlone Press.

O'Leary, B., & McGarry, J. (1995). Regulating Nations and Ethnic Communities. In A. Breton (Ed.), *Nationalism and Rationality.* Cambridge: Cambridge University Press.

O'Leary, B., et al. (1993). *Northern Ireland: Sharing Authority.* London: Institute of Public Policy Research.

Taylor, R. (1994). A Consociational Path to Peace in Northern Ireland and South Africa? In A. Guelke (Ed.), *New Perspectives on the Northern Ireland Conflict.* Aldershot: Avebury.

CHAPTER 5

Consociation, Conditionality, and Commitment: Making Peace in Northern Ireland

Timothy J. White

To achieve and keep peace between groups who have historically employed violence to pursue their political agenda requires convincing the parties in conflict that peace is more in their interest than continuing war (Werner and Yuen 2005). Increasingly, scholars have identified ethnic conflict as a major cause of conflict and in some cases war (Coakley 2010; Denny and Walter 2014). Historic rivalry, suspicion, and the legacy of past misdeeds make the transition in ethnically divided societies from war to peace exceedingly difficult. To convince those in conflict that violence does not achieve their aims requires the creation of political institutions that all sides trust and believe will provide for a stable means of peacefully pursuing their political agendas. Any potential political settlement that is seen as one-sided or provides asymmetric benefits to the warring parties or different ethnic groups is destined to fail. Many believe that power-sharing is the only means of providing the institutional guarantees that conflicting parties may agree to participate in a post-settlement peace. Consociationalism, as developed by Arend Lijphart, is one type of institutional mechanism that

T.J. White (✉)
Xavier University, Cincinnati, OH, USA

© The Author(s) 2018
M. Jakala et al. (eds.), *Consociationalism and Power-Sharing in Europe*, International Political Theory,
https://doi.org/10.1007/978-3-319-67098-0_5

allows historic rivals to share power. While there has been much debate over the definition of consociationalism and when institutional arrangements meet the precise conditions specified by Lijphart, the exact nature of the power-sharing arrangements and whether or not they meet certain specifications is less important than the political commitment of the warring groups to peace.

Scholars who have focused on the institutional arrangements of establishing governments and providing for social order believe that certain institutional arrangements are more likely to manage if not defuse ethnic conflict (Belmont et al. 2002: 1–3). This assumption builds on some of the most important post-World War II political science that focused on the contention that adaptable and effective political institutions provided stability and order in rapidly changing societies (Huntington 1968). As scholars focused more on the problem of differences within societies and not as much on change over time, they became more focused on specific institutional arrangements that could satiate ethnic tensions in society. Lijphart (1977) is famous for developing his theory of consociation as the institutional solution to highly divided societies. He contends that consociation is "the only feasible solution" to societies torn by ethnic divisions (Lijphart 2002: 37). While some critique power-sharing as a means of securing peace in ethnically divided societies (Horowitz 2014; Rothchild and Roeder 2005; Selway and Templeman 2012), there are many who contend that power-sharing arrangements provide stability after a negotiated settlement to a civil war between those historically divided by race, religion, or ethnicity (Hoddie and Hartzell 2005; Norris 2008: 211). But why do power-sharing arrangements persist and in some cases collapse? The thesis of this chapter is that consociational solutions to ethnic conflict have collapsed when the parties to the conflict no longer believe that the power-sharing arrangements associated with consociationalism are in their interest. Consociational or power-sharing arrangements endure when groups perceive it fruitful to continue under the institutional arrangements that allow them to pursue their interests peacefully. Using Northern Ireland as a case, I will illustrate how the key to achieving and maintaining peace under a consociational framework is to ensure that the groups historically in conflict see it in their interest to operate under the power-sharing institutions.

DEFINING CONSOCIATIONALISM

Most that use the concept of consociationalism associate it with power-sharing, but, as developed by Arend Lijphart, the concept has a more precise meaning. The concept was developed to define institutional arrangements for societies divided by ethnicity or some other social cleavage that provided assurances for fair governance for the major communities in a pluralistic society. The two "primary characteristics" of consociationalism are the sharing of executive power and group autonomy (Lijphart 2002: 39). Earlier, Lijphart (1977: 25–44) had identified grand coalition, mutual veto, proportionality, segmental autonomy, and federalism as the defining characteristics of consociationalism. Because relatively few states that had institutionalized power-sharing met all of the required conditions, scholars tended to equate many forms of power-sharing with consociationalism. As a result, many have stretched the meaning and definitional requirements of consociationalism so that the concept lost its meaning (Dixon 2005: 357–358; Lustick 1997). Despite this criticism, Lijphart (2002: 47) contends that the core meaning of consociationalism remains intact and those who critique how the concept has been applied are guilty of conceptual rigidity and timidity.

CONSOCIATIONALISM IN THE NORTHERN IRELAND CONTEXT

In his early work defining and developing the theory of consociationalism, Lijphart stressed the difficulties of achieving consociation in Northern Ireland in the 1970s. During the height of the troubles, it was easy to see Northern Ireland as a fundamentally unstable polity in an intractable conflict (Lijphart 1975: 96). Lijphart (1977: 140–141) argued that the geographic proximity and social isolation of each community only created animosity and power-sharing among Catholics and Protestants less likely. This assessment was built on identifying the Northern Ireland conflict as a sectarian one (Coakley 2002; Elliott 2009; Guelke 2015; Mitchell 2006). Rather than confront the problem of sectarianism directly, critics of Lijphart, such as Taylor (2011), suggest that managing the conflict through consociational institutions fails to address the underlying injustice of Northern Irish society. To be fair, Lijphart (1975: 99, 1977: 137) stressed that the ability of one community to exercise hegemonic power in

Northern Ireland made it unlikely they would concede to changes under-mining their historic dominant status. This meant that the historic advantage Protestants held both electorally and in governing arrange-ments would make them unwilling to share power with Catholics as envi-sioned by consociationalism. Moreover, Lijphart (1975: 100, 1977: 138) did not believe compulsory power-sharing could be imposed, nor were there "overarching solidarities" that could overcome the sectarian differ-ences. The unionist community so strongly identified with the British political tradition that they were unlikely to accept a political format of grand coalition or power-sharing which was alien to this tradition (Lijphart 1975: 100). In addition, Lijphart (1975: 100–101, 1977: 139) believed that Northern Ireland might be too small to create a viable consociational governing system, and he believed the external environment was threaten-ing the potential for consociationalism as the Republic of Ireland sought to marginalize the majority community in Northern Ireland by incorpo-rating Northern Ireland into the Republic (Lijphart 1975: 101). Despite these challenges for consociationalism in Northern Ireland, Lijphart (1975: 104–105) did recommend power-sharing, but he insisted that it could not be imposed. It should be agreed upon by the local parties in conflict.

Fortunately, the Northern Ireland peace process evolved beginning in the 1980s and through the 1990s overcoming the obstacles that Lijphart identified. Beginning with the Anglo-Irish Agreement, the British and Irish governments increasingly cooperated in a joint effort to negotiate a peaceful means of governing Northern Ireland (Aughey and Gormley-Heenan 2011; Hennessey 2011; McLoughlin 2014; O'Kane 2007; Tannam 2011; Todd 2011). By the late 1980s, secret indirect negotia-tions allowed the British government to engage with Sinn Féin, the politi-cal wing of the Irish Republican Army (IRA) (Arthur 1999; Ó Dochartaigh 2011; O'Kane 2015). This was based on an increasing recognition by the British government that Sinn Féin was not just a political arm of a terror-ist group but could become part of a peace settlement for Northern Ireland (Gupta 2007; Todd 2014). John Hume, as leader of the Social Democratic and Labour Party (SDLP), began engaging Sinn Féin in 1988 to explore the possibility of an IRA ceasefire that could lead to all-party talks including Sinn Féin and the British government (McLoughlin 2017: 83). By the 1990s, under the auspices of Fr. Alec Reid, the Irish government and its chief negotiator, Martin Mansergh, began to meet with Gerry Adams and others exploring the possibility of negotiations.

The Irish and British governments continued direct negotiations and reached important agreements, including the Downing Street Declaration which laid the groundwork for the first IRA ceasefire. By the 1990s, the United States of America began to play a more active role promoting a peace process in Northern Ireland (Arthur 1997; Cox 1999; Guelke 2012; Hazleton 2000; Mac Ginty 1997). After the failure of the first IRA ceasefire to lead to negotiations, George Mitchell established the ground rules for eligibility in all-party talks. By early 1998, all of the major parties in Northern Ireland with the important exception of the Democratic Unionist Party (DUP) agreed to negotiate directly with the British and Irish governments. Ultimately, on April 10th, 1998, Good Friday that year, the Irish and British governments as well as all of the parties to the negotiations agreed to a settlement.

Fundamentally, unionists, who had historically had political dominance in Northern Ireland agreed to share power with nationalists in exchange for peace, and a recognition that Northern Ireland's status within the United Kingdom could only be changed by democratic means. While this may be seen as a political trade-off, it was also based on what many perceive as making Northern Irish society fundamentally more fair or just. Critics of Lijphart, such as Taylor (2011), who focus on the fundamental injustices of Northern Irish society fail to recognize the important changes that have come with the peace process. Parties learned to trust each other to negotiate and came to understand what the differing groups would or would not accept (Tannam 2001). The 1998 Agreement stressed parity of esteem and that each community needed to be respected and that all citizens and groups should have their rights protected. In addition, a wide array of international players, including the Irish, British, and American governments became effective in providing guarantees and in supporting the peace process and a power-sharing governing arrangement for Northern Ireland. The Agreement also gained legitimacy because of a referendum process (Filardo-Llamas 2011) that has been found to support the effective implementation of peace agreements in other contexts (Loizides 2014).

Several scholars have attempted to apply Lijphart's model of consociationalism to the institutions that have been created by the Good Friday Agreement in Northern Ireland (Coakley 2011; McGarry and O'Leary 2008, 2016; O'Leary 2002: 296–329). More recently, some have moved beyond a narrow focus on consociationalism and its required elements as developed by Lijphart to focus more generally on power-sharing as an institutional mechanism to bring peace and stability as in Northern Ireland (McEvoy 2015: 39–104, 2017; McEvoy and O'Leary 2013; Norris 2008). The critical consociational condition for scholars who believe the Good Friday Agreement brought peace to Northern Ireland was the creation of a power-sharing executive. This executive requires the coordination of the highest level of executive power be shared by the first minister and deputy first minister who are to be the leaders from the largest parties in each community (unionist and nationalist). In addition, the cabinet ministries are to be distributed according to the d'Hondt system of allocating ministerial seats. Both the distribution of seats in the cabinet and the formal power-sharing among the first minister and deputy first minister are meant to guarantee that both communities' leaders are part of the decision-making process, and thus a formal power-sharing method is in place.

Recent efforts to analyze power-sharing in the Northern Ireland context no longer focus on the autonomy that was a critical defining characteristic of consociationalism in Lijphart's (2002) more recent formulation and analysis. There was no effort to provide formal autonomy for groups in the Agreement. However, Gallaher (2017) contends that the failure to provide for rapid decommissioning at the time of the Agreement in 1998 or soon thereafter and the slow process of implementing police reforms and establishing a justice ministry meant that paramilitaries were able to evolve to gain a foothold in policing their local communities. As a result, the Police Service of Northern Ireland (PSNI) deferred to the paramilitaries in certain neighborhoods. This process was informal autonomy and not what Lijphart envisions in his conceptualization of autonomy associated with consociationalism.

Much of the debate about the applicability of the consociational model to Northern Ireland contends that consociational institutions freeze ethnic conflict and prevent effective cross-community cooperation that eventually breaks down or reduces ethnic conflict in society (Coakley 2011: 490; Finlay 2011; Taylor 2006). Indeed, many have criticized the failure to overcome the sectarian divide after the Agreement (Jarman and Bell 2012; McEldowney et al. 2011; Morrow 2012). Dixon (2017: 26–27) claims that the problem with employing a consociational or what he identifies as a conservative realist approach to Northern Ireland is its inability to allow for change, especially as the peace process evolved and various actors modified their positions and identities. Despite these criticisms of consociationalism and the failure of politics in Northern Ireland to move beyond the sectarian divide, O'Flynn (2010) contends that leaders can learn to take into consideration members of ethnic groups in a consociational governing environment. This, has in fact, happened as even critics of consociationalism like Dixon (2002) point to the coordination of moves by the various political parties to move the peace process forward. Gormley-Heenan (2007) similarly interprets the ability of leaders to modify their positions based on their interaction with the other parties and leaders as critical to the success of the peace process. Thus, O'Leary (2005: 8) insists that consociational arrangements are based on a realistic understanding of durable conflicting identities and allow for these identities to change over time. Aitken (2010: 233–234) and Hancock (2013: 61–62) have argued that conflicts tend to heighten the salience of ethnic-based identities and perhaps a settlement (based on consociationalism or any other institutional arrangement that might bring political stability) might undermine heightened tensions based on ethnic conflict. If an agreement brings peace, those identities conceived in opposition to the other may recede as other bases of identity emerge to replace them.

Integrationists believe that peace can only be achieved when historic rivalries and cleavages erode and new identities emerge that transcend the traditional social divisions. Todd (2016: 92) has recently argued that "ethnic distinctions in Northern Ireland are not only embedded and polarized, but also fluid and permeable." This conception of ethnic conflict makes transformation possible where conflicting identities gradually give way to a politics based on difference that need not return to violence but where identity-based differences can be resolved through a normal democratic process. Thus, consociation may create a short-term ceasefire between historic rivals, but it does not lead to long-term peace if it does not effectively reduce the underlying conflict between the groups in a society. In order to achieve peace, critical cultural models of change and institutional incentives to further this process of cultural change are needed (Todd 2016: 101). This can occur because of a gradual process of contact and increased familiarity with others in the power-sharing setting (Cairns 2013). Party leaders and the political elites have learned to share power in the Stormont Assembly. The evidence is less clear whether the sectarian divide has been improved over the last two decades in local communities in Northern Ireland. The argument I make in this chapter is that focusing on whether consociation or any other form of power-sharing prevents societies from overcoming historic conflict misses the more proximate cause of peace and war and the stability of institutions that govern a society, namely the willingness of parties to continue to operate under consociational or power-sharing arrangements.

COMMITMENT AND THE ENDURANCE OF POWER-SHARING

The fundamental reason why a group in a state continues to operate under the extant governing arrangement is because they perceive it in their interest to do so. Typically, warring factions in a civil war choose a ceasefire when they have achieved what they can through fighting and believe they can pursue their objectives through a negotiated settlement (Bapat 2005; Greig 2001; Zartman 2000, 2008). In Northern Ireland early efforts at power-sharing like Sunningdale failed because some actors rejected the power-sharing institutions and believed that war or at least refusal to participate offered them the better option (Coakley 2011: 481; McCann and McGrattan 2017; McLoughlin 2009). As McEvoy (2015: 59) explains, "[a] fully inclusive coalition [power-sharing] may not be possible as some actors refuse to relinquish their violent methods."

The commitment to effective power-sharing is not just shaped by the parties to the conflict but the external actors who have influence over the parties to the conflict. Lijphart argues that when power-sharing failed in the 1970s in Lebanon it was not due just to domestic factors but international factors that impinged on the local ethnic conflict (Lijphart 2002: 42). If significant parties outside of the local ethnic groups undermine existing institutional arrangements for their own political interests, this reduces the likelihood of continuing success for consociational or power-sharing arrangements. Instead of undermining the local political process, international actors need to be supportive of local ethnic groups and leaders who are willing to share power and maintain peace. Wolff (2011: 120) has advocated for complex power-sharing as a theoretical approach to appreciate the "broad range of situations [where] neither territorial self-governance or power sharing on their own is sufficient to offer a viable solution to self-determination conflicts." Similarly, White (2017) has argued that a model of complex cooperation best explains the numerous actors who support, help achieve, and implement a peace agreement like in Northern Ireland. Understanding the context of the numerous actors and how they impinge upon or support a peace process is critical to understanding the potential for power-sharing arrangements to adapt and survive over time.

In the Northern Ireland context, McGarry and O'Leary have argued that the Good Friday Agreement does not represent solely a consociational settlement among the unionists and nationalists but also a settlement between the United Kingdom and the Republic of Ireland (McGarry and O'Leary 2008). McEvoy (2015: 86 and 104) demonstrates that in the case of Northern Ireland external actors helped shape the decisions of the parties in Northern Ireland to agree to the Good Friday or Belfast Agreement and were critical in creating conditions that supported its effective implantation. Given that local groups have little history of effective cooperation and have no history of trust, outside actors and international groups can play important roles in shaping the decisions of groups to remain within the power-sharing arrangements. This requires a long-lasting commitment by outside states and international organizations to support the power-sharing arrangements that bring peace, stability, and in many cases effective democracy to a region or state historically plagued by conflict. Northern Ireland has the peculiar status as a region where two states do not have aggressive non-democratic designs for incorporation. Since at least the Downing Street Declaration, the British government has made it clear that it has no selfish or strategic interest in Northern Ireland. Both the British government and the Irish government agreed in the Belfast Accords in 1998 that the future status of Northern Ireland should only be modified or changed based on the consent of the populations of Northern Ireland and the Republic of Ireland. This means that both states have committed themselves to a democratic process regarding the status of Northern Ireland. The key for both the Republic of Ireland and the British government to play a supporting role in the Northern Ireland peace process was for each government to come to this conclusion and convince the local parties to the conflict in the North that the only resolution to the conflict in Northern Ireland would come with the democratic consent of the people of Northern Ireland and the Republic of Ireland.

While the British government made their intentions clear going back to the Anglo-Irish Agreement in 1985 and especially in the Downing Street Declaration, the Irish government's commitment to a peaceful process of change was only made manifest in the Good Friday Agreement itself. Until then, the Irish government had claimed in Articles 2 and 3 of its constitution jurisdiction over all of Ireland, including the six counties that have remained in the United Kingdom since the Anglo-Irish Treaty of 1921. One of the neglected elements of the changing dynamics to the conflict was the ability of Irish nationalists, north and south of the border, to withdraw their territorial claim to Northern Ireland as a means of supporting a peace process. Owsiak (2017: 40) in recent research has highlighted how preferences for a united Ireland diminished as the Irish government and people became willing to forego this aspiration as a means of pursuing peace in Northern Ireland.

Like any other institutional approach to providing order, consociational arrangements are only likely to be successful if those who are in conflict see it in their interest to continue to pursue their agendas under the auspices of the consociational institutions. Politicians involved in the Northern Ireland peace process devised a political settlement not based on seeking a consociational settlement but as a result of diplomatic exchanges and a search for a diplomatic settlement acceptable to all (Bew 2006; Mansergh 2014). Each of the parties sought to advance their own interests but came to appreciate the constraints that other parties faced in negotiating a settlement and implementing it. Not only did political elites learn to understand the contours of what was acceptable to leaders of other groups, but the peace process required the evolution of the identities of nationalists and unionists in Northern Ireland which had been shaped by habit and had to be reformed to reconfigure inherited identities and interests.

ELECTORAL SYSTEMS, CONSOCIATIONALISM, AND THE PRESERVATION OF PEACE

Critics of consociationalism have often advocated electoral systems that promote accommodation across ethnic and cultural divisions in society. While these systems are contingent on a variety of structural factors in society to be successful, some evidence across a number of systems that utilize alternative or preferential voting suggests that parties across social cleavages can come together to cooperate and help bridge the historic divisions that separate groups in society (Reilly 2001). Clearly, promoting inter-ethnic cooperation is a noble goal, but is this a realistic option in societies like Northern Ireland where deep sectarian divisions prevent the pooling of votes or successful cross-community electoral strategies have not proven effective? Lijphart has argued against the claims that centripetal models can overcome divisions in society claiming that consociational arrangements are the only means of providing stable democracy in deeply divided societies (Lijphart 1994: 222).

Advocates of Consociationalism as a solution to the problem of ethnic conflict in democracy have advocated Party-List Proportional Representation as a means of providing opportunities and perhaps ensuring minority ethnic groups representation. Nevertheless, the evidence suggests that there is no direct correlation between higher levels of support for democracy in PR-List systems (Norris 2002). Empirical evidence does suggest that PR-List systems are associated with the preservation of peace (Cammett and Malesky 2012). The Northern Ireland Assembly elections after the Good Friday Agreement were conducted under Proportional Representation-Single Transferable Vote (PR-STV). This system does not guarantee proportionality as does the PR-List system and is therefore not preferred by consociationalists like Lijphart (1977: 136–137). However, PR-STV has tended to produce more proportional results than Single Member District or Majoritarian systems which tend to produce results unfavorable for minority groups. Even though PR-STV may seem encourage voters to select candidates lower on their ballot papers and thereby help overcome historic ethnic differences (O'Leary 2002: 313–315), the reality is that most analyses of voting behavior since 1998 in Northern Ireland does not suggest that many voters choose to select candidates from the other community with their lower preferences. There is some evidence of support for moderate parties across the communal divide in Northern Ireland (Garry 2014). In the end, the success or failure of the political institutions of Northern Ireland, whether they are the formal power-sharing arrangements in the executive, rules for passing legislation in the Northern Ireland Assembly, or the electoral system, will depend on the motivation of politicians to follow and lead their constituencies.

Conclusion

A common refrain in Northern Ireland since the signing of the Good Friday or Belfast Agreement has been the failure of political leadership (McGrattan 2017: 218–219; Wolff 2005: 45). This assumes that the power-sharing institutional arrangements are not the problem in Northern Ireland. While critics of consociationalism have correctly articulated the challenge of institutional mechanisms that tend to assume and thus cement communal differences are not likely to allow for and promote the kind of change those who advocate grassroots peacebuilding in Northern Ireland seek, I have argued that the most fundamental challenge to consociational or any other power-sharing arrangement is the unwillingness of those engaged in political conflict to choose to remain in such governing arrangements. Consociational power-sharing arrangements emerge when groups historically have been in conflict, and we cannot expect any institutional mechanism to make historic ethno-communal differences evanesce. Rather, the strength of the institutional arrangement is based on its ability to adapt to changing conditions so that all of the parties agree to continue to operate within the institutional framework. Often, conditions change so rapidly that it is impossible for any institutional arrangement to survive without changes. We can see this with how the fundamental political deal between unionists and nationalists to share power in Northern Ireland that came with the Good Friday Agreement has been updated and made to reflect the interests of various parties through the St. Andrew's Agreement and the Stormont House Agreement. What the peace process has allowed is the parties continue to pursue their interests through elections, bargaining, and other traditional democratic means. Clearly, the negotiations associated with Brexit will influence the second strand of the Good Friday Agreement, specifically the coordination across the border in Ireland. The ability of the existing governing arrangement in Northern Ireland to survive and adapt will be based on the willingness of the political parties and the governments to accede to whatever changes are necessary based on the results of the Brexit negotiations. Commitment to power-sharing and democratic processes is critical to the long-term success of governing institutions in highly divided societies like Northern Ireland.

BIBLIOGRAPHY

Aitken, R. (2010). Consociational Peace Processes and Ethnicity: The Implications of the Dayton and Good Friday Agreements for Ethnic Identities and Politics in Bosnia-Herzegovina and Northern Ireland. In A. Guelke (Ed.), *The Challenges of Ethno-Nationalism: Case Studies in Identity Politics* (pp. 232–253). Basingstoke: Palgrave Macmillan.

Arthur, P. (1997). American Intervention in the Anglo-Irish Peace Process: Incrementalism or Interference'. *Cambridge Review of International Affairs, 11*(1), 46–62.

Arthur, P. (1999). 'Quiet Diplomacy and Personal Conversation': Track Two Diplomacy and the Search for a Settlement in Northern Ireland. In J. Ruane & J. Todd (Eds.), *After the Good Friday Agreement: Analysing Political Change in Northern Ireland* (pp. 71–95). Dublin: University College Dublin Press.

Aughey, A., & Gormley-Heenan, C. (2011). The Anglo-Irish Agreement: 25 Years On. *The Political Quarterly, 82*(3), 389–397.

Bapat, N. A. (2005). Insurgency and the Opening of Peace Processes. *Journal of Peace Research, 42*(6), 699–717.

Belmont, K., Mainwaring, S., & Reynolds, A. (2002). Institutional Design, Conflict Management, and Democracy. In A. Reynolds (Ed.), *The Architecture of Democracy: Constitutional Design, Conflict Management, and Democracy* (pp. 1–11). Oxford: Oxford University Press.

Bew, P. (2006). Myths of Consociationalism: From Good Friday to Political Impasse. In M. Cox, A. Guelke, & F. Stephen (Eds.), *A Farewell to Arms? Beyond the Good Friday Agreement* (2nd ed., pp. 57–68). Manchester: Manchester University Press.

Cairns, E. (2013). Northern Ireland: Power Sharing, Contact, Identity, and Leadership. In J. McEvoy & B. O'Leary (Eds.), *Power Sharing in Deeply Divided Places* (pp. 278–294). Philadelphia: University of Pennsylvania Press.

Cammett, M., & Malesky, E. (2012). Power Sharing in Postconflict Societies: Implications for Peace and Governance. *Journal of Conflict Resolution, 56*(6), 982–1016.

Coakley, J. (2002). Religion, National Identity and Political Change in Modern Ireland. *Irish Political Studies, 17*(1), 4–28.

Coakley, J. (2010). Comparing Ethnic Conflicts: Common Patterns, Shared Challenges. In J. Coakley (Ed.), *Pathways from Ethnic Conflict: Institutional Redesign in Divided Societies* (pp. 1–19). London: Routledge.

Coakley, J. (2011). The Challenge of Consociation in Northern Ireland. *Parliamentary Affairs, 64*(3), 473–493.

Cox, M. (1999). The War that Came in from the Cold: Clinton and the Irish Question. *World Policy Journal, 16*(1), 41–68.

Denny, E. K., & Walter, B. F. (2014). Ethnicity and Civil War. *Journal of Peace Research, 51*(2), 199–212.

Dixon, P. (2002). Political Skills or Lying and Manipulation? The Choreography of the Northern Ireland Peace Process. *Political Studies, 50*(3), 725–741.

Dixon, P. (2005). Why the Good Friday Agreement in Northern Ireland Is Not Consociational. *Political Quarterly, 76*(3), 357–367.

Dixon, P. (2017). The 'Real' and 'Dirty' Politics of the Northern Ireland Peace Process: A Constructivist Realist Critique of Idealism and Conservative Realism. In T. J. White (Ed.), *Theories of International Relations and Northern Ireland* (pp. 36–54). Manchester: Manchester University Press.

Elliott, M. (2009). *When God Took Sides: Religion and Identity in Ireland— Unfinished History.* Oxford: Oxford University Press.

Filardo-Llamas, L. (2011). Discourse Worlds in Northern Ireland: The Legitimisation of the 1998 Agreement. In K. Hayward & C. O'Donnell (Eds.), *Political Discourse and Conflict Resolution: Debating Peace in Northern Ireland* (pp. 62–76). London: Routledge.

Finlay, A. (2011). *Governing Ethnic Conflict: Consociation, Identity and the Price of Peace.* London: Routledge.

Gallaher, C. (2017). Under the Gun: Northern Ireland's Unique History with DDR. In T. J. White (Ed.), *Theories of International Relations and Northern Ireland* (pp. 55–73). Madison: University of Wisconsin Press.

Garry, J. (2014). Potentially Voting Across the Divide in Deeply Divided Places: Ethnic Catch-All Voting in Consociational Northern Ireland. *Political Studies, 62*(S1), 2–19.

Gormley-Heenan, C. (2007). *Political Leadership and the Northern Ireland Peace Process: Role, Capacity and Effect.* New York: Palgrave.

Greig, J. M. (2001). Moments of Opportunity: Recognizing Conditions of Ripeness for International Mediation Between Enduring Rivals. *Journal of Conflict Resolution, 45*(6), 691–718.

Guelke, A. (2012). The USA and the Northern Ireland Peace Process. *Ethnopolitics, 11*(4), 424–438.

Guelke, A. (2015). Sectarianism, Ethno-National Conflict and the Northern Ireland Problem. In F. Requejo & K. J. Nagel (Eds.), *Politics of Religion and Nationalism: Federalism, Consociationalism and Secession* (pp. 106–120). London: Routledge.

Gupta, D. (2007). Selective Engagement and Its Consequences for Social Movement Organizations: Lessons from British Policy in Northern Ireland. *Comparative Politics, 39*(3), 331–351.

Hancock, L. (2013). Peace from the People: Identity Salience and the Northern Irish Peace Process. In T. J. White (Ed.), *Lessons from the Northern Ireland Peace Process* (pp. 61–93). Madison: University of Wisconsin Press.

Hazleton, W. (2000). Encouragement from the Sidelines: Clinton's Role in the Good Friday Agreement. *Irish Studies in International Affairs, 11*, 103–119.

Hennessey, T. (2011). The Origins of the Peace Process. In T. E. Hachey (Ed.), *Turning Points in Twentieth Century Irish History* (pp. 201–214). Dublin: Irish Academic Press.

Hoddie, M., & Hartzell, C. (2005). Power Sharing in Peace Settlements: Initiating the Transition from Civil War. In P. G. Roeder & D. Rothchild (Eds.), *Sustainable Peace: Power and Democracy After Civil Wars* (pp. 83–106). Ithaca: Cornell University Press.

Horowitz, D. L. (2014). Ethnic Power Sharing: Three Big Problems. *Journal of Democracy, 25*(2), 5–20.

Huntington, S. (1968). *Political Order in Changing Societies.* New Haven: Yale University Press.

Ikle, F. (2005). *Every War Must End* (Rev. 2nd ed., pp.10–16). New York: Columbia University Press.

Jarman, N., & Bell, J. (2012). Routine Divisions: Segregation and Daily Life in Northern Ireland. In C. McGrattan & E. Meehan (Eds.), *Everyday Life After the Conflict: The Impact of Devolution and North-South Cooperation* (pp. 39–53). Manchester: Manchester University Press.

Lijphart, A. (1975). The Northern Ireland Problem: Cases, Theories, and Solutions. *British Journal of Political Science, 5*(1), 83–106.

Lijphart, A. (1977). *Democracy in Plural Societies: A Comparative Exploration.* New Haven: Yale University Press.

Lijphart, A. (1994). Prospects for Power-Sharing in the New South Africa. In A. Reynolds (Ed.), *Election '94 South Africa: The Campaign, Results, and Future Prospects* (pp. 221–231). Claremont: David Phillip Publishers.

Lijphart, A. (2002). The Wave of Power-Sharing Democracy. In A. Reynolds (Ed.), *The Architecture of Democracy: Constitutional Design, Conflict Management, and Democracy* (pp. 37–54). Oxford: Oxford University Press.

Loizides, N. (2014). Negotiated Settlements and Peace Referendums. *European Journal of Political Research, 53*(2), 234–249.

Lustick, I. (1997). Lijphart, Lakatos, and Consociationalism. *World Politics, 50*(1), 88–117.

Mac Ginty, R. (1997). American Influences on the Northern Ireland Peace Process. *Journal of Conflict Studies, 17*(2), 31–50.

Mansergh, M. (2014, May 30). Remarks at the Launch of *Lessons from the Northern Ireland Peace Process* (T. J. White, Ed.). Cork: University College Cork.

McCann, D., & McGrattan, C. (Eds.). (2017). *Sunningdale, the Ulster's Worker's Council Strike, and the Struggle for Democracy in Northern Ireland.* Manchester: Manchester University Press.

McEldowney, O., Anderson, J., & Shuttleworth, I. (2011). Sectarian Demography: Dubious Discourses of Ethno-National Conflict. In K. Hayward & C. O'Donnell (Eds.), *Political Discourse and Conflict Resolution: Debating Peace in Northern Ireland* (pp. 160–176). London: Routledge.

McEvoy, J. (2015). *Power-Sharing Executives: Governing in Bosnia, Macedonia, and Northern Ireland.* Philadelphia: University of Pennsylvania Press.

McEvoy, J. (2017). Power Sharing and the Pursuit of Good Governance: Evidence from Northern Ireland. In A. McCulloch & J. McGarry (Eds.), *Power Sharing: Empirical and Normative Challenges.* London: Routledge.

McEvoy, J., & O'Leary, B. (Eds.). (2013). *Power Sharing in Deeply Divided Places.* Philadelphia: University of Pennsylvania Press.

McGarry, J., & O'Leary, B. (2008). Consociational Theory and Peace Agreements in Pluri-National Places: Northern Ireland and Other Cases. In G. Ben-Porat (Ed.), *The Failure of the Middle East Peace Process? A Comparative Analysis of Peace Implementation in Israel/Palestine, Northern Ireland and South Africa* (pp. 70–96). Basingstoke: Palgrave Macmillan.

McGarry, J., & O'Leary, B. (2016). Power-Sharing Executives: Consociational and Centripetal Formulae and the Case of Northern Ireland. *Ethnopolitics, 15*(5), 497–519.

McGrattan, C. (2017). Responsibility, Justice, and Reconciliation in Northern Ireland. In T. J. White (Ed.), *Theories of International Relations and Northern Ireland* (pp. 218–232). Manchester: Manchester University Press.

McLoughlin, P. J. (2009). Dublin Is Just a Sunningdale Away'? The SDLP and the Failure of Northern Ireland's Sunningdale Experiment. *Twentieth Century British History, 20*(1), 74–96.

McLoughlin, P. J. (2014). The First Major Step in the Peace Process'? Exploring the Impact of the Anglo-Irish Agreement on Republican Thinking. *Irish Political Studies, 29*(1), 116–133.

McLoughlin, P. J. (2017). Assessing the Importance of Ideas and Agency in the Northern Ireland Peace Process. In T. J. White (Ed.), *Theories of International Relations and the Northern Ireland Peace Process* (pp. 74–92). Manchester: Manchester University Press.

Mitchell, C. (2006). *Religion, Identity and Politics in Northern Ireland: Boundaries of Belonging and Belief.* Burlington: Ashgate.

Morrow, D. (2012). The Rocky Road from Enmity. In C. McGrattan & E. Meehan (Eds.), *Everyday Life After the Conflict: The Impact of Devolution and North-South Cooperation* (pp. 20–36). Manchester: Manchester University Press.

Norris, P. (2002). Ballots Not Bullets: Testing Consociational Theories of Ethnic Conflict, Electoral Systems, and Democratization. In A. Reynolds (Ed.), *The Architecture of Democracy: Constitutional Design, Conflict Management, and Democracy* (pp. 206–247). Oxford: Oxford University Press.

Norris, P. (2008). *Driving Democracy: Do Power-Sharing Institutions Work?* Cambridge: Cambridge University Press.

Ó Dochartaigh, N. (2011). Together in the Middle: Back-Channel Negotiation in the Irish Peace Process. *Journal of Peace Research, 48*(6), 767–780.

O'Flynn, I. (2010). Deliberative Democracy, the Public Interest and the Consociational Model. *Political Studies, 58*(3), 572–589.

O'Kane, E. (2007). Re-evaluating the Anglo Irish Agreement: Central or Incidental to the Northern Ireland Peace Process? *International Politics, 44*(1), 711–731.

O'Kane, E. (2015). Talking to the Enemy? The Role of the Back-Channel in the Development of the Northern Ireland Peace Process. *Contemporary British History, 29*(3), 401–420.

O'Leary, B. (2002). The Belfast Agreement and the British-Irish Agreement: Consociation, Confederal Institutions, a Federacy, and a Peace Process. In A. Reynolds (Ed.), *The Architecture of Democracy: Constitutional Design, Conflict Management, and Democracy* (pp. 293–356). Oxford: Oxford University Press.

O'Leary, B. (2005). Debating Consociational Politics: Normative and Explanatory Arguments. In S. Noel (Ed.), *From Power Sharing to Democracy: Post-conflict Institutions in Ethnically Divided Societies* (pp. 3–43). Montreal: McGill-Queen's University Press.

Owsiak, A. P. (2017). Issues, Leaders, and Regimes: Reaching Settlement in Northern Ireland. In T. J. White (Ed.), *Theories of International Relations and Northern Ireland* (pp. 36–54). Manchester: Manchester University Press.

Reilly, B. (2001). *Democracy in Divided Societies: Electoral Engineering for Conflict Management*. Cambridge: Cambridge University Press.

Rothchild, D., & Roeder, P. G. (2005). Power Sharing as an Impediment to Peace and Democracy. In P. G. Roeder & D. Rothchild (Eds.), *Sustainable Peace: Power and Democracy After Civil Wars* (pp. 29–50). Ithaca: Cornell University Press.

Selway, J., & Templeman, K. (2012). The Myth of Consociationalism? Conflict Reduction in Divided Societies. *Comparative Political Studies, 45*(12), 1542–1571.

Tannam, E. (2001). Explaining the Good Friday Agreement: A Learning Process. *Government and Opposition, 36*(4), 493–518.

Tannam, E. (2011). Explaining British-Irish Cooperation. *Review of International Studies, 37*(3), 1191–1214.

Taylor, R. (2006). The Belfast Agreement and the Politics of Consociationalism: A Critique. *The Political Quarterly, 77*(2), 217–226.

Taylor, R. (2011). The Injustice of a Consociational Solution to the Northern Ireland Problem. In R. Taylor (Ed.), *Consociational Theory: McGarry & O'Leary and the Northern Ireland Conflict* (pp. 309–329). New York: Routledge.

Todd, J. (2011). Institutional Change and Conflict Regulation: The Anglo-Irish Agreement (1985) and the Mechanisms of Change in Northern Ireland. *West European Politics, 34*(4), 838–858.

Todd, J. (2014). Thresholds of State Change: Changing British State Institutions and Practices in Northern Ireland After Direct Rule. *Political Studies 62*(3), 522–538.

Todd, J. (2016). Northern Ireland in a Balkan Perspective: The Cultural Dynamics of Complex Conflicts. In É. Ó. Ciardha & G. Vojvoda (Eds.), *Politics of Identity in Post-conflict States* (pp. 92–104). London: Routledge.

Werner, S., & Yuen, A. (2005). Making and Keeping Peace. *International Organization, 59*(2), 262–293.

White, T. J. (2017). Cooperation Theory and the Northern Ireland Peace Process. In T. J. White (Ed.), *Theories of International Relations and Northern Ireland* (pp. 201–217). Manchester: Manchester University Press.

Wolff, S. (2005). Between Stability and Collapse: Internal and External Dynamics of Post-agreement Institution Building in Northern Ireland. In S. Noel (Ed.), *From Power Sharing to Democracy: Post-conflict Institutions in Ethnically Divided Societies* (pp. 44–66). Montreal: McGill-Queen's University Press.

Wolff, S. (2011). Peace by Design? Towards 'Complex Power Sharing.'. In R. Taylor (Ed.), *Consociational Theory: McGarry and O'Leary and the Northern Ireland Conflict* (pp. 110–121). London: Routledge.

Zartman, I. W. (2000). Ripeness: The Hurting Stalemate and Beyond. In P. C. Stern & D. Druckman (Eds.), *International Conflict Resolution After the Cold War* (pp. 225–250). Washington: National Research Council Press.

Zartman, I. W. (2008). The Timing of Peace Initiatives: Hurting Stalemates and Ripe Moments. In J. Darby & R. Mac Ginty (Eds.), *Contemporary Peacemaking: Conflict, Violence and Peace Processes* (2nd ed., pp. 22–35). New York: Palgrave Macmillan.

CHAPTER 6

Dialogue, Democracy and Government Communication: Consociationalism in Northern Ireland

Charis Rice and Ian Somerville

Introduction

This chapter explores the implications of consociationalism for government communication in Northern Ireland. Our study used qualitative data from 33 semi-structured interviews with key actors in the government communication process: *Government Information Officers (GIOs), Ministerial Special Advisers (SpAds)* and *political journalists.* We use contemporary Northern Ireland as a strategic case study to investigate how these unelected elite actors experience the consociational system in their professional roles and relationships and to ascertain what impacts they perceive it to have on the government communication sphere. While the strengths and benefits of consociationalism as a form of political accommodation have been assessed

C. Rice (✉)
Coventry University, Coventry, UK

I. Somerville
University of Leicester, Leicester, UK

© The Author(s) 2018

M. Jakala et al. (eds.), *Consociationalism and Power-Sharing in Europe*, International Political Theory,
https://doi.org/10.1007/978-3-319-67098-0_6

through the lens of various disciplines, namely political science, we propose that a communication focus has much to offer the debate. We demonstrate that major limitations of the consociational model are evident if we focus on the communication sphere in the stable post-conflict phase.

Government Communication and Democracy

Despite the long-standing significance of the government communication process to evaluations of democratic health (Blumler and Gurevitch 1995; Davis 2010; Habermas 1989), scholars do not often give it precedence when examining the functioning of political systems. Moreover, the studies that do, have largely focused on communication from majoritarian (mostly American or Westminster) institutions (Canel and Sanders 2012). Such research highlights some of the political, practical and ethical complexities public relations practitioners face working in government settings that often require political responsiveness as well as impartial public service (Gaber 2007; Gregory 2012). These are particularly significant in complex power-sharing systems such as the UN (Center 2009) or the European Union (Laursen and Valentini 2013). Thus, the development and practice of government communication is influenced by the political system and media structures embedded in a particular society (Sriramesh and Verčič 2009). By focusing on Northern Ireland's relatively unique governmental system (at least for Western Europe), this research expands the traditional focus of government communication and in turn considers the impact of consociationalism on government communication.

Dialogue and Consociationalism

'Dialogue' is a nebulous term, informed by the theories and practices of various disciplines including philosophy, ethics, psychology and, perhaps most recently, public relations (Kent and Taylor 2002). Kent and Taylor (2002) define dialogue as:

> an orientation [which] includes five features: *mutuality*, or the recognition of organization–public relationships; *propinquity*, or the temporality and spontaneity of interactions with publics; *empathy*, or the supportiveness and confirmation of public goals and interests; *risk*, or the willingness to interact with individuals and publics on their own terms; and finally, *commitment*, or the extent to which an organization gives itself over to dialogue, interpretation, and understanding in its interactions with publics. (24–25)

When they characterise mutuality by an "inclusion or collaborative orientation" (p. 25), state that dialogue should be about the recognition of socially constructed reality and insist that it "involves an understanding of the past and the present, and...shared future for all participants" (pp. 25–26), Kent and Taylor's key features of dialogue speak directly to much of the theorising on (and discourse of) successful peace agreements and consociational accommodation. Thus, the key tenets of consociationalism—compromise and negotiation—which are "...institutionally anchored by the inclusion of representatives from all social segments" (Andeweg 2000, p. 512), arguably flow from dialogue. Indeed, Lijphart (1999) would contend that consociational democracy is a 'kinder', 'gentler' form of democracy that encourages deliberation and compromise between divided groups, vital for post-conflict cohabitation. The point here is not to become preoccupied with defining dialogue, but to use it as a point of departure for an examination of consociational government from a communication perspective. Thus, while we do not subscribe to the view that dialogue is necessarily 'better' or 'more ethical' than other strategies of communication—and indeed it may even act as a hindrance to effective and ethical communication in some cases (see Somerville and Kirby 2012)—we do argue that consideration of its role plays an important part in any assessment of government communication in a consociational context. This is because some form of dialogue between political elites has been highlighted as important in at least the path *towards* the consociational settlement in Northern Ireland (Byrne 2001; Hayward 2011; Hughes 2011; Somerville and Kirby 2012). Without discounting the power relations and manipulation that are often present in 'dialogue' (Roper 2005) or the poor conceptual clarity which dogs the term (Piezcka 2011; Kent and Taylor 2002), it can be considered a crucial part of the development of consociationalism in at least facilitating the *engagement* of diverse groups, if not consensus between them (Somerville and Kirby 2012).

Accordingly, what little research there is on government (rather than party political) communication in Northern Ireland tends to focus on Direct Rule governance (when Northern Ireland was governed by Britain via Westminster), or during times of unstable devolved governance when suspensions of the Northern Ireland legislature were ongoing (Fawcett 2002; Miller 1994). These tell us that during times of political conflict and institutional instability, relations between government and media institutions appeared fraught and characterised by mutual distrust. Northern

Ireland's consociational government has now functioned with relative stability since 2007[1]; for the first time in over 40 years, Northern Ireland now experiences (an uneasy) peace. In previous work (e.g. Rice and Somerville 2017), we have outlined some of the issues which arise for the communication professionals working in the current consociational Northern Ireland administration. We propose that the institutional design of government that has facilitated a stable post-conflict phase in Northern Ireland does not necessarily facilitate—and is arguably a barrier to—deliberative, accountable and public interest government communication. In this chapter, we concentrate specifically on analysing our interviewees' perspectives on the issue (the mechanisms, processes) of consociationalism in relation to government communication. Before doing so, we briefly explain some of the implications of consociationalism for the governance of Northern Ireland and contextualise the political and media background.

THE NORTHERN IRELAND CONTEXT

Devolution on a Consociational Basis

A number of factors make Northern Ireland distinctive (in Western European terms): the fact that a consociational power-sharing arrangement accompanied devolution[2] in Northern Ireland; the Northern Ireland Assembly has no provision for an opposition[3]—all parties with adequate electoral strength are in government; and it has a history of political violence. Northern Ireland is a country divided by religious differences between Catholics and Protestants, various political allegiances and constitutional attitudes, and diverse national identities[4] (Wilson and Stapleton 2006). Officially bringing the 30-year ethno-political violent conflict, known as *The Troubles*, to an end, the Good Friday Agreement (1998) recognised that parties representing the polar ends of the constitutional debate must be represented in government, because "...agreement between the middle ground was not going to solve the conflict" (McEvoy 2006, p. 454). Consociationalism's most important contemporary theorist, Arend Lijphart, explains: "Consociational democracy means government by elite cartel designed to turn a democracy with a fragmented political culture into a stable democracy" (2008, p. 31). Accordingly, the fundamentals of the consociational design in Northern Ireland are a joint First and Deputy First Minister Office and decision-making and voting procedures based on parallel consent, proportionality and a cross-community basis (Birrell 2012). Members of the Legislative Assembly (MLAs) must designate themselves 'Unionist' and 'Nationalist'—if they do not do so they are considered 'Others'[5]—and major decisions in the Assembly must be agreed by a majority of both Unionists and Nationalists to ensure cross-community consent. Parties representing the main designations also have the ability to veto (via the 'mutual veto' mechanism) government changes or proposals which are considered to "adversely affect their vital interests" (McGarry and O'Leary 2006a, p. 44). Likewise, McEvoy (2006) explains that d'Hondt rule[6] was the system agreed upon by the political parties in Northern Ireland to allocate ministerial departments due to its 'automatic nature' and because it was built on the principle of proportionality. Importantly, the d'Hondt mechanism also means that "no vote of confidence is required by the Assembly either for individual ministers or for the executive committee as a whole" (McGarry and O'Leary 2006b, p. 264).

Communication Roles in Consociational Northern Ireland

The *Executive Information Service (EIS)* is the official government communication system for the elected ministers and their departments in the Northern Ireland Executive. Each of the 12 departments[7] in the Executive comprises an assigned minister and a team of departmental communicators (GIOs) from the EIS. The EIS system is used to disseminate the information produced by each department and to monitor its propriety; it is also responsible for coordinating information across departments. Thus, in the Northern Ireland government communication arrangement (and indeed most 'Westminster style' government systems) there are two groups of interest, which we examine in our study: (1) GIOs, who assist the elected government of whichever political persuasion in communication and media relations in an *impartial* civil servant capacity. GIOs are appointed by the merit principle and work for one government department at a time (usually for a term of government/4–5 years), they are guided by a Code of Ethics prioritising political impartiality; (2) SpAds, 'temporary' civil servants who are personally appointed by a government minister to assist him/her in a *political* capacity. The SpAd is a link from the minister's government department to their political party, aiding the minister with departmental work and its media presentation while their minister is in office. While they have a specific Code of Conduct (DFP

2013), they are not bound by political impartiality, in fact they are *expected* to support the political (and increasingly also the communications) work of their minister when it is related to their minister's department.

Political neutrality is of fundamental importance in upholding normative standards of communication in impartial civil service governmental systems. However, within the UK, Northern Ireland and other Westminster style civil service governments, the role of SpAds and their relationships with both GIOs and journalists has come under scrutiny in this regard. SpAds are commonly depicted as powerful government figures, vital news sources for journalists and 'spin doctors' (Gaber 2004), carefully crafting policy language for political gain. At the same time, the increased use and influence of SpAds in Westminster systems is often linked to a desire to reassert political control over the civil service (Eichbaum and Shaw 2010). In this vein, SpAds are a necessary, invaluable and trusted aid to ministers in a demanding political environment (Yong and Hazell 2014). Importantly, in the UK legislatures, SpAds have no official authority over civil servants; in fact, they are specifically prohibited from 'managing' civil servants in their code of conduct. Nonetheless, several commentators have emphasised the need for clearer boundaries on government communication, and specifically on SpAds and their relationships with government press officers (see Sanders 2013).

Media Context
Our study also includes the perspectives of political journalists from the main press and broadcast organisations in Northern Ireland. These journalists regularly cover the work of the Executive and its representatives and interact with both GIOs and SpAds to source information. The main broadcast outlets in Northern Ireland are *BBC Northern Ireland*, *Ulster Television* and several independent radio channels; these organisations strive for impartiality in their news coverage of Northern Ireland and promote themselves as serving the whole population (Unionist/British and Nationalist/Irish). However, of the three national daily newspapers, only The *Belfast Telegraph* positions itself to appeal to both communities in Northern Ireland. The *Irish News* targets the Nationalist community while the *News Letter* is staunchly Unionist in its outlook, and this long-standing 'political parallelism' (Hallin and Mancini 2004) is also a feature of the local press. At the same time, the move to a devolved consociational government means that political journalism has changed over the past two decades. Namely, local politicians, their policies and their behaviour in

government come under more scrutiny now than they have done in the past 40 years (McLaughlin and Baker 2010).

Research Questions
Despite this distinctive environment, there is remarkably little empirical research examining the impact of consociational governance on government communication, from the perspectives of the *unelected* individuals who actually produce and disseminate government communication. Our research questions are, therefore:

1) *How does the consociational structure of government in Northern Ireland affect government communication?*
2) *What does Northern Ireland's government communication tell us about the dialogic quality of consociational democracy in post-conflict societies?*

METHODOLOGY

A combination of purposive and snowball sampling techniques were employed to recruit individuals for semi-structured in-depth interviews who could provide relevant data (Tansey 2007). Our sample consisted of 9 senior GIOs (69% of the total), 8 SpAds (42% of the total) and 16 political journalists, 33 interviewees in total. All GIOs interviewed held the rank of *Principal Information Officer* in the civil service and as with the SpAds who participated, worked across a number of different government departments for all five parties in government. The journalists who participated were from the main press and broadcast organisations in Northern Ireland outlined above, and all were at section editor or overall editor level. Interview questions focused on probing participants on their daily work routines and their interactions with the other participant groups. All interviews lasted around 60 minutes, were conducted in the participants' workplaces, were audio recorded and later transcribed in full. GIO responses are denoted by G1, G2 and so on; SpAd responses by S1, S2 and so on; and journalists' responses by J1, J2 and so on. In our findings section below representative quotations are italicised and have been edited (to remove repetitions, stutters and non-verbal sounds) for ease of understanding.

In line with recommended interpretative phenomenological analysis (IPA) procedures, our data analysis was inductive in nature with themes emerging from the narratives (Smith et al. 2009). This involved the process of 'close reading' wherein a detailed reading and re-reading of the text is conducted (Alvesson and Skoldberg 2009) and primacy is given to the perceptions of respondents, since the objective is to generate knowledge in relation to their lived experience of a phenomenon (Langdridge 2007). The content was then coded to identify and delineate themes. The final thematic structure was agreed following detailed collaboration between the two authors, who checked the transcripts to confirm themes and ensure that the selected quotes were reflective of them. Our analysis and conclusions were further derived from comparison with the thematic findings from all participant groups. Accordingly, we organise our Findings and Analysis section under the following headings: *designation*; *mandatory coalition*; *absence of political opposition*; *political control*. These themes of course overlap, but for the purposes of this section, we hold them conceptually apart to draw out some of the key implications, which we will return to in the Discussion and Conclusion section.

FINDINGS AND ANALYSIS

Designation: Making Divisions Salient

An issue raised by many in our study was the impact of designation on Northern Ireland government communication. Interviewees supported the view that Northern Ireland ministers focus on differentiation between themselves and other parties, rather than inclusiveness (McEvoy 2006), and that this was fueled by the fact that individual ministers and parties are allocated within the Assembly to different nationalist and unionist identities. This creates problems both in decision-making, in communicating issues or decisions, and trying to build consensus which often results in the 'gravest problem of consociationalism' (Andeweg 2000, p. 529), deadlock. For example, one SpAd commented:

> *designation means the majority in both communities have to agree. If you did away with that then just a simple majority could agree, or at least if you'd a weighted majority, so that one community couldn't agree and just ignore the other...on any serious policy issue, education, RPA [Review of Public Administration], look at them they just can't agree and it just falls apart... judged against violence, this is much better. But that's not to say it's a good system.* (S1)

Indeed, this arguably fuels the norm of identity-based politics recounted by another SpAd:

> *The conflict shaped our politics to the extent of, almost it didn't matter, who you were but what you were, and, I think in a truly post-conflict situation, that's what needs to change.* (S3)

Media Shaped by Conflict

Our GIO and SpAd participants also stressed the instrumental role of the print media in exacerbating cultural divides and accentuating social cleavages (Hallin and Mancini 2004). One GIO stated: *"Well the Irish News isn't gonna take a story about Ulster Scots...It's not their readership, the News Letter isn't gonna take a story about GAA, it's not their readership"* (G5). Additionally, some GIOs and the majority of SpAds contended that journalists are *"shaped by the conflict"* (S3), and so are overly interested in constitutional issues and political disputes over everyday government business. One SpAd explained:

> *there's criticism at election time that people talk about the constitutional issues, they don't talk about bread and butter policies but whenever you hold a press conference...on some matter of detailed policy, press don't cover it...they criticize us but don't always you know deliver whenever people do the worthy things.* (S2)

Media negativity and an over-concentration on 'soft' political issues over policy issues is a frequent complaint amongst political actors in various polities across the democratic world (Avery 2015). However, several SpAds perceived that Northern Irish journalists' historic lack of experience in engaging with policy issues contributes to journalists' poor reportage of these issues in the present context. For instance, one SpAd commented:

> *I find them really poor...with one or two exceptions...They don't understand policy issues, and in many cases don't want to...the media have had you know bombs and bullets and paramilitaries and gangsters and conflict, and they're struggling to get to deal with the detail of policy and normal stuff.* (S8)

Several journalists strongly argued that it was politicians' continual disputes over 'tribal-based' issues that fuel the media's focus on politically controversial issues. Journalists contended that the news agenda *had* changed considerably since a relatively stable government and post-conflict era had emerged. A typical statement was

> *up until about five or six years ago, I mean we were fixated by politics and vio-lence, now the news agenda has changed dramatically...journalists are paying far more attention to the social issues, health, welfare, the economy, education... we have to reflect that.* (J10)

Many journalists view their role as moving on from divisive politics and consider the politicians responsible for the perpetuation of division, one noted: "*with politics, it's a very tribal thing here, the democracy it really is still nascent, it's still developing*" (J9). Indeed, some commentators insist that politicians think that this approach may be necessary for parties' electoral success, since citizens' voting behaviour in Northern Ireland is perceived to be influenced by 'tribal'-based politics (Evans and Tonge 2009). This reflects the criticism that in this kind of consociational system, there is little incentive for elites to attract voters from other communities when support is based on ethno-national group identification and intra-community competition (Horowitz 2014). Overall, it is clear that designation is one example of how cultural identities and ethno-political antagonisms are compartmentalised, solidified and made salient in the consociational context (Andeweg 2000), rather than being restructured or reconceptualised in line with Lijphart's theory of accommodation.

Mandatory Coalition: Party Fiefdoms

The issue of designation is closely linked to interviewees' criticisms of mandatory coalition in Northern Ireland. Amongst SpAds and journalists in particular, there was a general sense that while the consociational system represented the significant political progress made since the peace process, it was not ultimately an effective system of government:

> *I suppose in some ways it's remarkable that they [parties of government] have done as much as they have...but, it is a kind of transition arrangement, and I think that it's not a sustainable way of doing government, everyone sitting at the Executive table, there's a good reason why they don't do it in other countries. You kind of need to have people who broadly agree on the same things and we certainly don't have that at the minute.* (J4)

However, the main issue with the system according to interviewees is that government departments are operated as 'party fiefdoms' (Wilford 2007). That is, because the parties have not voluntarily entered a coalition government but are in power due to the principles of inclusivity and proportionality, there is no incentive or legal requirement (Birrell 2012) for politicians to work together, nor is there a sense of collective responsibility for the governing administration. Our participants noted that while there is an incentive for parties/elites to dialogue and negotiate with each other in order to get into government (Horowitz 2002), this incentive decreases while they are in government where the need to differentiate becomes stronger (Martin and Vanberg 2008). Instead, departments become strongly identified with individual ministers and operated as individual entities (Birrell 2012) and public relations efforts revolve around promoting the minister (Rice and Somerville 2013). For this reason, it is particularly difficult to communicate a cohesive message which is agreed upon by the five parties and to coordinate messages across departments. Interviewees contended that this situation means that ministers, and by default GIOs, are in competition with each other for media coverage. One SpAd explained the common perception that each GIO:

> *works entirely to his or her minister, so there is a danger at times that you've no coordination. Now there is a central [communication and information] mechanism...but the will of the ministers will always over-rule this central mechanism...you get this silo mentality where people are doing separate things...it's almost a replication of the political structure that sits above it...a lot of them [ministers]...try and get the best piece of PR for themselves...rather than looking at the Executive as a whole.* (S6)

This point was corroborated by several journalists, with one stating: "*the EIS is a mirror image of a very monolithic, compulsory coalition that we have here*" (J15). Similarly, GIOs explained how the EIS design, based on the consociational structure, encourages the competition between ministers to infiltrate departmental information dissemination. One GIO said: "*I'm competing with ten or eleven other departments, to try and get my stuff in the papers*" (G3). While GIOs and SpAds commented that overtly party political information would not be disseminated via the EIS system, the fact that ministers 'time' announcements in this confrontational fashion, "*let's out-trump them*" (G8), illustrates a 'below the line' political public relations (PR) tactic (Gaber 2000) which arguably 'politicises' government information, albeit in a procedural rather than substantive manner (Eichbaum and Shaw 2008). The overall consensus across GIOs, SpAds and journalists was that inter-departmental/inter-ministerial rivalry and a deluge of uncoordinated EIS press releases portrays a very disjointed image of government.

Absence of Official Political Opposition

The situation interviewees describe above is intensified and reinforced by the absence of an official political opposition in the legislature. Up until 2016,[8] there was neither a provision nor any funding for opposition parties outside of the Executive, meaning that very strong forms of opposition exist *within* government (McGarry and O'Leary 2006b). According to interviewees this made any unity amongst government partners less likely and the 'government message' more contradictory, for example: *"here you've got four different parties all fighting like ferrets in a sack...I think official opposition would be better here, and it would create better, more mature government, as opposed to what we've got now"* (J9).

Private Dialogue Versus Public Dispute

However, an important distinction to be made about the opposition theme was that while public disagreements are frequent between the parties, when the parties decide it is in their mutual interests, the lack of an official political opposition makes it relatively easy to control the message journalists, and therefore the public, receive. Journalists viewed this as a significant problem for journalistic investigation and for democratic accountability. As one commented:

> we don't have an opposition here, so if something happens around the Executive table, it's often in all parties' priorities to keep that quiet, and you know if we had an opposition, I suppose they would be more likely to challenge things...to alert you to certain things. (J13)

Another explained the wider problem in terms of restricting political debate and facilitating political agenda setting:

> when they're all in government here you know there's no kind of debate to cover...it's all internalised. If there's a big Executive announcement on jobs, they'll all pretty much on board...so where do you go with that? It just kind of frustrates debate ...it's not great for journalism...Natural politics should be,

party A saying doing this to save the economy and party B saying bollocks do B, you know and then you have them both on [the media]. (J16)

For journalists, the opposite of consensus without debate was that when consensus was not reached, a lack of transparency around disagreements or decision-making was also a problem, which was aided through the tactics GIOs employed of withholding information. This was particularly evident in the shared Unionist-Nationalist OFMDFM[9] office:

[GIOs] feel their job is to protect their department rather than to build up relationships with journalists that can work in that quid quo pro way... OFMDFM statements are always horribly bland because you have to persuade two different parties to agree to the same statement...often because they cannot get it agreed between the two ministers, you just won't get any response. (J13)

One journalist suggested this approach reflected a legacy of unaccountable politics:

the tendency here is to be controlling and very conservative and hostile towards sort of external questions...you even look at the history of the peace process, it was actually an external hand that actually broke things up...they just think they can hunker down, just sort of shrug off external criticism or legitimate questions or exposition of wrongdoing. (J15)

However, these kinds of comments should be qualified by GIOs' accounts of the restrictions that their impartial role brings regardless of the political dynamics:

As a civil servant, I am not political and it doesn't matter who my minister is, I'm impartial...I operate as if it's a unified body, the ministers may not...it used to be that we knew who the government was and who the opposition was, the government was Direct Rule and the opposition was the local parties. Now, the government is the opposition...if you're responding to criticism from a government minister you know you're quite often hamstrung in what you can say. (G1)

Such sentiments bear out Birrell's explanation that: "without collective responsibility ministers were [and are] able to disagree in public, in the Assembly and its committees and in the media, both with the declared Executive policy and with other ministers...with no consequences for their place in government" (2012, p. 55).

The Media as Political Opposition

Moreover, in lieu of an official political opposition in Northern Ireland's consociational system, a significant issue topic was how the media act as a de facto political opposition. Typical statements were:

> *the press here, because there's no formal opposition at Stormont, probably take the view that they effectively are the opposition. Which creates a culture where people tend to think little or nothing's been achieved which can be a bit damaging for the political process…the difference is in the UK as a whole, you would have some of the large national papers be broadly sympathetic to one party, some sympathetic to another, most of them are just generally hostile here.* (S2)

While political actors have made similar comments in the UK Westminster context on the media even when an official opposition exists (e.g. Davis 2009), the fact that Northern Ireland has no official opposition party means that media 'opposition' to the government is more pronounced, at least according to SpAds. There was a range of journalist responses to whether or not they felt it was their role to act in an opposition capacity, with some journalists agreeing that this was an important part of their role given Northern Ireland's political system:

> *I think most journalists would see their role as, probably being in opposition actually…there's obviously not an opposition here at the moment politically…it is very important to have <u>someone</u> who's asking questions and not just accepting everything that's said.* (J4)

Several others stated that this was absolutely not their responsibility, for example:

> *all this crap you know that journalism has become the opposition, that's a ridiculous notion, nobody elected us…it is our job to ask the awkward questions but you know, it's not our job to formulate alternative policies.* (J16)

There are clear differences in how 'opposition' is being defined by different individuals. For example, opposition seems to be considered as hostility by S2, as scrutiny by J4 and as proposing alternative policies by J16. Indeed, one journalist offered a helpful explanation as to why this opposition perception may exist amongst government actors:

> *sometimes they'll probably see you as that [the opposition] simply by virtue of the fact that you're challenging them but…it's not that we're challenging them*

from a political point of view, we're challenging them to justify their actions, and that's our job on behalf of our audience...that's a function of a democracy and I think it's a pretty important one. (J7)

Conversely, some journalists commented that the media are often not critical enough of government. One journalist stated that

the worst aspect of the press here I think has been the tendency...to overbuy, to feel that they have to participate in the peace process...and therefore...that you can't come down too hard on the coalition and stuff...it's a new entity and that peace depends on it...it's just simply not our role to assume...that mantle. (J15)

This was a sentiment that journalists felt government actors reinforced at times to justify a lack of information.

Political Control

As a result of Northern Ireland's devolved consociational system, all inter-viewees discussed the significant growth in party political control over departmental functioning and thus departmental communication. Unsurprisingly devolution increased local party political power to the det-riment of civil service power (Knox 2010). However, interviewees from all groups explained that more than this, there is little trust from political parties in the civil service, meaning that government communication is strongly directed by political actors rather than civil servants. One journal-ist explained that:

what you find about this power-sharing administration, is that party press offi-cers tend to sometimes know more than the departmental press officers, so if you actually want the minister, sometimes you're better going to the party as opposed to the department...[with] the party, it goes up the food chain...straight up to the Special Adviser or to the minister, things work a bit faster. (J3)

Moreover, it was generally believed that the DUP and Sinn Féin, who hold the First Minister and Deputy First Minister positions, largely frame this approach to government communication. The two parties' positions as the largest parties in the Executive means that a consensus between them is enough to implement policy decisions and a disagreement enough to halt Assembly business (Knox 2010). This means according to inter-viewees that they can similarly control how Executive *and* departmental issues are communicated. One GIO commented that

DUP and Sinn Féin are in control of everything. They will come in and take your events if they're big events and they want to do them…because they are the main players so they will want to…take all the glory…that's the way it is and that's very clear now. (G9)

At the same time, there was acknowledgement that the DUP and Sinn Féin, especially under the leadership of Peter Robinson and Martin McGuinness, were working increasingly collaboratively: *"there's clearly a growing consensus between the DUP and Sinn Féin that 'we really run the show'. You know they seem to be not spinning against each other"* (J6).

Both past research (e.g. Gormley-Heenan 2006) and the current crisis situation after DUP leadership changed do indicate that relationships between political elites and political leadership in specific are crucial factors in a consociational system, a fundamental point made by Lijphart (1968).

SpAd Control

According to GIOs and journalists, the increased power of SpAds over departmental communication was another indication of the increase in party power over the civil service since the consociational political system was adopted. Interviewees explained that the system, in particular, leaves GIOs constrained but enables political actors to work relatively freely. Several SpAds discussed their role in managing departmental communication and explained this as vital in compensating for the limitations of the Executive Information System:

whenever you've four or five parties in the Executive, each of whom may have competing interests, it's hard to get one clear line that you know a government press officer is comfortable putting out…[therefore] most of the things which are of any interest…isn't put out by the government press office. You know I would have written it, [the minister] would amend it and then you know gone out through the party. (S2)

Thus, one could view the consociational structures in Northern Ireland as facilitating SpAd domination. While SpAds discuss their involvement in departmental communication in benign terms, a number of GIOs provided a more problematic reading of situation. They explained how SpAds can complicate their interactions with journalists by 'leaking' information to journalists, for political purposes. For example *they would leak an awful lot of stuff that they shouldn't really leak at all. So, it's unhelpful when they do speak to journalists because I'm in one room trying to sell something and he's in a room just over there talking to the same journalist about something else, it makes us look...moronic...but they all do it...it's just something we're faced with.* (G5)

Journalists also recognised this tension:

I think there's an uneasy relationship...between the Special Advisers and the civil servants...you might have an announcement that is coming out through the department, the department wants it portrayed in a certain way, the party wants it portrayed in another way. (J1)

At the same time, journalists understood that as close confidants of ministers, SpAds had more 'inside' knowledge on political issues and due to their role being free of political impartiality restrictions, they could reveal this information if they wished, making them preferred sources. Typical comments were, *"when you're speaking to the Special Adviser you know you're speaking to the minister...they can be more helpful in sort of steering you to and also to stories that are in their advantage"* (J13).

Interviewees from all three participant groups commented that 'leaking' was a frequent way of disseminating information from the government because it avoided the protracted process of the Executive Information System, which requires information to be politically neutral and often to have cross-departmental/party agreement in the consociational system (Rice and Somerville 2013).

SpAd Mediation and Protection

At the same time, SpAds illustrated how they have become particularly valued by politicians for their inter-party role as parties try to control communications in the context of a grand coalition (Rice et al. 2015). They explained that their role involved mediating and negotiating with SpAds from other departments/parties to agree on cross-departmental issues. Common sentiments were:

we are the negotiating contact with other parties...when there's cross-departmental issues, where there's areas of controversy, where there's blockages, Special Advisers are the people that are sent in to try and resolve those issues...that's how that's worked through day to day issues right through to the big, big peace stuff. (S4)

Similar findings have been found in other coalition governments such as the Republic of Ireland where political advisers were found to play a negotiating, centralising role (Connaughton 2010). In Scotland there was an increase in SpAd appointments during periods of coalition government to try to limit internal problems (Fawcett and Gay 2010); the same thing occurred in the Conservative-Liberal Democrat coalition in the UK, in part to improve the coalition's public communication (Walker 2012). There are however additional issues to manage in the Northern Ireland situation given that there is a lack of, as one SpAd put it: "*philosophical agreement on many areas*" (S2) and the reality that much of the inter-party relations are confrontational and lead to deadlock. As one SpAd noted: "*we have a political system that doesn't allow anything to be done if you're attitude is simply confrontational*" (S3).

DISCUSSION AND CONCLUSION

The Northern Ireland case demonstrates that institutional change brought about through conflict resolution can create new conflict in other spheres. In the government communication context, the consociational design has challenged existing practices and behaviours and legitimised new norms and antagonistic ways of working (Helms and Oliver 2015). It is useful at this point to reflect on an important issue, raised by Hughes (2011), which is, whether consociationalism should be viewed as an outcome or a process, in terms of how one judges its success. Clearly, a government in Northern Ireland that includes both of the main communities working through democratic means is better than violent conflict. However, Hughes (2011) usefully highlights the value of the "the process of mediation itself (the 'peace process', 'dialogue')" (p. 10). He contends that

> The endogenous actors, those former protagonists in the conflict, are embedded in the routine problems of making the engineering a "worked" example, but their expertise is also being called upon in mediation and dialogue in international conflicts. In contrast, the leading exogenous political actors show little interest in the engineering and emphasise the process of dialogue that led to the accommodation. (p. 11)

Byrne reminds us that "the 1988 Hume–Adams peace talks articulated the need for a healing process of dialogue and partnership that would create a civic society of vision and responsibility" (2001, p. 338). This is a useful point for both summing up our findings and in stressing the importance of assessing the quality of communication as part of the overall debate around consociationalism. It is clear that the consociational design in Northern Ireland impacts the flow of transparent and coordinated communication from the Northern Ireland government departments, which largely affects those civil servants working in an apolitical capacity by restricting their autonomy. The strategic control of communication is then annexed by political parties producing a largely divisive political discourse in public communication. This is exacerbated by the media's focus on areas of inter-party/inter-departmental tension and ministerial disagreement due to, in part, their socialisation in a conflict context. At the same time, a level of cooperation between the 'top', highly polarised parties, DUP and Sinn Féin, in the absence of an official political opposition, actually means that a significant amount of debate is internalised and kept from the media and thus the public.

It is important to note that the purpose of the implementation of consociational power-sharing in Northern Ireland was to enable two deeply divided communities to be represented in government, facilitating them in promoting and communicating their ideologies freely in the context of democratic debate (Tonge 2005). To this extent, consociationalism is working effectively, at least for the two largest parties, the DUP and Sinn Féin. However, if we consider the dialogic properties of Northern Ireland's government communication, we can question the success of the system in the current climate. Kent and Taylor's (2002) work on dialogue from a public relations perspective is apt and applicable here in defining how dialogue can be conceived of and operationalised in the consociational context:

> ""Genuine dialogue" involves more than just a commitment to a relationship. Dialogue occurs when individuals (and sometimes groups) agree to set aside their differences long enough to come to an understanding of the others' positions. Dialogue is not equivalent to agreement. Rather, dialogue is more akin to intersubjectivity where both parties attempt to understand and appreciate the values and interests of the other...Dialogue rests on a willingness to "continue the conversation"—not for purposes of swaying the other with the strength of one's erudition, but as a means of understanding the other and reaching mutually satisfying positions". (Kent and Taylor 2002, pp. 29–30)

Dialogue, from this perspective, thus reflects the successful foundation of accommodative politics. Our participants depicted a context where there is little dialogue of this nature between departments and that when there is, this is done in private by unelected SpAds, and most often between the two dominant parties, who negotiate the content of public messages. This not only goes against Lijphart's idea of consociationalism as an inclusive system for minorities which is useful for consensus building, but also detracts from the *public performance* of dialogue and consensus building which is vitally important for a developing post-conflict society where distrust of institutions pervasive (Gormley-Heenan and Devine 2010). Arguably, it seems the approach of the political elites in Northern Ireland is to reserve dialogue and negotiation to private quarters, at least when it is in the interests of their parties. This approach may play an important role in demonstrating political stability to Northern Ireland stakeholders, which cannot be disregarded given the importance of ensuring security. Indeed, our findings may confirm that the 'appearance of consensus' is all that is possible in this kind of democratic settlement (Dixon 2011). However, it may be that almost 20 years after the signing of the Good Friday Agreement when the Assembly has been suspended due to political breakdown, between the DUP and Sinn Féin,[10] that the time for *public* dialogue on difficult issues has arrived, where the need to see the 'trading' and concessions made between parties is pressing, alongside an open attempt to understand the 'other'. This may actually facilitate a move to more mature power-sharing and even reduce the reliance of the consociational mechanisms designed to protect against 'democratic perversions' (Olsen 1997). Currently, transparency around political decision-making is at the top of the public and media agenda, a re-focus on the foundational process of consociational power-sharing— elite dialogue—may prove timely and constructive. In these respects, Arend Lijphart's theory of accommodation fits well with normative theories of government communication which promote transparency, deliberation and rational consensus (Habermas 1989), and with those which speak to politically divided societies in need of bridging rhetoric and respect of difference (Dryzek 2010). While consociationalism may be best considered as a dynamic process, rather than a static model, the Northern Ireland case clearly demonstrates the problems of implementing mandatory consociationalism as a long-term solution to conflict (Rothchild and Roeder 2005). As Tonge notes, a consociational system: "when unaccompanied by a longer-term plan for societal integration, does not offer the promise of movement towards reconciliation, instead leading to the restatement of difference" (2014, p. 914). Our findings indicate that public dialogue between political elites, facilitated by the media, should be an integral part of such a longer-term plan.

Notes

1. Since the writing of this paper, the Northern Ireland government has collapsed and elections to the new legislature are scheduled for 2 March 2017—see the following link for an overview of the events leading to this and to new elections: http://www.bbc.co.uk/news/uk-northern-ireland-38612860.

2. As with the other 'nations' in the UK (Scotland and Wales) the Labour government in 1998 enacted legislation to devolve power over most domestic political decision-making to the national/regional legislature. The UK government did reserve power over several matters; foreign policy, defence and macro-economic policy.

3. Since the writing of this paper, provision has been made for an official opposition within the Assembly and an official opposition now exists; however, the constitutional arrangement with its consociational guarantees remains in place.

4. For a fuller explanation, see Roche, J. and Barton, B. (2013) (eds) *The Northern Ireland Question: Myth and Reality*. Tonbridge: Wordzworth.

5. http://education.niassembly.gov.uk/post_16/snapshots_of_devolution/gfa/designation.

6. In effect this means that the largest party in the Assembly gets 'first pick' of which departments to manage, with the next largest getting second pick, and so on.

7. Since the time of data collection, the number of government departments in Northern Ireland has been reduced from 12 to 9.

8. Our data is gathered before this period (2012–2013).

9. Now called the *Executive Office*.

10. As Horowitz (2014, pp. 16–17) notes: "The most likely route to serious change for a stalled consociation lies in some unpredictable crisis not necessarily related to the conflict that produced the consociational regime – a shock that makes stalemate intolerable, neutralizes minority objections, and renders quick action necessary. This is typical of agenda-setting events, and it provides an advantage to those who have solutions ready and are merely waiting for problems to develop that can make their solutions attractive. [However] Like most events that trigger major institutional changes, this kind of event may have too much urgency to allow much deliberation."

REFERENCES

Alvesson, M., & Skoldberg, K. (2009). *Reflexive Methodology: New Vistas for Qualitative Research* (2nd ed.). London: Sage.

Andeweg, R. B. (2000). Consociational Democracy. *Annual Review of Political Science, 3*(1), 509–536.

Avery, J. M. (2015). Videomalaise or Virtuous Circle? The Influence of the News Media on Political Trust. *International Journal of Press/Politics, 14*(4), 410–433.

Birrell, D. (2012). *Comparing Devolved Governance*. Basingstoke: Palgrave Macmillan.

Blumler, J. G., & Gurevitch, M. (1995). *The Crisis of Public Communication*. London: Routledge.

Byrne, S. (2001). Consociational and Civic Society Approaches to Peacebuilding in Northern Ireland. *Journal of Peace Research, 38*(3), 327–352.

Canel, M. J., & Sanders, K. (2012). Government Communication: An Emerging Field in Political Communication Research. In A. Semetko & M. Scammell (Eds.), *The SAGE Handbook of Political Communication* (pp. 85–96). London: Sage.

Center, S. A. (2009). The United Nations Department of Public Information: Intractable Dilemmas and Fundamental Contradictions. In K. Sriramesh & D. Verčič (Eds.), *The Global Public Relations Handbook: Theory, Research, and Practice* (2nd ed., pp. 886–903). Oxon: Routledge.

Connaughton, B. (2010). Ireland. In C. Eichbaum & R. Shaw (Eds.), *Partisan Appointees and Public Servants: An International Analysis of the Role of the Political Adviser* (pp. 151–179). Cheltenham: Edward Elgar.

Davis, A. (2009). Journalist-Source Relations, Mediated Reflexivity and the Politics of Politics. *Journalism Studies, 10*(2), 204–219.

Davis, A. (2010). *Political Communication and Social Theory*. Oxon: Routledge.

Department of Finance and Personnel. (2013). *Code of Conduct for Special Advisers*. Belfast: DFP.

Dixon, P. (2011). Is Consociational Theory the Answer to Global Conflict? From the Netherlands to Northern Ireland and Iraq. *Political Studies Review, 9*(3), 309–332.

Dryzek, J. S. (2010). Rhetoric in Democracy: A Systemic Appreciation. *Political Theory, 38*(3), 319–339.

Eichbaum, C., & Shaw, R. (2008). Revisiting Politicization: Political Advisers and Public Servants in Westminster Systems. *Governance: An International Journal of Policy, Administration and Institutions, 21*(3), 337–363.

Eichbaum, C., & Shaw, R. (Eds.). (2010). *Partisan Appointees and Public Servants: An International Analysis of the Role of the Political Adviser*. Cheltenham: Edward Elgar.

Evans, J., & Tonge, J. (2009). Social Class and Party Choice in Northern Ireland's Ethnic Blocs. *West European Politics, 32*(5), 1012–1030.

Fawcett, L. (2002). Who's Setting the Postdevolution Agenda in Northern Ireland? *The Harvard International Journal of Press/Politics, 7*(4), 14–33.

Fawcett, P., & Gay, O. (2010). The United Kingdom. In C. Eichbaum & R. Shaw (Eds.), *Partisan Appointees and Public Servants: An International Analysis of the Role of the Political Adviser* (pp. 24–63). Cheltenham: Edward Elgar.

Gaber, I. (2000). Government by Spin: An Analysis of the Process. *Media, Culture & Society, 22*(4), 507–518.

Gaber, O. (2004). Alastair Campbell, Exit Stage Left: Do the 'Phillis' Recommendations Represent a New Chapter in Political Communications or Is It 'Business as Usual'? *Journal of Public Affairs, 4*(4), 365–373.

Gaber, I. (2007). Too Much of a Good Thing: The 'Problem' of Political Communications in a Mass Media Democracy. *Journal of Public Affairs, 7*, 219–234.

Gormley-Heenan, C. (2006). Chameleonic Leadership: Towards a New Understanding of Political Leadership During the Northern Ireland Peace Process. *Leadership, 2*(1), 53–75.

Gormley-Heenan, C., & Devine, P. (2010). The 'Us' in Trust: Who Trusts Northern Ireland's Political Institutions and Actors? *Government and Opposition, 45*(2), 143–165.

Gregory, A. (2012). UK Government Communications: Full Circle in the 21st Century? *Public Relations Review, 38*, 367–375.

Habermas, J. (1989). *The Structural Transformation of the Public Sphere: An Inquiry into a Category of Bourgeois Society* (T. Burger & F. Lawrence, Trans.). Cambridge: Polity Press.

Hallin, D. C., & Mancini, P. (2004). *Comparing Media Systems: Three Models of Media and Politics*. Cambridge: Cambridge University Press.

Hayward, K. (2011). Convergence/Divergence: Party Political Discourse in Northern Ireland's Transition from Conflict. *Dynamics of Asymmetric Conflict, 4*(3), 196–213.

Helms, W. S., & Oliver, C. (2015). Radical Settlements to Conflict: Conflict Management and Its Implications for Institutional Change. *Journal of Management & Organization, 21*(4), 471–494.

Horowitz, D. L. (2002). Constitutional Design: Proposals Versus Processes. In A. Reynolds (Ed.), *The Architecture of Democracy: Constitutional Design, Conflict Management, and Democracy* (pp. 15–36). Oxford: Oxford University Press.

Horowitz, D. L. (2014). Ethnic Power Sharing: Three Big Problems. *Journal of Democracy, 25*(2), 5–20.

Hughes, J. (2011, March 29). Is Northern Ireland a "Model" for Conflict Resolution? *LSE Workshop on State Reconstruction After Civil War*. Available from: http://personal.lse.ac.uk/hughesj/images/NIModel.pdf

Kent, M. L., & Taylor, M. (2002). Toward a Dialogic Theory of Public Relations. *Public Relations Review, 28*(1), 21–37.

Knox, C. (2010). *Devolution and the Governance of Northern Ireland*. Manchester: Manchester University Press.

Langdridge, D. (2007). *Phenomenological Psychology: Theory, Research and Method*. Harlow: Pearson Prentice Hall.

Laursen, B., & Valentini, C. (2013). Media Relations in the Council of the European Union: Insights into the Council Press Officers' Professional Practices. *Journal of Public Affairs, 13*(3), 230–238.

Lijphart, A. (1968). Typologies of Democratic Systems. *Comparative Political Studies, 1*(1), 3–44.

Lijphart, A. (1999). *Patterns of Democracy: Government Forms and Performance in Thirty-Six Countries*. New Haven: Yale University Press.

Lijphart, A. (2008). *Thinking About Democracy: Power Sharing and Majority Rule in Theory and Practice*. Oxon: Routledge.

Martin, L. W., & Vanberg, G. (2008). Coalition Government and Political Communication. *Political Research Quarterly, 61*(3), 502–516.

McEvoy, J. (2006). Elite Interviewing in a Divided Society: Lessons from Northern Ireland. *Politics, 26*(3), 184–191.

McGarry, J., & O'Leary, B. (2006a). Consociational Theory, Northern Ireland's Conflict, and Its Agreement. Part 1: What Consociationalists Can Learn from Northern Ireland. *Government and Opposition, 41*(1), 43–63.

McGarry, J., & O'Leary, B. (2006b). Consociational Theory, Northern Ireland's Conflict, and Its Agreement. Part 2: What Critics of Consociation Can Learn from Northern Ireland. *Government and Opposition, 41*(2), 249–277.

McLaughlin, G., & Baker, S. (2010). *The Propaganda of Peace: The Role of Media and Culture in the Northern Ireland Peace Process*. Bristol: Intellect.

Miller, D. (1994). *Don't Mention the War: Northern Ireland, Propaganda, and the Media*. London: Pluto Press.

Olsen, J. P. (1997). Institutional Design in Democratic Contexts. *The Journal of Political Philosophy, 5*(3), 203–229.

Pieczka, M. (2011). Public Relations as Dialogic Expertise? *Journal of Communication Management, 15*(2), 108–124.

Rice, C., & Somerville, I. (2013). Power-Sharing and Political Public Relations: Government-Press Relationships in Northern Ireland's Developing Democratic Institutions. *Public Relations Review, 39*(4), 293–302.

Rice, C., & Somerville, I. (2017). Political Contest and Oppositional Voices in Post-conflict Democracy: The Impact of Institutional Design on Government-Media Relations. *International Journal of Press/Politics, 22*(1), 92–110.

Rice, C., Somerville, I., & Wilson, J. (2015). Democratic Communication and the Role of Special Advisers in Northern Ireland's Consociational Government. *International Journal of Public Administration, 38*(1), 4–14.

Roper, J. (2005). Symmetrical Communication: Excellent Public Relations or a Strategy for Hegemony? *Journal of Public Relations Research, 17*(1), 69–86.

Rothchild, D., & Roeder, P. G. (2005). Power Sharing as an Impediment to Peace and Democracy. In P. G. Roeder & D. Rothchild (Eds.), *Sustainable Peace: Power and Democracy After Civil Wars* (pp. 29–50). Ithaca: Cornell University Press.

Sanders, K. (2013). The Strategic Shift of UK Government Communication. In K. Sanders & M. J. Canel (Eds.), *Government Communication: Cases and Challenges* (pp. 79–98). London: Bloomsbury.

Smith, J., Flowers, P., & Larkin, M. (2009). *Interpretative Phenomenological Analysis: Theory, Method and Research.* London: Sage.

Somerville, I., & Kirby, S. (2012). Public Relations and the Northern Ireland Peace Process: Dissemination, Reconciliation and the 'Good Friday Agreement' Referendum Campaign. *Journal of Public Relations Inquiry, 1*(3), 231–255.

Sriramesh, K., & Verčič, D. (Eds.). (2009). *The Global Public Relations Handbook: Theory, Research, and Practice* (2nd ed.). Oxon: Routledge.

Tansey, O. (2007). Process Tracing and Elite Interviewing: A Case for Non-probability Sampling. *PS: Political Science and Politics, 40*(4), 765–772.

Tonge, J. (2005). *The New Northern Irish Politics?* Hampshire: Palgrave Macmillan.

Tonge, J. (2014). *Comparative Peace Processes.* Cambridge: Polity.

Walker, B. (2012). The Coalition and the Media. In R. Hazell & B. Yong (Eds.), *The Politics of Coalition: How the Conservative-Liberal Democrat Government Works* (pp. 135–154). Oxford: Hart.

Wilford, R. (2007). Inside Stormont: The Assembly and the Executive. In P. Carmichael, C. Knox, & R. Osborne (Eds.), *Devolution and Constitutional Change in Northern Ireland* (pp. 167–185). Manchester: Manchester University Press.

Wilson, J., & Stapleton, K. (2006). Identity Categories in Use: Britishness, Devolution, and the Ulster Scots Identity in Northern Ireland. In J. Wilson & K. Stapleton (Eds.), *Devolution and Identity* (pp. 11–31). Aldershot: Ashgate.

Yong, B., & Hazell, R. (2014). *Special Advisers: Who They Are, What They Do and Why They Matter.* Oxford: Hart Publishing.

CHAPTER 7

The 2016 European Union Referendum, Consociationalism and the Territorial Constitution of the UK

Andrew Blick

INTRODUCTION

The UK is a society marked by significant diversity: ethnic, religious, linguistic and political. This variety is often associated with political tension, or even—especially over issue of Ireland/Northern Ireland—violent conflict. Typically, the overall UK system is not classified fully as consociational[1] in nature. However, the challenges faced by the UK state arising from this heterogeneity are similar to those difficulties which consociationalism is intended to manage. Moreover, some administrative and constitutional mechanisms developed partly in response to these problems could be said to display characteristics of a consociational nature. Taking into account these overlaps with consociational analysis, the following chapter considers the developing UK polity through the prism of the diverse reactions to the European Union (EU) referendum of June 2016 from the different executives of the UK.

On 2 October 2016 Theresa May gave her inaugural speech as a leader—and newly installed Prime Minister—to the Conservative Party

A. Blick (✉)
King's College London, London, UK

© The Author(s) 2018
M. Jakala et al. (eds.), *Consociationalism and Power-Sharing in Europe*, International Political Theory,
https://doi.org/10.1007/978-3-319-67098-0_7

conference. Unavoidably, it focused on the event that had brought her to power: the 'leave' vote in the EU referendum of 23 June, and its consequences. She was insistent that she would interpret this result as an irresistible mandate to take the UK out of the EU. As she put it: '[t]he referendum result was clear. It was legitimate. It was the biggest vote for change this country has ever known. Brexit means Brexit – and we're going to make a success of it.' In executing this perceived mandate, May was determined that she and her ministers should dominate the process from the UK end: 'the negotiations between the United Kingdom and the European Union are the responsibility of the Government and nobody else.' She criticised those whom she saw as seeking to frustrate the verdict of the people through the courts or the UK Parliament. Moreover, for May, the decision to leave had been taken by the UK as a whole and should therefore be implemented by the UK-level executive. In her words:

> Because we voted in the referendum as one United Kingdom, we will negotiate as one United Kingdom, and we will leave the European Union as one United Kingdom. There is no opting out from Brexit. And I will never allow divisive nationalists to undermine the precious Union between the four nations of our United Kingdom. (May 2016)

This formulation was in part a response to a position of vulnerability. Unity around the decision to leave was manifestly lacking. The EU vote of 23 June 2016 both revealed and exacerbated divisions in the UK polity. The result was close in percentage terms—51.9 per cent 'leave' versus 48.1 per cent 'remain'.[2] In themselves, these figures made claims about a firm mandate harder to sustain. Moreover, underneath this overall figure, there was polarisation across multiple spectrums, suggesting further problems with the nature of the outcome. Sharp social divisions were apparent in voting patterns. Opinion research conducted by Ipsos-MORI showed, for instance, substantial age differentials. Older voters were broadly more likely to opt for 'leave'. The 18–24 age group was 75 per cent 'remain' and 25 per cent 'leave', while for the 65–74 age group the percentages were 34 remain and 66 leave, and for 75 and above 37 remain and 63 leave. When ethnicity is taken into account, whites were 46 per cent remain and 54 per cent leave, while those in the Black and Minority Ethnic category were 69 per cent remain to 31 per cent leave. The AB social class, including such groups as managers and professionals, was 59 to 41 per cent in favour of remain, while the DE group, comprising semi-skilled and unskilled workers, was 36 to 64 per cent in favour of leave. People with no educational qualifications were 30 per cent remain and 70 per cent leave, while those with a degree or above supported remain by 68 per cent to 32 per cent. Students were 80 per cent remain and 20 per cent leave (Ipsos-MORI 2016).

A further divergence with important political and constitutional ramifications was territorial. England voted by 53.4 per cent to 46.4 per cent to leave; though within England, in Greater London, there was a 59.9 per cent remain vote, to 40.1 per cent leave, with all but five of 33 London boroughs producing remain majorities. In Wales, the leave lead was 52.5 to 47.5 per cent. In Scotland, remain won by 62 per cent to 38 per cent, with every single counting area producing a remain majority; while in Northern Ireland, there was a 'remain' result, by 55.8 to 44.2 (BBC News 2016). Geographical divisions in voting patterns, then, were clear. In the case of Northern Ireland, as well as there being a majority that diverged from the whole UK outcome, there was a further cleavage within the territory itself (Garry 2016). To some extent the characteristics of leave and remain voters in Northern Ireland differentiated along similar lines to those elsewhere in the UK. Nonetheless, Garry concludes that there was, in Northern Ireland, strong evidence of 'a very strong ethno-national nature to this vote' (2016, p. 17). To a significant extent, preferences over EU membership reflected the long-standing constitutional dispute in the region. For instance, of those brought up in the Catholic religion, 85 per cent voted stay and 15 per cent voted leave; while of Protestants, the scores were 40 per cent remain and 60 per cent leave. Another, connected, way of differentiating voters was by constitutional preference. Of those who supported Northern Ireland remaining in the UK under direct rule, 40 per cent were in the remain group and 60 per cent leave. Advocates of continuing inside the UK under devolution were 58 per cent leave and 42 per cent leave, while those who wished to join with the Republic of Ireland were 85 per cent remain and 15 per cent leave. As Garry puts it: '[t]he referendum divided leavers from remainers; equally it divided Protestant unionists from Catholic nationalists' (2016, p. 3).

As this analysis of the Northern Ireland result demonstrates, territory and identity were important features of the EU vote, and they in turn had a connection to constitutional issues, pertaining not only to how the UK should be governed, but whether it should continue to exist in its present form. It was not only Northern Ireland to which these features of the EU referendum were important. Important and differing considerations arose for the whole UK. The present chapter seeks to place them in context and analyse them. First, it considers the historical background. Second, it analyses—with particular attention to their territorial content—policy papers issued by three governments: those of Scotland, Wales and the UK, setting out their post-referendum positions. No such equivalent document exists for Northern Ireland (HM Government 2017, p. 20). Third, the chapter considers the political setting within which each approach was formulated. Finally, it discusses the implications both of these stances and the differences between them, considering applicable modes of analysis, namely those of federalism and consociationalism.

Historic Trajectory

A long-term perspective is required if we are fully to appreciate the nature of the EU vote and the responses it prompted. Territorial and national divergence has been the essence of the UK throughout its existence. Its pre-history involves four distinct national units, each with its own culture and political tradition, sometimes overlapping in physical space. These patterns remain important today, in such forms as divisions within Northern Ireland or bilingualism in Wales, and the differences in the party systems prevailing across the UK (Blick 2014, 2015, 2016a). The UK proper was formed from a series of incorporations, each distinct in nature. First, Wales was legally absorbed into England in the sixteenth century (Morgan 1971; Roberts 1972). Then England (including Wales) and Scotland merged into Great Britain following the Treaty and Acts of Union of 1706–1707 (Ford 2007; Jackson 2012; Macinnes 2007; Wicks 2001). Great Britain and Ireland formed the UK under the Act of Union of 1800 (Brown et al. 2003; Smith 2001). Yet while affecting incorporation, both of the latter unions provided protections for the particularities of Scotland and (to a lesser extent) Ireland against English hegemony (Blick 2015). Consequently, the UK has been characterised by pronounced diversity: differences in official religion, in the organisation of local government (McConnell 2004), and even the continued operation of parallel legal systems (Dickson 2001; Manson-Smith 2004; Slapper and Kelly 2013).

The territorial variation built into the UK from the outset was elaborated upon during its existence. Funding mechanisms—the 'Goschen Formula' originating in the late nineteenth century and the 'Barnett Formula' dating from the 1970s—have provided different parts of the UK with their own privileges with respect to resource allocation (Heald and McLeod 2005; McCrone 1999; McLean 2005). Ministers and departments included within the UK government but with territorially specific functions were established (Gibson 1985). In Northern Ireland from the 1920s to the 1970s an elected tier of devolved government functioned (Birrell and Murie 1980; Mansergh 1936). These patterns have encouraged some scholars to conclude that, despite a more traditional view of the UK as a unitary constitution, the label 'union state' is more applicable. Indeed, one academic has argued that 'state of unions' is the most appropriate title, reflecting the composite of multiple and diverse mergers that have over time comprised the UK (Mitchell 2006, 2010). Given this uncertainty about the true historic nature of the UK state, various conceptual frameworks, including those offered by federalism and consociationalism, have potential value to an understanding of its qualities.

Some of the potential for tensions produced by the 2016 EU referendum, then, has existed in latent form throughout the history of the UK. Indeed, we can find a pre-echo of these difficulties from time of the popular vote on membership of the European Economic Community (EEC) of 1975. On this occasion, some commentators noted that problems might arise if different parts of the UK produced majorities in different directions (Mackintosh 1975). This outcome did not come about. In 2016, however, following similar warnings, it did (Bogdanor 2015). Moreover, developments in the intervening period gave the divergence in voting patterns a greater significance than it might have possessed four decades previously. Institutions with their own electoral legitimacy had been introduced to Wales and Scotland—and re-introduced to Northern Ireland (Bogdanor 2001). They were potentially in a position to make interventions in response to the referendum. Moreover, the advent of devolution expanded upon the geographical diversity of the UK constitution in such a way that might encourage the view that a qualitative change was underway or had taken place in its nature. For instance, some might view it as having developed increasingly federal characteristics, even if it had not yet become fully federal (Blick 2014, 2015, 2016a). Another possible interpretation was that the UK was partly responding to problems of a nature that had in other countries encouraged consociational responses and that it had to some extent followed this type of constitutional model.[3] For instance, devolved institutions afford the communities that come within their remit localised control over key policy areas such as health, education and culture and use electoral systems more proportionate than those employed to determine the membership of the House of Commons, the elected chamber of the Westminster Parliament. The EU referendum has prompted the advancement of models for the reconfiguration of the UK political system in which these federal or consociational qualities might become more pronounced still, for instance, through the introduction of consensus-based decision-making at the UK level.

Within this changed constitutional landscape, particular difficulties manifested themselves in relation to Northern Ireland and Scotland. The devolved institutions of Northern Ireland were themselves one facet of a wider peace process—more decisively consociational in character than any other feature of the UK political system—the most important encapsulation of which was found in the Belfast or 'Good Friday' Agreement of 1998 (McGarry and O'Leary 2004; Northern Ireland Office 1998). This document contained numerous references to the EU. They suggest that an important component of conciliation between conflicting groups was the assumption that both sides of the border in the island of Ireland, though separated for the time being into two states, would share membership of a wider entity, the EU (Morgan 2000; Meehan 2000). This arrangement was also crucial to trade and commercial activity. Departure from the EU presented the danger of erecting barriers between the Republic and the North if Northern Ireland, along with the rest of the UK, withdrew from the Single Market and the Customs Union (Blick 2016d; Burke 2016; Douglas-Scott 2014). Aware of such concerns and their implications for the maintenance of peace and prosperity in the island of Ireland, the UK government stressed its intention to avoid what was known as a 'hard' border (McHugh 2017).

A further current of change that has made different majorities within the UK more destabilising in 2016 than they might have been in 1975 is the rise of the independence movement in Scotland (Agatstein 2015). The Scottish National Party has held office at devolved level, either as a minority or majority administration, since 2007 (Lynch 2009; Mitchell et al. 2012). An independence referendum was held in 2014, and though a majority of those taking part supported continued participation in the UK, the episode seemed, initially at least, to add momentum to the cause of Scottish departure from the UK (McHarg 2016). Furthermore, a key part of the 'Better Together' platform had been that remaining within the UK was desirable since it would ensure continued membership of the EU. Exit from the UK, so the pro-union argument ran, would remove Scotland from the EU, with no guarantee of immediate or fast-track accession (Bourne 2014). The referendum of 2016 reversed this premise. Now it was possible to perceive being part of the UK as a threat to Scottish presence within the EU. Majorities in England and Wales, it could be held, were forcing Scotland out of the EU contrary to the wishes of a majority of those voting in Scotland (Blick 2016d). Appropriately, then, the following consideration of policy documents commences with that produced by the Scottish executive, the first body to issue its views in this form.

A View from Scotland

The (SNP) Scottish Government published *Scotland's Place in Europe* on 20 December 2016. In her foreword, the First Minister, Nicola Sturgeon, opened with the statement: 'On 23 June, the people of Scotland voted categorically and decisively to remain within the European Union' (Scottish Government 2016, p. v). The Scottish Government, she noted, remained firmly committed to the ideal of European integration (Scottish Government 2016, p. viii). Sturgeon recalled further that there was a 'remain' vote in Northern Ireland, while Wales and England favoured 'leave'. Her conclusion was that '[t]he stark divergence in the democratic will between the different nations of the United Kingdom…demands a reappraisal of how political power in the UK is exercised'.

Sturgeon described the position of the Scottish Government as being in favour of an independent Scotland that was a full member of the EU. However, she expressed a willingness to work 'in good faith and a spirit of compromise' to find ways, in the circumstances of UK exit from the EU, of protecting the interests of Scotland within the UK. Sturgeon presented the way in which the UK government approached the formulation of its policy as a test of how far the UK could be viewed as 'a partnership of equals' (Scottish Government 2016, p. v). The sole purpose of the Scottish Government would be to safeguard Scotland. It would seek both to ensure that Scotland was involved in the process and that it had a substantive influence on the UK approach. The paper acknowledged that responsibility for negotiating exit from the EU fell to UK ministers. However, the Scottish Government referred to a 'clear previous commitment' that Scotland would be engaged in policy formulation and execution. It expected the undertaking it identified to be abided by. If the necessary protections for Scotland could not be achieved, the paper cautioned, the Scottish people should be given the chance to opt for independence in a further referendum (Scottish Government 2016, p. viii).

The stated initial goal of the Scottish Government was that the UK as a whole should remain a member of the Single Market via the European Economic Area (EEA). This end, it was held, could be achieved at first through membership of the European Free Trade Association (EFTA). The Scottish Government also wanted the UK to remain within the EU Customs Union (Scottish Government 2016, pp. 24–5). However, the paper noted that it was unlikely that the UK government would find such approaches acceptable. In such a circumstance, the Scottish Government would seek to develop an arrangement enabling Scotland to participate in the EEA and Single Market despite the remainder of the UK being outside them (Scottish Government 2016, p. 26). At the same time, it would preserve free trade with the remainder of the UK (Scottish Government 2016, p. 27).

Scotland's Place in Europe sought to bolster the plausibility of this proposal on a number of grounds. It drew attention to the existence of special arrangements elsewhere in the EU. For instance, while Denmark was a Member State of the EU, the Faroe Islands and Greenland were part neither of the EU nor of the EEA. The Channel Islands were not members of the EU but were incorporated into the Customs Union and in some senses the Single Market. The UK government was also likely to seek flexibility in the approach taken to the status of Northern Ireland and Gibraltar as the UK left the EU. Moreover, the Mayor of London was hoping for differential arrangements for the city region he represented. The UK government might also try to obtain a degree of variation by sector within the domestic economy, as opposed to territorial differentiation. Leeway of different kinds, therefore, so the paper reasoned, was already on the agenda and consequently could be provided for Scotland (Scottish Government 2016, pp. 26–7). The Scottish Government also presented a particular view of the UK constitution in support of its proposal. It described a 'principle of differentiation' that was intrinsic to the UK from the outset and that had been augmented by the introduction and development of devolution. The paper depicted the model it proposed for Scotland—being within the Single Market while other parts of the UK were not—as an outgrowth of this historic and ongoing pattern of constitutional diversity (Scottish Government 2016, p. 27).

Another important theme of the paper was the constitutional implications for the UK of departure from the EU. The Scottish Government took the view that exit suggested the need for 'a fundamental reconsideration of the nature of the UK state, with different relationships between its constituent parts as well as changes to the detail of their powers' (Scottish Government 2016, p. 41). The crucial concern identified in the text was the division of powers between devolved and central level in the UK after leaving the EU. The Scottish Government asserted three broad principles. The first was that matters that had previously been subject to European law, if they fell within policy areas that were devolved, would come within the remit of the Scottish Parliament. These areas included health; protection of the environment; higher education and research; fisheries and the marine environment; agriculture, food and drink; and civil and criminal law and law enforcement. The paper held that locating these powers at the UK level would require the consent of the Scottish Parliament, and the Scottish Government would oppose its being provided (Scottish Government 2016, pp. 41–42). The second principle advanced by the Scottish Government was that there were some powers that did not currently fall within the devolved category, including equality, health and safety, protection of consumers, and employment, which should be transferred to Scotland to enable the protection of the rights of citizens once European law ceased to apply to the UK. Third, there were other areas of activity for which further devolution should be considered. Among them were responsibilities pertaining to freedom of movement of people, goods, capital and services and international relations (Scottish Government 2016, pp. 43–44).

In its discussion of powers covered by the first principle, *Scotland's Place in Europe* acknowledged that there might be a need for a 'crossborder framework' for some areas of activity that were devolved. But—in an assertion that was of a consociational flavour—the document insisted that decisions made under this arrangement would be subject to consensus between the devolved and UK executives involved and 'not...imposition from Westminster' (Scottish Government 2016, p. 41). This passage addressed the wider constitutional system of the UK. Largely, however, the text was focused on Scotland and how much control it could exert. As the paper put it, the issues it engaged with respect to devolved powers were likely to 'have resonance in other parts of the UK' but 'the governance and constitutional arrangements of England, Wales and Northern Ireland are matters for the people of those countries' (Scottish Government 2016, p. 40). Yet, though not generally directly concerned with broader issues for the UK, the Scottish Government nonetheless pledged to promote its approach to new constitutional arrangements in its interactions with the devolved and UK executives and other bodies including the

London Assembly (Scottish Government 2016, p. 44). The implication was that there might be some kind of joint exertion of pressure for the introduction of mechanisms ensuring UK government was conducted by territorial consent.

A View from Wales

The second entrant in the field after the Scottish Government was its Welsh devolved counterpart. On 23 January 2017 the (Labour) Welsh Government launched a statement jointly with the Welsh nationalist party, Plaid Cymru, entitled *Securing Wales' Future: Transition from the European Union to a New Relationship with Europe*. Both parties to the document had supported 'remain'. But their position, as presented in this text, was that referendum result must lead to departure from the EU in some form. The preface by the First Minister, Carwyn Jones, opened with the statement that 'A majority in Wales voted to leave the European Union...and the Welsh Government has been clear from the outset that this democratic decision must be respected.' (Welsh Government 2017, p. 4). In this sense, there was some alignment with the stance of the UK government, which treated the referendum as obliging it to implement exit from the EU. Yet there was no reference in the Welsh account of the referendum mandate to the UK as a whole. Rather it was the 'majority in Wales' that created this imperative to leave. This phrasing might lead to the question: what if a 'majority in Wales' had voted in a different direction to the majority in the UK?

While sharing the broad platform that the referendum created a requirement to depart from the EU, *Securing Wales' Future* contained policy propositions that were, as we will see, difficult to reconcile with the outlook of the UK government or were at least markedly different in emphasis. In its preferences for the type of exit the UK should secure, the Welsh executive took a similar stance to the Scottish. Most importantly, the Welsh Government stated that '[t]he case for continuing Single Market participation is overwhelming and we can agree to no other position' (Welsh Government 2017, p. 9). This outcome, the document held, could be achieved through membership of EFTA and via this organisation a place in the EEA. Otherwise there might be a special agreement tailored specifically for the UK. There would be 'a continuing need to ensure that the domestic regulatory regime for goods and services within the UK are [sic] compatible with those of the EU' (Welsh Government 2017, p. 10).

The paper also favoured—albeit only on balance—continued membership of the Customs Union (p. 14). It insisted that the UK government should make a firm guarantee to all EU migrants currently present within the country that their rights would be preserved following departure from the EU (Welsh Government 2017, p. 15). The value of freedom of movement within Europe was stressed (Welsh Government 2017, p. 16). The paper noted that in contrast to the UK generally Wales was a net recipient of EU funds. It asserted that Wales should continue to receive support at equivalent levels to those it would have received had the UK remained within the EU (Welsh Government 2017, p. 25).

Alongside the substantive agenda it contained, *Securing Wales' Future* presented views about the constitutional framework within which policy should be formulated. The thrust of the text was that given the development of devolution in the years since the UK acceded to the then EEC in 1973, after departure it would not be possible to return to arrangements that prevailed before the UK joined. The paper reiterated the already-existing policy of the Welsh Government for the establishment of a constitutional convention to consider arrangements for the governance of the UK. In the context of departure from the EU, a shift to a 'more federal' system for the UK was, it held, appropriate. In promoting this model, the Welsh Government and Plaid Cymru addressed an important conundrum that the prospect of removal from the EU raised for the UK political system, with which the Scottish Government had also concerned itself. A range of powers such as fisheries, agriculture, economic development and the environment were technically devolved but were subject to EU-level regulation. The Welsh Government paper presented the assumption that 'At the point of UK exit from the EU, when EU regulatory and administrative frameworks cease to apply, these powers will continue to be devolved in Wales.' There were other areas of operation due to be repatriated, in which, while they were not devolved, Wales also had an 'active interest'. This latter category included international trade, employment law and policy on competition. Some of these authorities might in future become devolved. The handling all of them would, post-exit, require 'a new approach to the UK's governance structure that reflects the interdependencies and interests between devolved and non-devolved' layers (Welsh Government 2017, p. 26).

The text recognised a need to ensure that the devolved institutions, in utilising the powers they possessed that had been released from the EU remit, did not undermine the uniformity of regulation within the

UK required for it to function as a single market. The Welsh Government offered to participate in the development of mechanisms to ensure the necessary standardisation, but subject to certain conditions. The devolved legislatures of Wales, Scotland and Northern Ireland would take part 'on equal terms' with the government of the UK, which would represent England (Welsh Government 2017, p. 26). At least current levels of discretion for the devolved institutions to pursue their own distinctive policies would be maintained. There would be a need for 'robust, and genuinely independent arbitration mechanisms' to determine disagreements over whether the overall UK framework was being adhered to in particular instances. The paper concluded that 'wholly new intergovernmental machinery' was needed, both to ensure that devolved powers were aligned with each other in cases where the different executives of the UK agreed they needed to be and for the handling of matters that were not devolved, but had important consequences for devolved operations. The paper also held that there should be an independent means of resolving disputes between the devolved and UK levels if there was disagreement at devolved level with the use being made of a non-devolved power by the UK government, if it had significant impact at devolved level (Welsh Government 2017, p. 27). It contended that the Joint Ministerial Committee (JMC), a non-statutory body for consultation between the UK and devolved administrations (Blick, 2016c), might be developed into a 'UK Council of Ministers' dealing with spheres of action where the consent of all the executives was necessary (Welsh Government 2017, p. 28).

While the Welsh Government preferred the term 'federal' to describe the direction of development it projected, 'consociational' might also have been applied. It was clear from the positions set out by both the Welsh and Scottish executives that departure from the EU created the prospect of constitutional controversy and disruption. Membership of this supranational organisation had provided a means of preventing conflicts about how particular powers should be deployed, through removing them from immediate UK control. This means of dispute resolution—or avoidance—was no longer possible, and other methods had to be found: a context in which consociationalism was relevant.

The Position of the UK Government

On 2 February 2017 the UK government published *The United Kingdom's Exit from and New Partnership with the European Union*. The foreword by May claimed the support of '65 million people willing us' to make exit negotiations a success. She went on to assert that 'after all the division and discord, the country is coming together.' While conceding that '[t]he referendum was divisive at times', she emphasised the importance of 'the strength of our identity as one nation' (HM Government 2017, p. 3). For May, therefore, the emphasis at this point was on a single UK identity, rather than multiple polities with territorial and other connections. This approach represented a firm distinction from that presented from the Scottish and Welsh perspectives. The constitutional outlook of *The United Kingdom's exit*...largely matched this less differentiated perception of the UK state.

Early passages of the paper dealt with a proposed Great Repeal Bill intended to provide continuity through translating EU law into domestic legislation at the point of exit. From this point, the text explained, Parliament 'and, where appropriate, the devolved legislatures' would be able to make choices about retaining, altering or expunging former European law (HM Government 2017, p. 9). The government then described the various ways in which outside groups would be involved in the process of leaving the EU. They included 'organisations, companies and institutions' from across the UK. The Westminster Parliament would be engaged in providing the required statutory powers. There would also be an ongoing role for the JMC, including as it did within its membership the devolved executives and the UK government. It would meet in its full incarnation with the Prime Minister in the chair, and in the form of a sub-committee on EU Negotiations—abbreviated to JMC (EN)—chaired by the Secretary of State for Exiting the EU (HM Government 2017, pp. 10–11). However, while the UK government sought to make use of the JMC, it did not share the view of the Welsh administration that the JMC might be developed as part of a shift towards a more federal constitutional structure for the UK.

The text then turned to the crucial issue that the plan to leave the EU created in relation to the territorial governance of the UK, that both the Scottish and Welsh Government/Plaid Cymru had addressed. The UK government white paper noted that devolution had been introduced within the framework of the UK being an EU member state. The law-making power of the devolved legislatures was exercised subject to a legal requirement that it remain compatible with European law. Consequently, the powers these legislatures possessed—in areas such as transport, the environment and agriculture—operated within a framework of 'rules... devised and agreed in Brussels'. After departure from the EU, the white paper explained, 'these rules will be set here in the UK by democratically elected representatives.' But at what level within the UK? The return of authorities to the UK from the EU would create the possibility to discern the most appropriate tier at which to locate them, 'ensuring power sits closer to the people of the UK than ever before'. The government stressed 'that no decisions currently taken by the devolved administrations will be removed from them'. It would also take the opportunity of repatriation of powers 'to ensure that more decisions are devolved' (HM Government 2017, p. 18).

This wording presented a clear challenge to other perceptions of the post-EU position. The Scottish and Welsh documents had presented the idea of a default assumption that powers within devolved remits would be devolved once returned from the EU. While group decision-making might be possible in some areas, it would be subject to consent and might potentially be extended to involve the devolved institutions in previously non-devolved remits. Underpinning its differing outlook, the UK government then emphasised the significance of the internal market of the UK, noting a calculation that Scottish exports to the remainder of the UK exceeded those to the EU by a multiple of four. It was therefore vital, the text held, that 'no new barriers to living and doing business within our own Union' were erected. The UK would retain the appropriate 'common standards and frameworks for our own domestic market', creating a firm basis for the agreement of international trade deals. The government would apply these values when collaborating with the devolved executives 'on an approach to returning powers from the EU that works for the whole of the UK' and for Wales, Scotland and Northern Ireland. It would also promote the expansion of the autonomy of local authorities in circumstances where there was a sound economic basis for such changes (HM Government 2017, p. 19).

Further territorial issues arose in connection with the Isle of Man, the Channel Islands and the Overseas Territories, the links of which with the EU would alter following UK exit. Special considerations applied in the case of Gibraltar where the EU treaties had extensive application, though it was not a member of the Customs Union. Various mechanisms had been formed to take the interests and views of these territories into account (HM Government 2017, p. 20). Another significant concern was the island of Ireland, both Northern Ireland, a part of the UK, and the Republic (HM Government 2017, p. 22). A particular apprehension raised by the prospect of UK exit from the EU, discussed above, was whether it might entail the restoration of the 'hard' land border between the North and the Republic and of trade barriers between the two. There were serious economic implications, and possibly a threat to the peace process in an area that had been a site of tension and conflict for centuries. The UK government pledged to cooperate with the Northern Ireland executive and the government of the Republic to develop a workable approach that took into account these special circumstances (HM Government 2017, p. 23).

The white paper took a firm stance in certain policy areas. Control over inward migration and therefore exemption from the Free Movement Directive was essential (HM Government 2017, p. 25). Partly as a consequence of this position, the UK would 'not be seeking membership of the Single Market'. Rather it would attempt to acquire a Free Trade Agreement with the EU, and a 'new customs agreement'—implying exit from the Customs Union as well as the Single Market (p. 35). These objectives were clearly in opposition to the Scottish and Welsh executives and demonstrated an outlook on the part of the UK government that it was not required to proceed by consensus: a definite limitation on the extent to which consociationalism had applicability in the UK.

Political Contexts

Each of the government responses to the EU referendum considered here—those of Scotland, Wales and the whole UK—presented distinctive views of the territorial constitution of the state. In all three cases, it is possible to detect tactical calculations as playing a part in their formulation. The EU referendum presented the Scottish Government with both opportunities and dangers. That Scotland had voted 'remain' by 68 per cent to 32 per cent was a clear divergence from the full UK result. It also suggested that Scotland was firmer in its resolve to continue EU membership than the UK was in its intention to depart, with a 'leave' lead in the UK overall of only 51.9 to 48.1 per cent. Moreover, there was a coalescence between the view of a decisive majority of Scottish voters and that of the SNP, with an established position of support for participation in the EU, whether as part of the UK or as an independent nation. This circumstance strengthened the political authority of the Scottish Government in asserting a need to maximise continuity in areas such as the Single Market. The divergence between the whole UK and Scottish votes also enabled the SNP to present Scotland as distinct from the UK. It provided a basis, too, for turning the rhetoric of inclusive union on those who deployed it. The Scottish Government felt able to insist upon an influential role in the policy of leaving the EU; that the substantive outcome should reflect particular Scottish requirements and that it should operate in the form of new constitutional arrangements that enhanced the autonomy of a devolved Scotland further still. The Scottish Government acknowledged that the perspective it took might have significant implications for the constitutional framework of the whole UK. It suggested that other devolved territories might wish to insist on conditions similar to those which it demanded. Yet primarily the white paper was focused on Scotland: what the EU referendum meant from its perspective and its relationship with the UK.

However, while in many ways the EU referendum created political dynamics advantageous to the SNP as a promoter of Scottish particularity within—or possibly outside—the UK, it brought with it potential difficulties. A failure satisfactorily to exploit this opportunity might cause the SNP to suffer a substantial loss in momentum. If it did not demand or secure an independence referendum, it might be regarded as having squandered the best chance it could hope for to achieve the historic objective of exit from the UK. Yet to obtain such a vote and to lose it would then mean that the independence cause had suffered two such defeats in less than a decade. Serious questions might be raised—perhaps even within the SNP—regarding whether it would ever be possible to secure a win, and many might regard the matter as settled for the foreseeable future.

The available post-referendum evidence did not provide convincing evidence of a popular upsurge in support for independence. Opinion research conducted by YouGov between August and December 2016, for instance, suggested that the balance of opinion—with 46 per cent favouring exit from the UK and 54 per cent opposing it—was roughly where it had been at the time of the 2014 referendum. The EU was an important shaping factor, but not in a straightforward sense. According to the polling, among those who voted in both the independence and EU referendums, 28 per cent voted 'no' to independence from the UK and to 'remain' in the EU, and 14 per cent voted to leave both the UK and the EU. In other words, supporters of EU membership were not necessarily previously committed to independence, and those inclined towards independence were not necessarily favourable towards EU membership. The core support group from the perspective of the Scottish Government/ SNP position, those who voted for independence and for 'remain', made up just 21 per cent of those who participated in both referendums. A further bloc of 16 per cent was the least promising from this perspective, comprising those who voted 'no' in 2014 and 'leave' in 2016. As the journalist Chris Curtis noted, the challenge for the SNP was to win over 'no' and remain voters without losing the backing of 'yes' and 'leave' supporters. The 2016 research suggested that while some 'no' and 'remain' voters had moved over to the SNP side since June 2016, at the same time members of the 'yes' and 'leave' group moved in the opposite direction, leading to little change in the overall balance of support for and against Scottish independence (Curtis 2017).

The SNP response to the EU referendum might be regarded partly as an attempt to manage the countervailing risks this circumstance produced. The Scottish Government made it clear that its preferred position was for an independent Scotland within the EU. But it was far from certain it had sufficient support to secure this outcome. Therefore, it advanced a set of principles that it could present as representing a constructive attempt to achieve a compromise between the desire of Scotland to remain within the EU and the determination of the UK government to leave it. Yet behind the outward semblance of reasonableness, it always stretched plausibility to suppose that the substantive requirements of the Scottish Government would be politically tolerable to the UK government. Furthermore, some of the possibilities advanced for special arrangements for Scotland within a post-EU UK might be practically unattainable. Finally, the proposed allocation of repatriated powers, maximising devolution, was likely to meet with resistance. The approach of the Scottish Government could, therefore, be seen as a means of progressing to a demand for an independence referendum. Rather than adopting this position from the outset, arguably the Scottish Government chose to seek to engineer a scenario in which it appeared to have had its conciliatory efforts rejected by a UK government that was not serious about inclusive decision-making. It could therefore plausibly claim that it had been left with no reasonable option other than to call for an independence referendum, as it duly did in March 2017.

For the Welsh Government (cooperating to establish a shared platform with Plaid Cymru) different considerations prevailed. Like the SNP, both Labour and Plaid had supported 'remain'. But Wales, like the UK as a whole, voted 'leave' (by 52.5 per cent to 47.5). Moreover, Labour was opposed to Welsh independence, and Plaid—though a Welsh nationalist party—did not tend to prioritise this outcome in the way that the SNP did, reflecting the low levels of support for independence detected in opinion research. Independent Communications and Marketing (ICM) polls published in 2015 and 2016 (before the EU referendum) both showed that when voters were presented with a range of constitutional options from abolition of the Welsh Assembly to independence, only 6 per cent favoured independence (in 2014 it was 3 per cent) (Scully 2016). YouGov data released in July 2016, however, recorded 26 per cent supporting independence if it made it possible for Wales to remain within the EU; though when the EU was not mentioned in relation to this issue, the figure for those favouring independence was lower, at 16 per cent. The timing of the polling, shortly after the EU referendum, should be taken into account when assessing the significance of such figures. Furthermore, they fell well short of a majority, and objections to departure from the EU would not be a motive to support independence for those who had voted leave (Stone 2016).

While independence did not have the same traction in Wales it had achieved in Scotland, neither was retention of the status quo necessarily the most popular option. The ICM surveys consistently found that of the possible constitutional options for Wales, a plurality favoured a strengthened Assembly (2014: 49 per cent; 2015: 40; 2016: 43) (Scully 2016). The Welsh Government/Plaid agreed position seemed to play to fairly broad currents in Welsh opinion: accepting that the UK was, in some form, leaving the EU; not making independence an issue, but suggesting enhancements to the Welsh devolved institutions. The Welsh constitutional programme was presented firmly within the context of a wider recalibration of the system of governance of the UK. Here was an important distinction from the stance of the Scottish Government that emphasised Scotland and its place within the UK more than the overall constitutional framework of the UK.

The UK government position was shaped by a different set of political considerations again. Like the Welsh Government, the official position of the UK government had been to advocate 'remain', but the result for the territory over which it presided as a whole had been 'leave'. In percentage terms the lead was slim, though measured in numbers of votes was more than 1.2 million (Electoral Commission 2016, p. 17). During the campaign a special exemption had applied, allowing for ministers to opt out of collective Cabinet responsibility and publicly advocate leave. May, who was Home Secretary at the time, had not exercised this exemption and had supported remain, along with the majority of members of her Cabinet. While the referendum result was not legally binding, May, as we have seen, chose—notwithstanding her previous remain stance—to interpret it as creating a decisive political obligation to leave. Moreover, the particular variant of leaving she and her government adopted involved placing an emphasis upon exit from the Single Market and no longer participating in the Customs Union: a maximisation of discontinuity. This approach seems in part to have reflected a political judgement that it was the most plausible means of uniting the governing Conservative Party, which had been severely divided over the EU for a quarter of a century. May probably judged that Eurosceptics within her own ranks would accept nothing less than a swift move towards departure from the EU, in an abrupt form (Blick 2016b; 2017). Her position, then, was not one of strength. She and other ministers who were previously remain supporters were driven by forces they felt unable to resist. Yet the position was more complex still. Among Conservative voters, a significant minority had voted for continued membership of the EU in June. Opinion research suggest that 41 per cent of Conservative voters at the 2015 General Election backed 'remain' in June 2016, as against to 59 per cent 'leave' (Ipsos-MORI 2016).

Another facet of the May approach to leaving the EU, which probably also partially reflected the political pressure to which she was subject, was her determination forcefully to drive through her policy. In her view as initially expressed, the task of implementing the verdict of the electorate was largely the business of the UK executive, subject to some consultation with outside groups such as the devolved institutions. The information flow to the outside would be restricted (May 2016). This approach had to be substantially modified following political resistance and the judgement of the Supreme Court of 24 January 2017, which confirmed finally that specific statutory authorisation was required from the UK Parliament for the activation of Article 50 of the Treaty on European Union, formally commencing the exit process.

But the Supreme Court rejected the idea that the devolved legislatures had legally enforceable rights in this process. In the words of the judgement 'the devolved legislatures do not have a parallel legislative competence [to the UK Parliament] in relation to withdrawal from the European Union.' Two further decisions arose specifically in relation to the position of Northern Ireland. There was no obligation for 'the consent of a majority of the people of Northern Ireland to the withdrawal of the United Kingdom from the European Union.' Furthermore, 'the consent of the Northern Ireland Assembly is not a legal requirement before the relevant Act of the UK Parliament is passed.' This latter conclusion meant that, by extension, the Welsh and Scottish legislatures also lacked this right.[4]

The combined consequence of the UK government approach, then, was that the referendum results in Scotland and Northern Ireland (and Greater London) were not treated as invalidating or qualifying the leave result and that the stated desires of Welsh and Scottish governments to retain continuity with respect to the Single Market were eschewed. In presenting its approach the UK government stressed the idea that the UK as a whole had taken a decision. It sought to create an impression of post-referendum consensus around leaving the EU to an extent that defied credulity. While describing in some detail the mechanisms it had initiated for consultation with the devolved executives, only the UK Parliament would have the power to approve a final deal. Furthermore, the UK government was far less inclined than the Welsh and Scottish governments to treat departure from the EU as a moment for the expansion of devolved powers and potentially saw an opportunity to augment its own scope of authority.

CONCLUSION: PARALLEL MODELS

The EU referendum of June 2016 helped illuminate both the extent to which the UK had always been a diverse polity in territorial and other senses and how far it had developed in this respect since 1973 when the UK acceded to the EEC. Devolution had been introduced (or reintroduced in the case of Northern Ireland) to Wales, Scotland and Northern Ireland (and Greater London). Changes had taken place in the party political complexion of these territories. The SNP, for instance, had become dominant in Scotland, with parties that operated across Great Britain eclipsed. In the process, Scottish independence had become a serious proposition. A peace agreement came into force in Northern Ireland. All of these developments had taken place against a background of ongoing EU membership. The prospect of exit revealed certain assumptions that had formed about territorial aspects of the UK constitution. The devolved governments themselves were able to promote these views, though they might differ from each other and from the position of the UK government.

It is significant that the two devolved governments considered here even felt able to advance comprehensive prospectuses for exit from the EU and for constitutional arrangements post-departure that would entrench their rights. The positions of the Welsh and Scottish governments—as with that taken by UK government—were influenced by the particular political circumstances, threats and opportunities that the referendum created. But nonetheless they amounted to coherent models for the UK system. The Scottish proposal was perhaps suggestive of a loose confederation or federacy, while the Welsh advanced concepts that avowedly had a federal dimension to them. The UK government promoted a neo-unitary ideal, which sought to contain the transformations that had occurred since 1973 within a system in which the UK continued to be characterised by a single central pole of superior political authority. In legal terms it retained the ability to operate along these lines. Interest in the Article 50 case has tended to focus on its implications for the balance of power at the centre, between the UK executive and the Westminster Parliament. But it also had connotations for the territorial dispersal of authority. Whatever role the devolved executives or legislatures thought they should have in exit from the EU, it did not seem fully to exist in law. Yet—as we have seen—the political environment can have a powerful impact upon behaviour and decisions. If the circumstances that influenced different players at the turn of 2016–2017 shifted, the prevailing views, and even the legal framework, might do also.

If such a change took place, the federal model would be one useful comparator in assessment of the emerging arrangements. But also of value could be the consociational school. The process of devolution might be seen as an attempt to manage divisions within the UK through a partial adoption of consociational devices: predominantly, those that grant autonomy in significant policy areas to some territories within the state, in recognition of and providing expression to their diversity. But there has been less attention to how the inbuilt pressures of the UK might be handled through central mechanisms. The devolved institutions do not have a firm legal role in the conduct of policy at UK level. Perhaps membership of the EU has served to diffuse some of tensions that might otherwise have existed, through transferring responsibility to a supranational sphere. Exit from the EU might remove this means of release and necessitate further steps in a consociational direction.

NOTES

1. For examples of the body of work exploring this concept of a sustained period of decades, see Lijphart (1968, 1969, 2004).
2. There were 33,577,342 voters, representing 72.2 per cent of those who were eligible to take part. Of them, 16,141,241—48.1 per cent—opted for 'remain', while 17,410,742—51.9 per cent—voted 'leave' (23,359 ballot papers were rejected) (Electoral Commission 2016, p. 17).

3. For a comparison between consociationalism and federalism, see Lijphart (1985).
4. R (on the application of Miller and another) v Secretary of State for exiting the European Union [2017] UKSC 5; paras 130; 135; 150.

REFERENCES

Agatstein, Z. P. (2015). *And Be the Nation Again: A Consideration of the Scottish Nationalist Movement and Scottish National Party.* Boston: Northeastern University.

BBC News. (2016). *EU Referendum Results: UK Votes to Leave EU* [online]. Available at: http://www.bbc.co.uk/news/politics/eu_referendum/results

Birrell, D., & Murie, A. (1980). *Policy and Government in Northern Ireland: Lessons of Devolution.* New York: Barnes & Noble Imports.

Blick, A. (2014). *Devolution in England: A New Approach* [online]. Available at: http://fedtrust.co.uk/wp-content/uploads/2014/12/Devolution_in_England.pdf

Blick, A. (2015). *Beyond Magna Carta: A Constitution for the United Kingdom.* Oxford: Bloomsbury Publishing.

Blick, A. (2016a). *Federalism: The UK's Future?* [online]. Available at: http://fedtrust.co.uk/wp-content/uploads/2016/05/FEDERALISM_THE_UKS_FUTURE.pdf. Accessed 19 Mar 2017.

Blick, A. (2016b). *Taking Back Control? The EU Referendum, Parliament and the 'May Doctrine'* [online]. Available at: http://fedtrust.co.uk/wp-content/uploads/2016/10/Taking_back_control_Andrew_Blick.pdf. Accessed 19 Mar 2017.

Blick, A. (2016c). *The Codes of the Constitution.* Oxford: Bloomsbury Publishing.

Blick, A. (2016d). *The EU Referendum, Devolution and the Union* [online]. Available at: http://fedtrust.co.uk/our-work-on-europe/the-eu-referendum-devolution-and-the-union/. Accessed 19 Mar 2017.

Blick, A. (2017). *Deal or No Deal? The Article 50 Process in Context* [online]. Available at: http://fedtrust.co.uk/our-work-on-europe/deal-or-no-deal/. Accessed 23 Mar 2017.

Bogdanor, V. (2001). *Devolution in the United Kingdom.* Oxford: Oxford University Press.

Bogdanor, V. (2015). *The Crisis of the Constitution: 2nd Edition* [online]. Available at: https://consoc.org.uk/wp-content/uploads/2016/02/COSJ4072-Crisis-of-Constitution-2nd-Ed-12_15-WEB.pdf. Accessed 29 Mar 2017.

Bourne, A. K. (2014). Europeanization and Secession: The Cases of Catalonia and Scotland. *JEMIE, 13,* 94.

Brown, M., Geoghegan, P. M., & Kelly, J. (2003). *The Irish Act of Union, 1800: Bicentennial Essays.* Dublin: Irish Academic Press.

Burke, E. (2016). Who Will Speak for Northern Ireland? The Looming Danger of an Ulster Brexit. *The RUSI Journal, 161*(2), 4–12.

Curtis, C. (2017, January 27). Why Hasn't Scotland Changed Its Mind on Independence? *The Guardian*, [online]. Available at: https://www.theguardian.com/commentisfree/2017/jan/27/shift-scottish-independence-yougov-nicola-sturgeon-balancing-act. Accessed 24 Mar 2017.

Dickson, B. (2001). *The Legal System of Northern Ireland*. Belfast: SLS Publications.

Douglas-Scott, S. (2014). British Withdrawal from the EU: An Existential Threat to the United Kingdom. *Future of UK and Scotland blog,20*.

Electoral Commission. (2016). *The 2016 EU Referendum* [online]. Available at: http://www.electoralcommission.org.uk/__data/assets/pdf_file/0008/215279/2016-EU-referendum-report.pdf. Accessed 19 Mar 2017.

Ford, J. D. (2007). The Legal Provisions in the Acts of Union. *The Cambridge Law Journal, 66*(01), 106–141.

Garry, J. (2016). *The EU Referendum Vote in Northern Ireland: Implications for Our Understanding of Citizens' Political View and Behaviour* [online]. Available at: https://www.qub.ac.uk/home/EUReferendum/Brexitfilestore/Filetoupload,728121,en.pdf

Gibson, J. S. (1985). *The Thistle and the Crown: A History of the Scottish Office*. Edinburgh: HM Stationery Office.

H.M. Government. (2017). *The United Kingdom's Exit from and New Partnership with the European Union*, Cm 9417 [online]. Available at: https://www.gov.uk/government/uploads/system/uploads/attachment_data/file/589191/The_United_Kingdoms_exit_from_and_partnership_with_the_EU_Web.pdf. Accessed 19 Mar 2017.

Heald, D., & McLeod, A. (2005, January). Scotland's Fiscal Relationships with England and the United Kingdom. In *Proceedings-British Academy* (Vol. 128, p. 95). Oxford: Oxford University Press Inc.

Ipsos-MORI. (2016). *The 2016 EU Referendum—Who Was in and Who Was Out? How Britain Voted in the 2016 Referendum* [online]. Available at: https://www.ipsos-mori.com/researchpublications/researcharchive/3774/The-2016-EU-referendum-who-was-in-and-who-was-out.aspx. Accessed 19 Mar 2017.

Jackson, A. (2012). *The Two Unions: Ireland, Scotland, and the Survival of the United Kingdom, 1707–2007*. Oxford: Oxford University Press.

Lijphart, A. (1968). Typologies of Democratic Systems. *Comparative Political Studies, 1*(1), 3–44.

Lijphart, A. (1969). Consociational Democracy. *World Politics, 21*(2), 207–225.

Lijphart, A. (1985). Non-majoritarian Democracy: A Comparison of Federal and Consociational Theories. *Publius: The Journal of Federalism, 15*(2), 3–15.

Lijphart, A. (2004). Constitutional Design for Divided Societies. *Journal of Democracy, 15*(2), 96–109.

Lynch, P. (2009). From Social Democracy Back to No Ideology?—The Scottish National Party and Ideological Change in a Multi-level Electoral Setting. *Regional and Federal Studies, 19*(4–5), 619–637.

Macinnes, A. I. (2007). *Union and Empire: The Making of the United Kingdom in 1707*. Cambridge: Cambridge University Press.

Mackintosh, J. P. (1975). The Case Against a Referendum. *The Political Quarterly, 46*(1), 73–82.

Mansergh, N. (1936). *The Government of Northern Ireland: A Study in Devolution*. London: Allen.

Manson-Smith, D. (2004). *The Legal System of Scotland*. London: Stationery office.

May, T. (2016). *Britain After Brexit: A Vision of a Global Britain* [online]. Available at: https://www.politicshome.com/news/uk/political-parties/conservative-party/news/79517/read-full-theresa-mays-conservative. Accessed 19 Mar 2017.

McConnell, A. (2004). *Scottish Local Government*. Edinburgh: Edinburgh University Press.

McCrone, G. (1999). Scotland's Public Finances from Goschen to Barnett. *Quarterly Economic Commentary, 24*(2), 30–46.

McGarry, J., & O'Leary, B. (2004). *The Northern Ireland Conflict: Consociational Engagements*. Oxford: Oxford University Press on Demand.

McHarg, A. (2016). The Future of the United Kingdom's Territorial Constitution: Can the Union Survive? [online]. Available at: https://papers.ssrn.com/sol3/papers.cfm?abstract_id=2771614. Accessed 19 Mar 2017.

McHugh, M. (2017, March 15). Hard Border Between Northern Ireland and Republic Ruled Out. *The Scotsman*, [online]. Available at http://www.scotsman.com/news/hard-border-between-northern-ireland-and-republic-ruled-out-1-4392773. Accessed 19 Mar 2017.

McLean, I. (2005, January). Financing the Union: Goschen, Barnett, and Beyond. In *Proceedings-British Academy* (Vol. 1, No. 128, pp. 81–94). Oxford: Oxford University Press.

Meehan, E. (2000). 'Britain's Irish Question: Britain's European Question?' British-Irish Relations in the Context of European Union and the Belfast Agreement. *Review of International Studies, 26*(01), 83–97.

Mitchell, J. (2006). Evolution and Devolution: Citizenship, Institutions, and Public Policy. *Publius: The Journal of Federalism, 36*(1), 153–168.

Mitchell, J. (2010). Introduction: The Westminster Model and the State of Unions. *Parliamentary Affairs, 63*(1), 85–88.

Mitchell, J., Bennie, L., & Johns, R. (2012). *The Scottish National Party: Transition to Power*. Oxford/New York: Oxford University Press.

Morgan, K. O. (1971). Welsh Nationalism: The Historical Background. *Journal of Contemporary History, 6*(1), 153–172.

Morgan, A. (2000). *The Belfast Agreement: A Practical Legal Analysis*. London: Belfast Press Ltd.

Northern Ireland Office. (1998). *The Belfast Agreement* [online]. Available at: https://www.gov.uk/government/uploads/system/uploads/attachment_data/file/136652/agreement.pdf. Accessed 19 Mar 2017.

Roberts, P. R. (1972). The Union with England and the Identity of 'Anglican' Wales. *Transactions of the Royal Historical Society (Fifth Series), 22*, 49–70.

Scottish Government. (2016). *Scotland's Place in Europe* [online]. Available at: http://www.gov.scot/Resource/0051/00512073.pdf. Accessed 19 Mar 2017.

Scully, R. (2016). *The BBC/ICM St. David's Day Poll* [online]. Available at: http://blogs.cardiff.ac.uk/electionsinwales/2016/03/07/the-bbcicm-st-davids-day-poll/. Accessed 24 Mar 2017.

Slapper, G., & Kelly, D. (2013). *The English Legal System: 2012–2013*. London: Routledge.

Smyth, J. (2001). *The Making of the United Kingdom, 1660–1800: State, Religion and Identity in Britain and Ireland*. Harlow/New York: Prentice Hall.

Stone, J. (2016, July 18). Brexit Boosts Support for Welsh Independence, Poll Finds. *Independent* [online]. Available at: http://www.independent.co.uk/news/uk/politics/welsh-independence-poll-brexit-eu-referendum-plaid-cymru-leanne-wood-a7142856.html. Accessed 24 Mar 2017.

Welsh Government. (2017). *Securing Wales's Future: Transition from the European Union to a New Relationship with Europe* [online]. Available at: https://beta.gov.wales/sites/default/files/2017-02/31139%20Securing%20Wales%C2%B9%20Future_Version%202_WEB.pdf. Accessed 19 Mar 2017.

Wicks, E. (2001). A New Constitution for a New State? The 1707 Union of England and Scotland. *LQR, 117*, 109.

CHAPTER 8

Arend Lijphart and Consociationalism in Cyprus

Neophytos Loizides

INTRODUCTION

This chapter applies Arend Lijphart's theory of consociationalism to Cyprus. It begins by considering the failure of Cypriot consociationalism in the early 1960s, just three years after the island's newly established independence. It argues that the case of Cyprus offers useful empirical insights into how power-sharing arrangements fail in deeply divided societies. At the same time, the chapter explains why the Cypriot experience does not refute Lijphart's consociational reasoning and also examines the degree to which past United Nations (UN) proposals for Cyprus have failed to take into consideration some of the key prescriptions of the Dutch political scientist. It goes on to demonstrate the critical importance of consociationalism for Cyprus and the ongoing peace talks to reunify the island and then concludes with a set of recommendations for the "kinder and gentler democracy" Lijphart has advocated in his defence of consensus democracy.

N. Loizides (✉)
School of Politics & International Relations, University of Kent, Canterbury, UK

© The Author(s) 2018
M. Jakala et al. (eds.), *Consociationalism and Power-Sharing in Europe*, International Political Theory,
https://doi.org/10.1007/978-3-319-67098-0_8

155

The Cypriot Context and Lijphart's Terminology

The decades-long negotiations in Cyprus have taken place in a conceptual vacuum as definitions and terminologies have been inevitably contested in post-conflict and divided places. To eliminate some of the confusion, Lijphart and other leading scholars in consociational theory have attempted to define and distinguish amongst consociationalism, federalism and power-sharing (Lijphart 1979; McGarry and O'Leary 2005). Amongst other features, consociationalism stipulates that power be shared by majorities and minorities, and it implies formal or informal veto rights for all parties (Lijphart 1977, 1979; McGarry and O'Leary 1993). Consociationalism involves power-sharing at the centre, for instance, the collective presidency in Bosnia, the allocation of certain key posts to members of specific groups in Lebanon or the voluntary proportional representation of all political parties in the Cabinet as in Northern Ireland (McGarry and Loizides 2015). In contrast, federalism refers to situations where authority is territorially divided between central and provincial governments, with both enjoying constitutionally separate competencies (O'Leary 2001: 49–52). To muddy the waters somewhat, federations can also be consociations, as in Belgium and Switzerland, but not all federations are consociations, as in the United States and Australia, or semi-consociations, as in Canada and India (Lijphart 1977: 513). Semi-consociations include some elements of consociations but not others, for instance, proportionality and community autonomy but no guarantees for long-term power-sharing or fully effective veto rights (McCrudden and O'Leary 2013: 9–10). There are also consociational agreements with territorially intermingled populations that do not take a federal form, such as post-1960 Cyprus, Lebanon or Northern Ireland after the 1998 Good Friday Agreement (O'Leary 2001: 44). Finally, by definition, power-sharing includes alternative forms of dividing authorities, either territorial or administrative, at the executive level. Following McGarry and O'Leary (2009a: 16–17), the chapter treats power-sharing as an umbrella term encompassing both federal and consociational forms of accommodation.

Since 1974, UN proposals and resolutions for a negotiated settlement in Cyprus have included federal and consociational provisions. It has been generally assumed that a settlement will incorporate two federal units and a shared administration at the central government. Terms such as "bizonal" and "bicommunal" federation (BBF), as well as references to "political equality" included in framework agreements already signed by the leaders of the two communities (see Loizides 2016), point to a convergence on power-sharing, although, admittedly, the details and substance of a future settlement after four decades of *de facto* partition remain unresolved.

As early as the late 1970s, Cypriot leaders on both sides signed two High-Level Agreements signifying initial convergence towards a bicommunal federal compromise. However, the 1977–1979 High-Level Agreements were not clearly defined; for instance, they emphasized adherence to human rights for all citizens, but the issue of Greek Cypriots returning to their properties in the North became subject to overcoming the "practical difficulties" for the Turkish Cypriot community (Ker-Lindsay 2011: 49–51; Loizides 2016). Moreover, the decision on whether the two communities should be territorially re-integrated to meet Greek Cypriot expectations or whether federal boundaries would be more rigid to satisfy the Turkish Cypriot positions was left for the future. As for power-sharing, the types of possible consociational arrangements have long been debated by the leaders of the two communities. While the inability to settle the Cyprus issue is unfortunate, it gives us useful material to assess how majority and minority leaders frame and endorse related peace proposals (see, for instance, McGarry 2011).

International experience suggests that power-sharing in the form of federalism can be adapted for various purposes and conditions, and, as Sisk demonstrates, the opportunities for innovation are so extensive that federalism can be structured to serve alternative needs for shared and separated powers (1996: 49; see also Jarstad and Sisk 2008). Yet in the past decades, the incentives of European Union (EU) accession for both Cyprus and Turkey have failed to effect a comprehensive settlement in the island (Demetriou 2004; Tocci 2007; Ker-Lindsay 2012). Regardless of the promise of federalism within the EU, despite the absence of major incidents of violence following the de facto partition of 1974 and in defiance of UN mediation attempts, negotiations have failed in Cyprus. The divided island has not managed to achieve a comprehensive peace settlement.

Oddly enough, both communities have, at times, voted for pro-federal politicians or rallied in support of the reunification of the island, as, for example, the pro-peace Turkish Cypriot rallies of 2002–2004. Historically, two-thirds of the Greek Cypriot public has voted for pro-settlement politicians hailing from either the nominally communist AKEL (Progressive Party of the Working People) or the centre-right DISY (Democratic Rally). Yet the two parties have so far failed to articulate a shared agenda on the Cyprus issue. As described below, this is largely because of intra-group antagonism dating to the Cold War, the 1955–1959 EOKA struggle and the 1974 coup against Makarios as well as the nature of the two-round presidential system that preserved the antagonism between the two largest and pro-settlement political parties in the Greek Cypriot community.

Overall, the Cypriot experience poses puzzles as to why societies choose or fail to negotiate power-sharing settlements as prescribed by Lijphart and consociational theorists. Signs have pointed at times to settlement and progress, but the larger picture in the island says otherwise, indicating, as in Lijphart's extensive reasoning, the limitations of consociationalism.

CYPRIOT HISTORY AND CONSOCIATIONAL NARRATIVES

Cyprus escaped the devastating wars of the late Ottoman era, as it was transferred to the British following the 1878 Berlin Congress. Turkey recognized the 1914 annexation of the island by the British in the 1923 Treaty of Lausanne (Article 20), and it became a Crown Colony in 1925. The first decades of colonial rule saw minimal conflict, but both communities gradually developed stronger attachments to their respective "motherlands" and became more assertive in their ethnopolitical demands (Demetriou 2012).

Unsurprisingly, the narratives of the two communities diverge in their explanations of the origins of the bicommunal violence. Greek Cypriots have historically taken a majoritarian view of recent history pointing not only to their demographic statues but also to the massive participation of Greek Cypriots (and Greece) in World War II (WWII) on the side of the British. Following Britain's subsequent refusal to end colonial rule, Greek Cypriots, under the leadership of Archbishop Makarios, started an active campaign for *enosis* (union) with Greece. Like other colonial subjects, Greek Cypriots had fought as allies to the British and felt eligible for freedom and self-determination. They also cited their demographic majority status—about 80 per cent of the population. In January 1950, 95.73 per cent of Greek Cypriots voted in favour of union with Greece in a "plebiscite" (in the form of signature collections) led by the Church (Crawshaw 1978: 34–56; Averoff-Tossizza 1986: 8–9).

Turkish Cypriot counter-mobilization developed almost simultaneously and emphasized geographic proximity to Turkey, as well as previous ownership of the island. Turkish Cypriots saw an existential threat to *enosis* and unsurprisingly still see it as such today as demonstrated in the recent

Cyprus parliament vote to commemorate the 1950 *enosis* plebiscite that led to the collapse of the power-sharing talks in 2017. In response to the post-WWII *enosis* movement, Turkish Cypriots, with the backing of Turkey, sought *taksim* (partition) of Cyprus into two separate territories (Bahcheli 1972: 60; Attalides 1977: 78–86). In a massive demonstration in December 1949, attended by 15,000 people, Turkish Cypriots demanded the island be returned to Turkey, if Britain decided to leave (Gazioğlu 1996: 455).

Between 1955 and 1959, the National Organization of Cypriot Fighters (EOKA) attempted to end colonial rule and to unite the island with Greece. The EOKA leadership initially promised not to target the Turkish Cypriot community and avoided bicommunal incidents. Despite EOKA promises, however, in the eyes of Turkish Cypriots, maintaining colonial rule was preferable to living under a potentially hostile Greek administration. Following the start of the EOKA campaign, Turkish Cypriots actively sided with colonial authorities, filling in for Greek Cypriot police officers who had resigned from their positions (Ker-Lindsay 2004: 16). According to Turkish Cypriot accounts, many expected that "sooner or later the campaign of terror would be directed against the Turkish Cypriot community" (Necatigil 1998: 7). Indeed, three years later in 1958, the conflict took increasingly a bicommunal character as EOKA retaliated against Turkish Cypriots supporting the British authorities, triggering, in turn, further attacks and counterattacks (Bahcheli 1972: 55).

Turkey added its strategic interests to the equation and insisted that any change in the status quo would necessitate a revision of the 1923 Lausanne Treaty (Bahcheli 1972: 71). Ankara and the Turkish Cypriots aimed at preventing the island from being dominated by Greeks insisting on no change to the status quo without their consent (Ertekün 1984: 1–5; Necatigil 1998: 7–8). For the Greek Cypriots such consent was unnecessary given the demographic, historical and cultural arguments for *enosis*. As a result, Turkish Cypriots were not included in the anti-colonial campaign, in what Greek Cypriots considered their national struggle for self-determination (Papadakis 1999: 25).

Theorists of consociationalism emphasize the potentially moderating role of alternative cleavages and political elites (Arend Lijphart 1979; Ulrich Schneckener 2002; Erkem 2016). Cross-cutting ideological linkages between elites, but more importantly, the capacity of moderates to draw a line between themselves and hardliners, are seen as important elements in the success of consociational arrangements. A critical test of/

factor in the success of a power-sharing agreement, missing from the colonial and the immediate post-colonial eras in Cyprus history, is the presence of elites whose thinking is independent of community politics. Also important are civil society networks, with both media and ordinary people eager to take major political risks or to face social marginalization—to the point of being labelled "traitors."

EOKA's military leader, Georgios Grivas, was a controversial figure of the Greek Civil War who saw communists as outside the national community and obstacles to the attainment of nationalist goals (Holland 1998: 29–30; Crawshaw 1978: 42–91). He found strong allies in the ultra-conservative Church of Cyprus which was threatened by the rise of the communist left amongst the working classes (Markides 1977; Servas 1997). Even though it occasionally emphasized a shared Cypriot identity, the left chose not to challenge the major tenets of Greek nationalism; in fact, even after independence, AKEL followed the mainstream Greek Cypriot position and, at times, supported union with Greece (Markides 1977: 63; Averoff-Tossizza 1986: 7; Drousiotis 1998: 40–46; Diglis 2010).

In clash with consociational reasoning, the 1959–1960 Zürich-London Agreements were seen as a "forced partnership" imposed on the two communities by their respective "motherlands" in the prevailing climate of the Cold War (Xydis 1973). The Agreements constituted the first and only power-sharing attempt and lasted for just three years. Critics point to consociationalism itself as a cause of the failure, particularly the separate election of community leaders (i.e. a Greek Cypriot President and Turkish Cypriot Vice-President voted on only in their respective communities), the mutual vetoes of the two leaders and the over-representation of the minority Turkish Cypriots in Cabinet and the civil service (Adams 1966; Polyviou 1980; Anderson 2008).

Yet attributing the failure of the 1959–1960 Zürich-London Agreements to consociationalism per has significant flaws. To begin with, the "presidential consociationalism" of the Zürich-London Agreements would not have been the preferred institutional choice of consociational theorists (Lijphart 1984; Linz 1990; Lijphart 1994; McGarry 2011). Following Lijphart's consociational reasoning, Juan Linz made one of the most significant contributions to comparative politics by demonstrating how "presidentialism is less likely than parliamentarism to sustain stable democratic regimes" (Mainwaring and Shugart 1997: 449). Presidentialism tends to introduce a majoritarian ("winner-take-all") logic into democratic politics which is often incompatible with the very essence of power-sharing. The view that ethnically diverse societies are better served by parliamentarianism than by presidentialism is now widely accepted amongst consociational theorists and illustrated in recent failures of presidential regimes to secure democratic transitions in Egypt, Zimbabwe and Kyrgyzstan (McGarry 2013).

More importantly, as Lijphart (1977: 160) argues, the main reason for the failure of consociationalism in Cyprus is that it could not be imposed against the wishes of one or more segments of a plural society, in particular, against the majority community. In this respect, the Cypriot case parallels the Northern Irish one, with a dual imbalance of power constituting the crucially unfavourable factor (ibid; see also Trimikliniotis 2009). But as the example of Northern Ireland suggests, structural disadvantages do not predetermine consociational failures, if institutions are designed to address such weaknesses and win ratification by majorities in peace referendums. In Cyprus, the unfavourable "dual imbalance of power" factor could have been mitigated by improving incentives for cooperation, making better security arrangements within the island and the region and eliminating unconstructive ambiguities about decentralization (e.g. the issue of separate municipalities was of immediate importance to both sides).

A number of broader geopolitical factors militated against consociational success in Cyprus as well. Both Greece and Turkey had already joined NATO in 1952, but membership did not mitigate the security dilemmas in the Greece-Turkey-Cyprus triangle (Krebs 1999: 357; Güney 2004). In fact, the Zürich-London Agreements institutionalized the military presence of Greece and Turkey in Cyprus as guarantor powers without their having to cooperate within the institutionalized structures of NATO or with the limited UN forces post-1964 (Joseph 1997: 21; Necatigil 1998: 9–20). Despite an earlier informal agreement between Turkey and Greece on Cyprus joining NATO, the Cypriot Republic became a member of the Non-Aligned Movement (Xydis 1973: 413). And while the decision was made against the wishes of Turkish Cypriot leaders, they did not use their constitutional veto (Ker-Lindsay 2004: 20). In fact, the Turkish government opted against Cyprus joining NATO, as membership would have severely curtailed Turkey's ability to act in the island (ibid: 20).

Given all these factors, it was only a matter of time before ethnic nationalism trumped power-sharing and visions of shared citizenship.

Besides the institutional and security reasons noted above, the collapse of the agreement was over-determined domestically by the fact that Greek Cypriots saw the Agreements as the first step towards *enosis*, while Turkish Cypriots continued to hold *taksim* as their priority. Moreover, both EOKA and the Turkish Resistance Organization (TMT) had already established strong organizational networks throughout the island. Finally, (unconstructive) ambiguities in the Constitution on municipal decentralization fuelled grievances about the "forced nature" of the partnership. The Agreements provided for separate municipalities in major cities. Article 173 made those provisions subject to the future approvals of the President and Vice-President, with no clarity as to the extent of their authority or territorial boundaries. As Dianne Markides argues, the strong Greek Cypriot reactions to the realities of municipal partition, the ambiguity of the wording of Article 173 and the failure of the guarantor powers to make the necessary clarifications fuelled the constitutional breakdown of the early 1960s (Markides 2001). In the absence of effective and credible external guarantees, both communities remained captive to their fears of being pre-empted by the other (or by the "motherlands"). As a result, both engaged in pre-emptive militarization and violence, leading to the breakdown of consociational arrangements in 1963–1964.

Just as the communities' respective narratives of the start of bicommunal violence differ, so too do their narratives of the collapse of power-sharing arrangements. The story told by Turkish Cypriots is stark: several thousand members of the community were displaced into enclaves, and the community was economically isolated for more than a decade (Patrick 1976), forcing it to rely on Turkey for protection and international representation (Vural and Rustemli 2006: 338). For their part, Greek Cypriots interpret events as a revolt against the legitimate state. As such, they gained the exclusive right to represent the Republic of Cyprus in international organizations, including the UN (Joseph 1997: 100; Necatigil 1998: 48–51). Nonetheless, in the 1968–1974 period, the two communities came close to a compromise combining limited regional autonomy for Turkish Cypriots in exchange for accommodating most amendments proposed by Greek Cypriot leaders in 1963.

According to Glafkos Clerides who led these negotiations for the Greek Cypriot side, President Makarios rejected the proposed settlement because of Denktaş's demand that Greek Cypriots renounce their aspirations for *enosis* (Clerides 1989–1992, 2007). As argued elsewhere (Loizides 2015, 2016), ethnocentric rhetoric, particularly with regard to national entitlements, could constrain leaders from negotiating necessary and mutually beneficial institutional compromises. The power of symbols, emotions and mental frames is extremely important in mediating power-sharing; while admittedly consociationalist theorists recognize those extensively, studies explicitly linking the two are still rare (and necessary as demonstrated by the near collapse of the Cyprus peace talks due to a Greek Cypriot decision to commemorate the 1950 *enosis* referendum). Likewise Clerides in 1973 recognized the necessity of a new consociational compromise but admitted that he could not confront Makarios or the dominant narratives in his own community (ibid).

The pre-war negotiations to restore power-sharing were interrupted by the Turkish invasion of the island on 20 July 1974. Turkey intervened militarily to prevent what it saw as an attempt by the Greek Junta to unite Cyprus with Greece in a coup against Makarios five days earlier. During the invasion, approximately 140,000 Greek Cypriots were forced by the Turkish military to flee from the North, while around 40,000 Turkish Cypriots living in the South chose or were coerced to abandon their houses and move to the North (Fisher 2001: 311). Since then, Cyprus has remained divided, despite efforts to renegotiate power-sharing in a new federal territorial arrangement between Greek Cypriot and Turkish Cypriot communities.

Elite Traditions and Consociational Culture

Conventional wisdom assumes that countries with first-hand experience of war and the collapse of power-sharing agreements, such as Cyprus, will be more reluctant to adopt renewed federal or consociational arrangements. As the case of Cypriot conflict suggests, societies that have experienced federal and consociational collapses or have witnessed failures in their immediate neighbourhood tend to hesitate when debating their own power-sharing transitions. In any event, failures in its immediate region have (*mis*)informed political debates at home in Cyprus, and no "regional or international model" has been identified in the public discourse to inspire the island's reunification process.

Lijphart pays close attention to the importance of past institutional legacies in the success of subsequent power-sharing arrangements. Specifically, his "tradition of elite accommodation" argument identifies such legacies as a favourable condition for consociationalism (1977: 99–104). However, he does not elaborate on alternative (*mis*)uses of historical traditions, nor does he explain how memories or competing nationalist interpretations of the past might matter. In the past decades, the examples of Lebanon, the former Yugoslavia, and post-1960 Cyprus have further consolidated the view of federalism and consociationalism as dysfunctional, if not catastrophic. Faced with comparable challenges, other post-colonial leaders, as in India, for example, have successfully countered imperial and colonial legacies by "crafting a pragmatic, political secularism that offered symmetrical treatment to various religious communities" (Kohli 2001: 5). In contrast, in the Eastern Mediterranean, coercive power-sharing turned the region's "early advantage" of relative tolerance into an unfortunate demonstration of how community rights and ethnic power-sharing lack viability.

A dominant frame of reference in the region is that power-sharing cannot resolve issues of multi-ethnicity. Critics of federalism and consociationalism say they can have devastating effects and may worsen ethnic and religious conflicts. They argue that power-sharing in various forms has failed in the region, in the late phases of the Ottoman Empire and in the post-colonial societies. The Cyprus experience is not unique for its region. More recently, in Iraq, external and domestic critics of consociationalism have emphasized the absence of a relevant federal example. For instance, both Muslim religious leaders and "liberal and democratic" politicians have stressed the need to preserve the country's unity and have frequently "urged the Kurds not to rush into formulae like federalism and confederalism with which *the region is not familiar*" (Mideast Mirror 2004; emphasis added). Likewise, in Turkey, similar perceptions preclude any discussion of federalism, in either the official Turkish Republican ideology or the broader majority discourses, including AKP's (Justice and Development Party) foreign policy initiatives in Cyprus and elsewhere. Sadly, the region lacks an indisputably successful consociational or federal model which could inspire others to follow. Looking at the interwar period in the Balkans, Ramet points out that while Norway and Finland in Europe provided models of what newly independent states could be, there was no similar model for the region (2006: 3).

Lijphart's most important distinction of majoritarian versus consensus in describing political systems involves some very important lessons for Cyprus and its region particularly the two "motherlands." In majoritarian democracies decisions are usually determined by a plurality of voters while in consensus democracies by "as many people as possible." Both options claim to foster moderation and effective decision-making either by privileging single governing parties as in Turkey and Greece or by encouraging regional decentralization and nationwide party coalitions as in most continental European political systems.

Despite the general liberalization of Turkish discourse on its domestic and regional identity representation since the 1990s (Somer 2005; Fokas 2008), institutional transformation through power-sharing has been almost non-existent in the country's political discourse. Instead since 2015, Turkey has moved towards an increasingly majoritarian (presidential) system, paradoxically, with the support of Kurdish voters following the 2008 referendum. In theory, the country could have evolved into a federation of eight administrative provinces as originally planned in the late phases of its military dictatorship in 1983 (Yucel 2007). In the case of Turkey, one could point to the size of the population and suggest the possibility of introducing "informal" federal or consociational arrangements, as in South Africa or Spain, to regulate conflict with the Kurdish minority. Instead, despite its early reliance on the Kurdish vote in the Southeast provinces, AKP has governed the country with little formal or informal power-sharing with either the Kurds or rival Kemalist political parties.

Likewise, according to Lijphart et al.'s measures and in the context of international or Southern European comparisons, Cyprus' second "motherland," Greece, has been extremely majoritarian (or eccentric, according to Lijphart et al. 1988). While other southern European countries, such as Spain and Portugal, have combined majoritarian-consensual institutional mechanisms, Greece has been "literally the most eccentric" in the region, a close "approximation of the majoritarian model" (Lijphart et al. 1988: 19–20). Kovras and Loizides (2014) argue that Greece, the country that relied most extensively on majoritarian institutions, entered the post-2008 crisis in the most vulnerable position while subsequently faced insurmountable obstacles in the management of the global financial meltdown. Yet as in the case of Turkey, debt-ridden Greece resisted attempts to form broader coalitions and to decentralize.

Inevitably, the political cultures of Greece and Turkey have also influenced decisions in Cyprus; lack of regional models in addition to the long history of bilateral antagonisms have constrained power-sharing prospects and negated the prospect of mediating a successful consociational arrangement in the island.

LIJPHART AND THE ANNAN PLAN

So far, the Annan Plan of 2002–2004 has been the best chance at reunification since 1974. Although the leaders failed initially to reach an agreement, they allowed UN Secretary-General Kofi Annan to prepare a plan for reunification. Drawing from elsewhere, particularly Switzerland and Bosnia (De Soto and del Castillo 1994; Jones 2003; Cox and Garlick 2003), the Annan Plan produced a set of noteworthy consociational innovations. For one thing, Greek and Turkish Cypriot leaders were the first to allow the UN Secretary-General the final arbitration role in completing the peace settlement, introducing it directly to the public in parallel referendums without prior endorsement at the leadership level. In addition, under the proposed Plan, Greek and Turkish Cypriots would have retained autonomy over most of their affairs under a decentralized federal system. Turkish Cypriots promised to return land to Greek Cypriot displaced persons in exchange for power-sharing, EU membership and federal status within a reunited Cyprus (Michael 2009; Pericleous 2009; Sözen and Özersay 2007).

Although the Annan Plan initially had the support of the two main Greek Cypriot political parties (AKEL and DISY) representing two-thirds of the electorate, it was rejected by a landslide 76 per cent of Greek Cypriots, while 65 per cent of Turkish Cypriots approved it during the twin April 2004 referendums. Surprisingly, DISY, whose ideological origins go back to the *enosis* movement, supported the Plan under the leadership of Nicos Anastasiades, while traditionally pro-settlement AKEL rejected it in a last minute *volte-face* (Trimikliniotis 2006). Reunification did not take place, but in the following month, Cyprus formally joined the EU. Yet the benefits of EU membership applied primarily to the Greek Cypriot community; the North has been officially in the EU, but the *acquis communautaire* (European body of law) does not apply to the areas outside the control of the Republic of Cyprus (Ker-Lindsay 2011). The majority of Turkish Cypriots maintained citizenship in the Republic of Cyprus and are entitled to travel and work in Europe, but the northern part of the island cannot initiate direct trade with or flights to third countries. Following the 2004 referendum, Turkish Cypriots argued for further economic and political integration of the northern part of the island with the EU, while Greek Cypriots accommodated this demand only partly. Although both aimed for a comprehensive settlement, they were unsuccessful despite the election of moderate leaders on both sides of the divide.

Foreign mediation, arbitration and peacekeeping are arguably essential elements of power-sharing settlements; they can resolve internal tensions and eliminate the negative influence of hostile neighbouring countries. Yet as cases like Cyprus reveal, particularly the experience of the Annan Plan in 2004, even small groups are frequently hesitant to welcome the involvement of major international organizations, opting to sustain a political culture that frowns on internationally endorsed arrangements. This is an unsurprising in the case of the Annan Plan as the UN proposal had "predictable adoptability problems" and many of its "provisions on power-sharing, sovereignty and human rights issues failed to create timely and credible incentives to secure the support of undecided voters and elected political elites" (McGarry and Loizides 2015).

Despite its failure, the Annan Plan of 2004 was undeniably a turning point in the history of negotiations in Cyprus and has become a broadly examined case study in the wider academic literature. So far, scholarly studies have concentrated on structural or institutional dimensions in explaining successes and failures of accommodation systems (Lijphart 1977; Horowitz 1993; Schneckener 2002). They have not considered the oppositional framing of advocates and critics in the context of peacemaking, something central to the Cypriot case.

A fundamental argument of the anti-federalist critics in the Annan Plan is that power-sharing arrangements which include vetoes and other power-sharing mechanisms as prescribed by Arend Lijphart are blatantly unfair and ultimately dysfunctional. But as we argued elsewhere the UN at the time decided to proceed to the twin referendums without securing the support of elected representatives. On the one hand, Lijphart defines consociational democracy as "government by elite cartel designed to turn a democracy with a fragmented political culture into a stable democracy."[1] On the other, the Annan Plan clashed with consociational theory in its mediation process through its "extreme arbitration provision" effectively sideling elected representatives. Overall, the Annan plan and its referendum process undermined the role of the elected leadership in Cyprus, thereby contradicting a key premise in the design of consociational arrangements (McGarry and Loizides 2015).

Moreover, at the time, critics pointed out that the Annan provisions on power-sharing were dysfunctional, given the apparent veto powers granted to Turkish Cypriots (Coufoudakis 2004: 10). This majoritarian view of politics contradicts international experience highlighting that majorities almost always oppress or at the best-case scenario ignore minority views while cases with minority vetoes almost never led to their repetitive use or abuse. In Cyprus, community vetoes are an essential characteristic of any consociational agreement aiming to protect both the Greek Cypriots and the Turkish Cypriots. Moreover, they are a central feature of the 1959 Agreements and reiterated in the references to political equality supported by the UN as well as endorsed by the Greek and Turkish Cypriot leaders Papadopoulos and Talat on 8 July 2006. As Turkish Cypriots consider their veto right an inalienable and established right through legal international agreements, ending those will legitimize demands for partition instead. Therefore, the challenge is to provide incentives within power-sharing for both sides to accept shared decision-making rather than opt for the continuation of the status quo.

Decentralization and Power-Sharing: An Addendum to Lijphart

To address some of these challenges, a future settlement in Cyprus could benefit from institutional designs broadly available in comparative peace processes. Looking at the design of federal and consociational arrangements around the world and adapting them to Cyprus would be admittedly a challenge. But contrary to Horowitz's claim that power-sharing democracy is a crude "one-size-fits-all" model (1999; see also criticisms in Lijphart 2004), this edited volume demonstrates the enormous variation in the design and application of federal and consociational models upon which Cyprus could draw. This applies at both the macro and micro levels of governance and, as this chapter demonstrates, a decentralized federation has better prospects, judging from recent Cypriot history. The reunification of Cyprus should not be the exclusive responsibility of the federal state; constituent states, municipalities, businesses and civil society should play a part.

Rather than creating a dysfunctional centralized administration, aspiring federations could rely on constitutional provisions and external security guarantees to prevent secession or the breakdown of intercommunal relations. But as the experience of the Zürich-London Agreements suggests, such guarantees could be ineffective, even highly detrimental, if the two sides fail to incentivize each other's cooperation in a settlement. Thus, it is more important in a future Cypriot settlement to have limited but secure and effective areas of authority, endowed with the necessary financial resources and competent public sector officials to meet long-term challenges. In other words, public expectations and competences should not exceed the resources available to the federal government. Likewise, central governments should not entertain unrealistic expectations of eliminating, for instance, per capita income inequalities, as such inequalities have not vanished in mature federations with centuries of experience in managing ethnofederal tensions.

The principle of subsidiarity and decentralization does not merely apply to federal units; it applies equally well to other levels of regional government. Unlike "loose federations," a decentralized federation does not eliminate effective governance in areas of security, citizenship and foreign policy. Indeed, as the Swiss experience illustrates, to implement municipal decentralization, central governments often must have the designated authority to do so (Steiner 2003; Mueller 2012).

Some scholars argue that the "medicine" of decentralization could end up being "poison," if decentralization becomes so excessive that any interaction amongst constituent states is restricted (Hechter 2000: 151–152; see also critique in Stefanovic 2008). Yet this argument is problematic, as it assumes central governments are the only agents responsible for maintaining a unified federation; in fact, in Cyprus, citizen initiatives, non-governmental organizations, multi-ethnic political parties, local governments, cross-community universities and joint economic ventures might be equally important and possibly more effective venues within which to express the federal identity of the reunified island. And as the chapter demonstrates, in post-colonial Cyprus, the failure to accept decentralization, even for municipalities, triggered the collapse of power-sharing in 1963–1964 and was responsible for the failure to restart it between 1968 and 1974 suggesting the potential linkages between decentralization and power-sharing.

If we are looking for lessons to shape a decentralized Cyprus, the literature and international experience could be rather limited in their recommendations. As Lijphart admits, "Experts have no clear advice to offer on how much decentralization is desirable within the federation, and there is no consensus amongst them as to whether the American, Canadian, Indian, Australian, German, Swiss, or Austrian model is most worthy of being emulated" (2008: 84). Thresholds cannot be determined from international experience, as federations decentralize in different forms (i.e. budgetary, territorial, administrative). These forms are difficult to quantify, so we are left with an important gap in the peace and conflict literature.

However, important recent additions to the literature on the application of Lijphart's criteria to Cyprus (see Yakinthou 2009; Erkem 2016; Kyriakou and Skoutaris 2016), as well as the direct involvement of consociational theorist John McGarry (2017) in the Cyprus peace talks, has opened new possibilities for theoretical and empirical precision specifically in integrating Lijphart's consociational vision to the micro-institutional variables in aspiring federations.

Conclusion: A Federal Cyprus?

Fostering consensus is a formidable task in post-conflict societies; yet power-sharing arrangements have been negotiated and implemented, even amidst heightened intercommunal mistrust. In often comparable conflicts such as Northern Ireland, the Good Friday Agreement addressed the problem of power-sharing by giving each political party automatic representation in Cabinet in accordance with the party's electoral strength. Northern Ireland is not the only potentially transferable example of power-sharing based on Lijphart's reasoning. Similar models have been introduced in other societies emerging from violent conflict (e.g. South Africa), in consolidated democracies (e.g. Switzerland, the Netherlands, post-WWII Austria), local governments (e.g. Danish municipal councils) and international organizations (e.g. committee chairs in the European Parliament). Consensus democracies, according to several academic studies (e.g. Lijphart 1977), are not only better at managing diversity; they also run more effective economic policies, something critically important in the immediate future in Cyprus. In his influential *Patterns of Democracy*, Lijphart also identifies a set of fiscal indicators in which consociational democracies outperform majoritarian ones (Lijphart 1999), an issue of key relevance for countries affected by the post-2008 financial crisis. Beyond healing historical divisions, power-sharing could allow a post-conflict society to embrace novel understandings of public responsibility, whereby the more parties share power, the better the prospects are for effective and sustainable management.

Consensus democracies have several other advantages: facilitating decision-making, increasing the durability of policies and strengthening grassroots support while allowing the representation of anti-systemic elements. Switzerland demonstrates that economic vitality and consensual decision-making go hand-in-hand. The country's so-called magic formula (Linder 1994) enables each party to propose specific candidates to the federal council. They are put under parliamentary scrutiny and only those receiving the support of Parliament can take up ministerial positions. This procedure facilitates the selection of broadly respected leaders and the exclusion of extremists on the far right. Likewise, South Africa prevented a breakdown into racial violence by negotiating an inclusive power-sharing arrangement amongst all major political parties during the post-apartheid period (Guelke 1999). In other words, power-sharing can bolster trust in times of transition and break the intercommunal deadlocks. As this chapter demonstrates, Lijphart's reasoning for divided societies could provide the grounds for a reasonable compromise between Greek and Turkish Cypriots as well as bring the two sides together in reconciling ethnic nationalism and power-sharing.

NOTES

1. Arend Lijphart. 1969. 'Consociational Democracy'. *World Politics* 21 (2): 207–225. p. 216.

BIBLIOGRAPHY

Adams, T. W. (1966). The First Republic of Cyprus: A Review of an Unworkable Constitution. *Western Political Quarterly, 19*(3), 475–490.

Anderson, P. (2008). The Divisions of Cyprus. *London Review of Books, 30*(8), 7–16.

Attalides, M. (1977). The Turkish Cypriots: Their Relations to the Greek Cypriots in Perspective. In M. Attalides (Ed.), *Cyprus Reviewed* (pp. 71–101). Nicosia: Jus Cypri.

Attalides, M. (1979). *Cyprus, Nationalism and International Politics.* New York: St. Martin's.

Averoff-Tossizza, E. (1986). *Lost Opportunities: The Cyprus Question, 1950–1963* (T. Cullen & S. Kyriakides, Trans.). New York: Aristide D. Caratzas.

Bahcheli, T. (1972). *Communal Discord and the State of Interested Governments in Cyprus, 1955–70* (Doctoral Thesis). University of London.

Bermeo, N. (1992). Democracy and the Lessons of Dictatorship. *Comparative Politics, 24*(3), 273–291.

Clerides, G. (1989–1992). *Cyprus, My Deposition.* Nicosia: Alithia.

Clerides, G. (2007). *Ντοκουμέντα Μιας Εποχής 1993–2003* (Documents of an Era 1993–2003). Nicosia: Politia.

Coufoudakis, V. (2004). The Case Against the Annan Plan. In V. Coufoudakis & K. Kyriakides (Eds.), *The Case Against the Annan Plan.* London: Lobby for Cyprus.

Cox, M., & Garlick, M. (2003). Musical Chairs: Property Repossession and Return Strategies in Bosnia and Herzegovina. In S. Leckie (Ed.), *Returning Home: Housing and Property Restitution Rights of Refugees and Displaced Persons* (pp. 65–83). Ardsley: Transnational.

Crawshaw, N. (1978). *The Cyprus Revolt: An Account of the Struggle for Union with Greece*. London: Allen & Unwin.

De Soto, A., & del Castillo, G. (1994). Obstacles to Peacebuilding. *Foreign Policy, 94*(Spring), 69–83.

Demetriou, O. (2004). *EU and the Cyprus Conflict: The View of Political Actors in Cyprus* (Working Paper Series in EU Border Conflicts Studies 9). Birmingham: Department of Political Science and International Studies, University of Birmingham.

Demetriou, C. (2012). Political Radicalization and Political Violence in Palestine, Ireland and Cyprus. *Social Science History, 36*(3), 391–420.

Denktash, R. R. (1982). *The Cyprus Triangle*. London: Rustem and Allen & Unwin.

Diglis, P. (2010). *AKEL: Personal Testimonies with Courage* [in Greek]. Nicosia: Epifaniou Publications.

Drousiotis, M. (1998). *EOKA: The Dark Face* [in Greek]. Athens: Ekdosis Stahi.

Erkem, P. (2016). Ethnic Nationalism and Consociational Democracy in Cyprus. *Beykent Üniversitesi Sosyal Bilimler Dergisi, 9*, 2.

Ertekün, M. N. (1984). *The Cyprus Dispute and the Birth of the Turkish Republic of Northern Cyprus*. Northern Cyprus: K. Rustem.

Fisher, R. (2001). Cyprus: The Failure of Mediation and the Escalation of an Identity-Based Conflict to an Adversarial Impasse. *Journal of Peace Research, 38*(3), 307–326.

Fokas, E. (2008). Islam in the Framework of Turkey-EU Relations: Situations in Flux and Moving Targets. *Global Change Peace & Security, 20*(1), 87–98.

Gazioğlu, C. A. (1996). *Enosis Çemberinde Türkler [Turks in the Circle of Union]*. Istanbul: Cyrep.

Guelke, A. (1999). *South Africa in Transition: The Misunderstood Miracle*. London: Tauris.

Güney, A. (2004). The USA's Role in Mediating the Cyprus Conflict: A Story of Success or Failure? *Security Dialogue, 35*(1), 27–42.

Hechter, M. (2000). *Containing Nationalism*. Oxford: Oxford University Press.

Holland, R. (1998). *Britain and the Revolt in Cyprus, 1954–1959*. New York: Oxford University Press.

Horowitz, D. (1993). The Challenge of Ethnic Conflict: Democracy in Divided Societies. *Journal of Democracy, 4*(4), 18–38.

Horowitz, D. (1999, December 9–11). "Constitutional Design: Proposals vs. Processes" Prepared for Delivery at Kellogg Institute Conference, *Constitutional Design 2000: Institutional Design, Conflict Management, and Democracy in the Late Twentieth Century*. University of Notre Dame. kellogg.nd.edu/faculty/research/pdfs/Horowitz.pdf. Accessed 12 Oct 2012.

Jarstad, A., & Sisk, T. (Eds.). (2008). *From War to Democracy: Dilemmas of Peacebuilding*. Cambridge: Cambridge University Press.

Jones, L. (2003). Property Restitution in Rwanda. In S. Leckie (Ed.), *Returning Home: Housing and Property Restitution Rights of Refugees and Displaced Persons* (pp. 105–125). Ardsley: Transnational.

Joseph, J. S. (1997). *Cyprus: Ethnic Conflict and International Politics: From Independence to the Threshold of the European Union*. New York: St. Martin's.

Ker-Lindsay, J. (2004). *Britain and the Cyprus Crisis, 1963–1964*. Mannheim: Bibliopolis.

Ker-Lindsay, J. (2005). *EU Accession and UN Peacemaking in Cyprus*. Basingstoke: Palgrave.

Ker-Lindsay, J. (2007). *Crisis and Conciliation: A Year of Rapprochement Between Greece and Turkey*. London: Tauris.

Ker-Lindsay, J. (2011). *The Cyprus Problem: What Everyone Needs to Know*. Oxford: Oxford University Press.

Ker-Lindsay, J. (2012). The Role of the EU as Conflict Manager in Cyprus. In R. Whitman & S. Wolff (Eds.), *The European Union as a Global Conflict Manager* (pp. 53–66). London: Routledge.

Kızılyürek, N. (1999). *Cyprus: The Impasse of Nationalisms* [in Greek]. Athens: Mauri Lista.

Kohli, A. (Ed.). (2001). *The Success of India's Democracy*. Cambridge: Cambridge University Press.

Kovras, I., & Loizides, N. (2014). The Greek Debt Crisis and Southern Europe: Majoritarian Pitfalls? *Comparative Politics, 47*(1), 1–20.

Krebs, R. R. (1999). Perverse Institutionalism: NATO and the Greco-Turkish Conflict. *International Organization, 53*(1–2), 343–377.

Kyriakou, N., & Skoutaris, N. (2016). The Birth of a Republic, but Not of a Nation: The Case of State-Building in Cyprus. *Nationalism and Ethnic Politics, 22*(4), 456–477.

Lijphart, A. (1968). *The Politics of Accommodation: Pluralism and Democracy in the Netherlands*. Berkeley: University of California Press.

Lijphart, A. (1977). *Democracy in Plural Societies: A Comparative Exploration*. New Haven: Yale University Press.

Lijphart, A. (1979). Consociation and Federation: Conceptual and Empirical Link. *Canadian Journal of Political Science/Revue canadienne de science politique, 12*(3), 499–515.

Lijphart, A. (1984). Proportionality by Non-PR Methods: Ethnic Representation in Belgium, Cyprus, Lebanon, New Zealand, West Germany, and Zimbabwe. In *Choosing an Electoral System: Issues and Alternatives*. New York: Praeger.

Lijphart, A. (1994). *Electoral Systems and Party Systems (A Study of Twenty-Seven Democracies 1945–1990)*. Oxford/New York: Oxford University Press.

Lijphart, A. (1996). The Puzzle of Indian Democracy: A Consociational Interpretation. *The American Political Science Review, 90*(2), 258–268.

Lijphart, A. (1999/2012). *Patterns of Democracy: Government Forms and Performance in Thirty-Six Countries*. New Haven: Yale University Press.

Lijphart, A. (2004). Constitutional Design for Divided Societies. *Journal of Democracy, 15*(2), 96–109.

Lijphart, A. (2008). *Thinking About Democracy: Power Sharing and Majority Rule in Theory*. London: Routledge.

Lijphart, A., Thomas, B., Nikiforos, D., & Richard, G. (1988). A Mediterranean Model of Democracy? The Southern European Democracies in Comparative Perspective. *West European Politics, 11*(1), 7–25.

Linder, W. (1994). *Swiss Democracy: Possible Solutions to Conflict in Multicultural Societies*. New York: St. Martin's.

Linz, J. J. (1990). The Perils of Presidentialism. *Journal of Democracy, 1*(1), 51–69.

Loizides, N. (2015). *The Politics of Majority Nationalism: Framing Peace Stalemates and Crises*. Stanford: Stanford University Press.

Loizides, N. (2016). *Designing Peace: Cyprus and Institutional Innovations in Divided Societies*. Philadelphia: University of Pennsylvania Press.

Mainwaring, S., & Shugart, M. S. (1997). Juan Linz, Presidentialism and Democracy: A Critical Appraisal. *Comparative Politics, 29*(4), 449–471.

Markides, K. (1977). *The Rise and Fall of the Cyprus Republic*. New Haven: Yale University Press.

Markides, D. W. (2001). *Cyprus 1957–1963: From Colonial Conflict to Constitutional Crisis; The Key Role of the Municipal Issue*. Minnesota Mediterranean and East European Monographs 8, University of Minnesota.

McCrudden, C., & O'Leary, B. (2013). *Courts and Consociations: Human Rights Versus Power-Sharing*. Oxford: Oxford University Press.

McGarry, J. (2011, November 17). *Centripetal Theory and the Cyprus Conflict*. Paper Presented at Workshop on Power-Sharing, Organized by the Ethnicity and Democratic Governance Project, Munk Centre, University of Toronto.

McGarry, J. (2013). Is Presidentialism Necessarily Non-collegial? *Ethnopolitics, 12*(1), 93–97.

McGarry, J. (2017). Centripetalism, Consociationalism and Cyprus: The "Adoptability" Question. *Political Studies, 65*(2), 512–529.

McGarry, J., & Loizides, N. (2015). Power-Sharing in a Re-united Cyprus: Centripetal Coalitions vs. Proportional Sequential Coalitions. *International Journal of Constitutional Law, 13*(4), 847–872.

McGarry, J., & O'Leary, B. (Eds.). (1993). *The Politics of Ethnic Conflict Regulation: Case Studies of Protracted Ethnic Conflicts*. London: Routledge.

McGarry, J., & O'Leary, B. (2005). *Federation as a Method of Ethnic Conflict Regulation*, Forum of Federations. www.forumfed. Accessed 18 Oct 2012.

McGarry, J., & O'Leary, B. (2009a). Power Shared After the Deaths of Thousands. In R. Taylor (Ed.), *Consociational Theory: McGarry and O'Leary and the Northern Ireland Conflict* (pp. 15–85). London: Routledge.

McGarry, J., & O'Leary, B. (2009b). Must Pluri-National Federations Fail? *Ethnopolitics*, *8*(1), 5–25.

Michael, M. S. (2009). *Resolving the Cyprus Conflict: Negotiating History*. Basingstoke: Palgrave Macmillan.

Mideast Mirror. (2004, January). The Challenge of Federalism in Iraq.

Mueller, Sean. 2012. *Why Decentralisation? A Sociocultural Explanation with Evidence from Subnational Switzerland*, Paper presented at the University of Kent, January.

Necatigil, Z. (1998). *The Cyprus Question and the Turkish Position in International Law*. Oxford: Oxford University Press.

O'Leary, B. (2001). An Iron Law of Nationalism and Federation? A (Neo-Diceyian) Theory of the Necessity of a Federal Staatsvolk, and of Consociational Rescue. *Nations and Nationalism*, *7*(3), 273–296.

Papadakis, Y. (1999). Enosis and Turkish Expansionism: Real Myths or Mythical Realities? In V. Calotychos (Ed.), *Cyprus and Its People: Nation, Identity, and Experience in an Unimaginable Community, 1955–1997* (pp. 69–84). Boulder: Westview.

Patrick, R. A. (1976). *Political Geography and the Cyprus Conflict, 1963–1971* (Doctoral Dissertation). Department of Geography, Faculty of Environmental Studies, University of Waterloo.

Pericleous, C. (2009). *The Cyprus Referendum: A Divided Island and the Challenge of the Annan Plan*. London: Tauris.

Polyviou, P. (1980). *Cyprus, Conflict and Negotiations, 1960–1980*. New York: Holmes and Meier Publishers.

Ramet, S. (2006). *The Three Yugoslavias: State-Building and Legitimation, 1918–2005*. Bloomington: Indiana University Press.

Schneckener, U. (2002). Making Power-Sharing Work: Lessons from Successes and Failures in Ethnic Conflict Regulation. *Journal of Peace Research*, *39*(2), 203–228.

Servas, P. (1997). *Common Homeland* [in Greek]. Nicosia: Proodos.

Sisk, T. (1996). *Power Sharing and International Mediation in Ethnic Conflicts*. New York: U.S. Institute for Peace.

Somer, M. (2005). Resurgence and Remaking of Identity: Civil Beliefs, Domestic and External Dynamics, and the Turkish Mainstream Discourse on Kurds. *Comparative Political Studies*, *38*(6), 591–622.

Sözen, A., & Özersay, K. (2007). The Annan Plan: State Succession or Continuity. *Middle Eastern Studies*, *43*(1), 125–141.

Stefanovic, D. (2008). *What Killed Yugoslavia? Social Causes of Political Disintegration* (Doctoral Dissertation). Department of Sociology, University of Toronto.

Steiner, R. (2003). The Causes, Spread and Effects of Intermunicipal Cooperation and Municipal Mergers in Switzerland. *Public Management Review*, *5*(4), 551–571.

Tocci, N. (2007). *The EU and Conflict Resolution. Promoting Peace in the Backyard.* London: Routledge.

Trimikliniotis, N. (2006). A Communist's Post-modern Power Dilemma: One Step Back, Two Steps Forward, "Soft No" and Hard Choices. *Cyprus Review,* *18*(1), 1–49.

Trimikliniotis, N. (2009). Interview with the author at University of Nicosia, Cyprus.

Vural, Y., & Rustemli, A. (2006). Identity Fluctuations in the Turkish Cypriot Community. *Mediterranean Politics, 11*(3), 329–348.

Xydis, S. G. (1973). *Cyprus: Reluctant Republic* (Vol. 2). The Hague: Mouton.

Yakinthou, C. (2009). *Political Settlements in Divided Societies: Consociationalism and Cyprus.* New York: Palgrave Macmillan.

Yucel, G. (2007, August 3). Don't Hold Your Breath About Evren's Federalism. *Hurriyet Daily News.*

CHAPTER 9

The Paradox of Direct Democracy and Elite Accommodation: The Case of Switzerland

Matt Qvortrup

Referendums are rare in consociational democracies. This is not surprising as consociationalism is essentially a system of elite accommodation. Drawing on Lijphart's classic model of consociationalism, the article outlines the relationship between consociationalism and referendums and presents a *tour d'horizon* of referendums in consociational systems with a special reference to Switzerland. While referendums on policy issues are rare outside Switzerland, a case study of this country suggests that mechanisms of direct democracy have facilitated consociation, provided a mechanism through which political parties in the grand coalition can distinguish themselves and has given civic and civil society groups a vehicle for providing input into the elite-dominated system. The referendum has not undermined consociationalism; rather the direct democracy device has strengthened the system's legitimacy.

The aim of this chapter is to explore the relationship between referendums and consociationalism. Are the two compatible and might the former even be used to strengthen the latter? The chapter first analyses the treatment of referendums in Lijphart's *oeuvre*; it then looks at the use of referendums to instigate consociational systems. After concluding that referendums under

M. Qvortrup (✉)
CTPSR, Coventry University, Coventry, UK

© The Author(s) 2018   177
M. Jakala et al. (eds.), *Consociationalism and Power-Sharing in Europe*, International Political Theory,
https://doi.org/10.1007/978-3-319-67098-0_9

consociationalism are rare, the article turns to the cases of Switzerland. Often and adequately described as a "special case" or *Sonderfall* (Eberle 2007), Switzerland is unique among consociational systems for having extremely frequent referendums—often up to a dozen per year (Serdült 2014).

LIJPHART'S CONSOCIATIONALISM

Arend Lijphart originally introduced the concept of consociationalism in his classic article *Typologies of Democratic Systems* (Lijphart 1968b). Inspired by Johannes Althusius, he conceptualised and formalised a concept used in earlier writings by, among others, Gerhard Lehmbruch, Sir David Lewis and the Austro-Marxists Otto Bauer and Karl Renner (Lijphart 2008: 4–5). The fundamental argument of these early works was that divided democracies—societies without cross-cutting cleavages—could survive if the elites accepted the "agreement to disagree" (Lijphart 1969) in a system where "pragmatic solutions are forged for all problems, even those with clear religious-ideological overtones" (Lijphart 1968a: 103).

The *Politics of Accommodation* was a great example of how a case study implicitly had implications for a larger N-analysis. Having analysed the political power-sharing between different "*zuilen*" (literally "pillars") (Lijphart 1968a: 17) in the Dutch political system, Lijphart was able to show more generally that even deeply divided societies could have relatively stable democracies provided that the "leaders of rival subcultures… make *deliberate efforts to counteract the immobilizing and unstabalizing effects of cultural fragmentation*" (Lijphart 1968b: 212, italics in the original). The role of the people in this system was *de minimis*. Indeed, in many ways, consociationalism was at odds with the normative ideal of participation as espoused by the likes of John Stuart Mill, namely that "nothing less can be ultimately desirable than the admission of all to share in the sovereign power of the state" (Mill 1991: 256).

Under the Dutch system as it existed in its heyday, "popular apathy and disinterest in politics and its apparent dullness [had] a positive value" (Lijphart 1968a: 138). In an article from the subsequent year, Lijphart would describe consociationalism as "government by elite cartel designed to turn a democracy with a fragmented political culture into a stable democracy" (Lijphart 1969: 216). The *verzuiling* in the Netherlands, described in *Politics of Accommodation*, was an extreme example of this. Indeed, one of the patterns singled out by Lijphart was "the pre-eminent role of the top-leaders in recognizing problems and in realistically finding solutions in spite of ideological disagreements – a process in which the rank and file were largely ignored" (Lijphart 1968a: 111). It follows from this elite focus that referendums can expect to be rare under consociationalism. This assumption is partly supported by a cursory look at Lijphart's classic texts on consociationalism. The referendum is absent from the indices of both *The Politics of Accommodation* (Lijphart 1968a, b) and *Thinking about Democracy* (Lijphart 2008). The referendum was, however, given a passing mention in *Democracy in Plural Societies*, where the case of Switzerland was briefly considered as a "curious mixture of proportional delegation of decisions to the level of the national executive with occasional lapses into the polar opposite, direct democracy and majority rule" (Lijphart 1977: 40). Is there a role for referendums in such systems?

At first glance, the descriptions of consociationalism seem to leave little room for referendums. Given that the referendum has been described as "the most majoritarian of policy making device" (Shugart and Carey 1992: 66) it is not surprising that the number of referendums held in consociational democracies is very low.

As Table 9.1 shows, the number of referendums held in consociational systems is in single digits with the notable exception of the perennial out-

Table 9.1 Number of referendums in consociational democracies excluding Switzerland[a]

Country	Number of referendums
Austria (1945–1966)	0
Belgium (1945–)	1 (1950)
Bosnia-Herzegovina (1996–)	0
Columbia (1958–1974)	1
India (1948–)	0
Lebanon (1943–1975)	0
Malaysia (1955–1969)	0
Netherlands (1917–1971)	0
Northern Ireland (1999–)	0 (1998)
Switzerland	611
Uruguay (1917–1934, 1952–1967)	2 (1917, 1951)

Source: Qvortrup et al. (2014). The list of consociational democracies is based on Lijphart (1996) with the addition of Northern Ireland (O'Leary 2001) and Bosnia-Hercegovina (Bose 2002)

[a]Switzerland held a total of 611 referendums since 1848. The vast majority of these were held after the establishment of a consociational system. The periods of consociationalism are based on Lijphart (1977) and Lijphart (2008)

lier that is the Helvetic Confederation. The average number of referendums per country since 1800 has been 9.5 (5.9 excluding Switzerland). With an average of 0.8 for countries with consociational systems, this is well below the average; they range from "very frequent referendums, as in Switzerland, to no national referendums at all" (Lijphart 1985).

POUVOIR CONSTITUENT REFERENDUMS AND CONSOCIATIONALISM

Before analysing the seemingly deviant case of Switzerland, it is instructive to distinguish between two types of referendums, namely constitutional referendums that establish the consociational system and policy referendums. In Uruguay (1917 and 1951), in Colombia (1957) and in Northern Ireland (1998) referendums were held to give the consociational systems a seal of popular legitimacy; these might be termed *pouvoir constituent* referendums (Klein 1996).

It is only in Belgium and Switzerland that referendums of the latter type have been held. Before moving on to the Swiss referendum, it is worth reflecting on why some countries have held referendums on the establishment of a consociational system.

These *pouvoir constituent* referendums were held in Colombia, Northern Ireland and Uruguay but not in Bosnia-Herzegovina, India, Lebanon, Malaysia and the Netherlands. Why were there no referendums in the latter countries? The reason for this is probably a consequence of the controversial nature of politics in divided societies. One of the dangers in such countries is that the elites "may engage in competitive behaviour and thus further aggravate mutual tensions and political instability" (Lijphart 1969: 212).

That referendums due to its majoritarian nature lend themselves to such tensions was one of the explicit reasons why referendums were deemed to be undesirable in Belgium after the 1950 referendum on the return of the King split the country along linguistic lines and this why the *Tripartite Constitutional Reform* decided to reject the future use of referendums as these "risiquerait de provoquer et d'ancer de grave oppositions entre les communautés" (quoted in Morel 1992: 858).

The negative experiences with referendums in Bosnia-Herzegovina— they once described as an "anarchy of referendums" (Brady and Kaplan 1994: 180)—were considered to be responsible for the outbreak of the

Bosnian war and explain why a referendum was considered undesirable after the signing of the *Dayton Agreement* (Brady and Kaplan, ibid). That referendums can be divisive can be abused (Mac Ginty 2003) might explain why they are not held. Another reason might be that such consultations were simply not considered at the time. Thus at the time of the establishment of the Lebanese and Malaysian consociational systems in, respectively, 1943 and 1955, referendums were relatively rare and neither of the systems was ratified through referendums, though it should be noted that Singapore merged with Malaysia following a referendum in 1963, only to secede two years later without a referendum (Smith 1986). Considerations regarding the suitability of submitting the issue to a referendum do seem to have played a major role in either case (see Dekmejian 1978) (Mauzy 1993).

Moreover, not all referendums held in consociational societies are the result of elite bargaining. For example, the establishment of the consociational system in Colombia that lasted from 1958 to 1974 was not the result of an elite agreement, rather the 1957 Constitution was initiated by the military junta and bore the hallmarks of an authoritarian plebiscite (see Dieter Nohlen 2005: 317).

This leaves us with the referendum in Northern Ireland in 1998 and the referendums in Uruguay in 1917 and 1951, respectively.

While referendums seem to run counter to the "spirit of accommodation" (Lijphart 1968a: 103), and thus exacerbate conflict in a society due to its majoritarian and winner-take-it-all nature, this is logically less likely to happen if the referendum is on an agreement reached by *both* or *all* of the blocs or groups in society. Thus *pouvoir constituent* referendums in which the elites of the communities seek the ratification of what Lijphart called "a deliberate joint effort by the elites to stabilize the system" (Lijphart 1969: 213) might even serve to strengthen rather than weaken "the spirit of accommodation" as it proves the elites can cooperate and lead the way for cooperation among and between the blocs in society. This was the case in Northern Ireland, where the legitimacy of the agreement was deemed to depend upon majority support in both unionist and nationalist communities (Hayes and McAllister 2001).

It might be suggested that this perceived need to win approval among the population is a novel phenomenon. While it is true that the original systems of consociationalism, as described by Lijphart, involved a somewhat breath-taking lack regard for popular legitimacy, which even involved "the rigging of an important election" (Lijphart 1968a: 111), it is noteworthy that the referendum on the *Constitución* in 1917 was submitted to a referendum. The logic of holding a referendum was not dissimilar to the logic of the Northern Ireland referendum 81 years later. According to Uruguayan political scientist David Altman, the referendum was the result of a "bargaining process," which followed "extensive negotiations" between the elites (Altman 2011: 142). José Batlle y Ordóñez was explicitly inspired by Switzerland, and it seems that this fascination with Swiss consensual institutions not only inspired him to advocate the establishment of a nine-member *colegiado* along the lines of the collective executive in Switzerland but also to follow the Swiss example of requiring that constitutional changes are ratified by the people (Altman 2011: 143). This precedent led to a constitutional convention of holding referendums on other constitutional changes in Uruguay in 1934, 1942, 1951, 1967, 1980 and 1996. That there was a referendum on the consociational constitution in 1954 seems to have been a result of this constitutional convention (Altman 2011: 148).

Referendums in consociational systems are generally rare but a case can perhaps be made for the view that ratifications of elite agreements add to the legitimacy of the consociational system and that such referendums contribute to fulfilling one of the major conditions for consociationalism, namely that the elites show they are able "to cooperate and compromise with each other without losing the allegiance and support of their own rank and file" (Lijphart 1969: 221).

Ratifications of consociational elite agreements might be consistent with and even conducive to consociational democracy but what about policy referendums? To answer this question we need to analyse the seemingly *sui generis* case of Switzerland.

And what can the case of Switzerland teach us about the relationship between referendums and consociationalism?

CONSOCIATIONALISM IN SWITZERLAND

To engage in a case study and to seek to draw general conclusions from this is fraught with difficulty. According to Eckstein's much cited study, "crucial case-studies…must closely fit a theory if one is to have confidence in the theory's validity" (Eckstein 1975: 119). Consequently, if we are to conclude that referendums can be compatible with consociationalism, we must show that the Alpine country can be described as falling within this category of political systems.

"Switzerland is generally considered an important example of this [consociational] pattern of policymaking and governing, which was, for a long time, characteristic of a plurality of smaller European countries." Though he goes on to qualify this statement by the observation that "Swiss 'consociationalism' is, however, a special case in several respects" (Lehmbruch 1993: 44). The reason for this uniqueness is the use of the referendum (Linder 2008: 92).

To understand the use of the referendum in Switzerland it is necessary to outline the basic features of the country's political system. Switzerland is not a classic parliamentary system, as the Cabinet cannot be removed by a vote in the legislature. But the system is not a presidential system either. The executive is elected by the representatives of the bicameral legislature (which comprises the lower house) and the *Ständerat*, to which the largest 20 states (*Kantone*) elect two representatives and the smaller states elect one representative.[1]

The distinguishing feature of the Swiss political system is the Federal Council (*Bundesrat*), a collective executive of seven members representing the four largest parties in the Federal Assembly. Since 1959, the parties in the executive have been the Free-Market Liberal FDP (*Freisinnig-Demokratische Partei*), the centre-left and pro-European Labour party SP (*Sozialdemokratische Partei der Schweiz*), the right-wing and Eurosceptic Swiss People's Party (*Schweizerische Volkspartei*, SVP) and Christian Democrats, *Christlichdemokratische Volkspartei der Schweiz*, CVP, which largely represents the Catholic minority (Hug and Schulz 2007).

Each of the federal councillors head one of the seven ministries, respectively (foreign affairs, Justice, Defence, Finance, Public Economy and Transport). It is a convention of the constitution that at least two of the ministers French or Italian regions (Linder 2008: 10). The president of the council is a purely ceremonial post that alternates between the four parties every year (Linder ibid).

The Referendum in Switzerland

The referendum exists in several forms in Switzerland. Art. 140 of the constitution provides for mandatory referendums on revisions of the constitution and Art. 138 allows 100,000 to initiate and propose changes to the constitution.

In addition to constitutional referendums and initiatives, the Swiss voters may request referendums on laws passed by the Federal Assembly if

50,000 citizens request this within 100 days after the publication of the law in official Gazette (Art. 89). Such a referendum on a recently enacted law can also be triggered by eight of the twenty-five cantons.

How then has the referendum been compatible with elite accommodation and consociational democracy? The answer is twofold and depends on the type of referendum and initiative. We will analyse them in turn.

MINORITY VETO: CONSTITUTIONAL REFERENDUMS AND INITIATIVES

Although the referendum in Swiss politics can be traced back to the late middle ages,[2] the modern use of this device is a result of a compromise that emerged in the period after the *Sonderbund War* (1848).[3] Partly inspired by referendums held at the cantonal level in the 1830s (Auer 1996), both Protestant and Catholic cantons wanted to introduce the referendum for fear that the majority would enact legislation, which would limit their autonomy and confessional rights.

Consistent with the political theory, Swiss referendums and initiatives on changes of the constitution were (and are) consociationally speaking an example of a minority veto (Qvortrup 1999). But it differs from other such requirements. For while "the minority veto in power sharing democracies," in Lijphart's words, "usually consists of merely an informal understanding that minorities can effectively protect their autonomy by blocking any attempt to eliminate or reduce it" (Lijphart 2008: 49), the Swiss referendum is highly institutionalised due to the so-called double-majority requirement (*doppelte Mehrheit*). Both mandatory constitutional referendums initiated by the representatives and constitutional initiatives initiated by the voters require *both* a majority of the participating voters (*Volksmehr*) and a majority of more than half of the 25 Cantons (*Ständemehr*).

This double-majority requirement means that fundamental policies cannot be passed by simple plurality and serves to safeguard the religious and linguistic minorities, who would otherwise be in danger of being overruled by the German-speaking or the protestant majority in the country, who constitute 63.7 per cent of the population (Linder 2008: 2). The minority veto is thus an example of how, "consociational democracy violates the principle of majority rule...[although] it does not deviate much from normative democratic theory" (Lijphart 1969: 214).

The majority requirement provided protection for the religious minorities in the late nineteenth century when the Protestant majority was keen to impose restrictions on the practice of the Catholic religion, for example, in the form of a prohibition against Jesuit activities (Linder 2008: 22). Has this requirement contributed to establishing a consociational system? It could be argued that very few constitutional proposals have failed as a result of the double-majority requirements. To wit, there have been a total of 413 constitutional referendums and initiatives in the period 1866–2015. Out of these, a total of 228 resulted in defeat. But only nine of the referendums failed due to the double-majority requirement, namely in 1866, 1955, 1970, 1973, 1975, 1983, 1994 (2) and 2013 (Serdült 2014: 88) (Table 9.2).

Apart from the referendums on, respectively, education in 1973 and family policy in 2013, the issues put to a vote have not been divisive issues dealing with confessional or linguistic differences. Based on this statistical evidence it could be questioned if the referendum has performed the function of a popular minority veto.

Yet, we should never overlook what Sherlock Holmes called the "dog that didn't bark." The fact that no referendums were held on religious or linguistic issues does not mean that the institution ipso facto was without effect. Governments have often refrained from enacting a law for fear that the voters might veto it (Luthardt 1994: 70). It is not inconceivable that the latent threat of defeat has dissuaded a government from enacting legislation that would have had detrimental effects on minorities.

Table 9.2 Swiss referendums that failed to win a double majority

Year	Type	Subject	Popular vote (%)	Cantons (%)
1866	Constitutional referendum	Metric system	50.4	9
1955	Constitutional initiative	Price control	50.2	7
1970	Constitutional referendum	Federal finances	55.4	9
1973	Constitutional referendum	Education	52.8	10
1975	Constitutional referendum	Economic policy	52.8	11
1983	Constitutional referendum	Federal energy policy	50.9	11
1994	Constitutional referendum	Promotion of arts and culture	51	11
1994	Constitutional referendum	Naturalization for young foreigners	52.8	10
2013	Constitutional referendum	Family policy	54.3	10

C2D: Centre for Research in Direct Democracy 2015

Overall, the referendum has contributed to establishing a consensus democracy. The function of a safeguard has prevented the enactment of legislation that was only supported by a parliamentary majority.

OPTIONAL REFERENDUMS AND CONSOCIATIONAL DEMOCRACY

Is the same true for the so-called optional referendums (*Fakultatives Referendum*)? Optional referendums constitute 171 out of a total number of 611 votes.[4] Given that these referendums only require a simple majority, it is surprising that they frequently have been described for enabling minorities to protect their rights. In a 1999 study, Arend Lijphart noted *en passant* that "the potential of calling a referendum...is a strong stimulus for the majority to be heedful of minority views" (1999: 231).

This seems paradoxical, for how is it possible for a minority to use a majoritarian device to defeat the policies of the majority? Isn't a minority vulnerable by the very fact that they constitute less than 50 per cent?

The answer is that we need to distinguish between parliamentary majorities and popular majorities as well as we need to distinguish between the period before 1919 and the period after.

The Period of Radicalism 1848–1919

The *Radical Party* (from 1894 renamed the FDP) was the dominant force in Swiss politics. The party pursued a twin-track of muscular secularism and free-market, laissez-faire liberalism. Under the majoritarian First-Past-the-Post (FPTP) electoral system the party was able to win a majority of the seats in the *Bundesrat* without winning a majority of the votes. Though the party was constrained by the majority in the *Ständerat*, it was able to enact legislation that was perceived to be a threat to both Protestants and Catholics. Following a constitutional revision in 1874, it became possible for citizens to challenge ordinary legislation through optional referendums. This changed the use for the referendum in Switzerland. The device "was used by the Catholic conservative opposition to their own advantage and the projects of the radical liberal majority (in the legislature) were shot down as if with a machine gun" (Linder 2008: 103). (See also Aubert 1974: 43–44.) How did this come about?

Realising that the Radical majority in the *Bundesrat* did not always have the support of the voters at large, and that Catholics and Protestants shared some of the same interests their confessional disagreements notwithstanding, the confessional groups began to challenge legislation passed by the government. This resulted in a number of important changes that challenged the Radicals' virtual monopoly on legislative power in the period before the First World War. For example, the rejection of a law on the establishment of federal ministry of education in 1884, the introduction of the Constitutional initiative in 1891 and the rejection of a more liberal temperance law in 1903 are all examples of how non-liberal groups prevented radical legislation.

Through the referendum, parties in opposition were able to shape public policy. In the view of one observer, "strong political minorities were able to threaten and mobilize for an activation of the optional referendum, until they were eventually co-opted into the government" (Serdült 2014: 85). This tendency became stronger after Switzerland became a multi-party system.

The Referendum After 1919

The FDP (formerly Radical Party) majority in the legislature was effectively broken after the introduction of List-PR in 1919. This changed the dynamics of the referendum. Since the early 1920, the referendum has provided a mechanism through which parties can distinguish themselves within the consociational system. This can take three forms. We shall analyse each in turn.

The Referendum as Means of Distinguishing Parties in the Grand Coalition

To win representation in multi-party systems, parties have to appeal to a relatively narrow section of the electorate. To understand how this influenced the use of the referendum it can be illustrative to look at the case of the Swiss People's Party (SVP). In recent years the SVP—once a party representing small businesses and farmers (Linder 2008: 146)—has courted more populist policies (McGann and Kitschelt 2005). However, as a result of their failure to win support for tougher immigration policies through parliamentary channels, the party has increasingly turned to the referendum to win popular approval for stricter immigration controls in a country where 23 per cent of the population are foreign born (Linder 2008: 2). While most of these referendums have been unsuccessful (11 out of 12 have been lost), the use of the referendum has provided the SVP with a means of distinguishing itself in a system where a grand coalition of the largest parties is the norm.

This effect has served to rejuvenate the consociational system. Parties in the permanent grand coalition often risk becoming indistinguishable. By forcing issues to referendums—even if these are not successful—serves to convince voters that political parties are still relevant. Direct democracy makes representative politics more relevant by allowing political parties to appeal directly to the voters.

The Referendum as a Mechanism for Opposition Parties
The other problem in a consociational system is that some smaller parties are not members of the executive. These parties, nevertheless, want to distinguish themselves and they want to influence the legislative process. They can do this through the referendum. By using the referendum, a party can become "known and can build up a base of potential followers for the next election" (Serdült 2014: 86). This use of the referendum to force issues on the agenda, which would otherwise have become "non-decisions" (Bachrach and Baratz 1962), has had legislative effect. Thus in the 1990s, 31 per cent of the referendums initiated by opposition parties resulted in rejection of legislation passed by the government (Serdült 2014) (Table 9.3).

Referendums as Mechanism for Civil Society Involvement
The problem in an elite-dominated consociational system is that the grand coalition becomes incapable of overcoming differences and that this leads to political petrification. This has to some degree been the case in Switzerland since the SVP's turn to the right. In the early 2000, the initia-

Table 9.3   Initiators of referendums in Switzerland 1980–2010

Decade	Government parties	Opposition parties	Civil society groups
1981–1990	7	3	31
1991–2000	10	13	47
2001–2010	17	4	41

Based on C2D Archives and Serdült (2014)

tive began to serve the function of a political aggregator that put issues on the agenda, which the political parties are unwilling to touch or unable to agree on (Papadopoulos 2001: 38). By putting issues such as drug policies on the agenda, through initiatives, civil society groups can get access to the political system and get the stamp of approval as legitimate negotiation partners for the government (Wälti et al. 2004).

CONCLUSION

The aim of all politics, Immanuel Kant observed, is to find a solution to the problem of out "unsocial sociability" (Kant 2006: 6), how we can live with other people whom we can "neither endure nor do without" (Kant 2006: 7). Consociationalism provides a mechanism for this problem of how individuals can live together. Needless to say consociationalism is not a perfect solution, "nothing straight can be fashioned from the crooked wood of which humankind is made" (Kant 2006: 9). Referendums on elite agreements (as in Northern Ireland in 1998) can add legitimacy to an elite consensus forged by leaders of different communities.

The case of Switzerland suggests that consociationalism and referendums can be compatible. One of the distinguishing characteristics of Swiss referendums is the double-majority requirement for constitutional initiatives and referendums. While few referendums have been invalidated due to the special majority requirement, the double-majority provision arguably prevented the Radical Party from enacting legislation that would have discriminated against the catholic minority. This facilitated the establishment of a consociational political system.

The referendum served as a constitutional safeguard for the minority until the introduction of proportional representation.

After Switzerland became a multi-party system—and especially after the establishment of the permanent four-party coalition in 1958—the referendum played a different role. Three effects have been identified; first of all, the referendum rejuvenated consociationalism by providing a mechanism through which political parties in the grand coalition can distinguish themselves. This has especially been true for the Swiss People's Party's sponsoring of referendums since the 1990s.

Secondly, the referendum has provided a vehicle for opposition parties to stay relevant. Parties outside government, such as the Green Party, have been able to use the referendum to get issues on the agenda, which would otherwise not have been discussed in the federal parliament.

Lastly, the referendum is not—despite its appearance—a majoritarian device. The way it has been used in Switzerland the referendum has provided a valuable mechanism for keeping consociationalism alive and relevant. It has given civic and civil society groups a vehicle for providing input into the elite-dominated system. This was most spectacular in the case of the constitutional initiative to abolish the army in Switzerland. While the initiative failed, it spurred the government to enact reform.

APPENDIX A: NUMBER OF REFERENDUMS PER COUNTRY
1800–2015

Country	Number of referendums
Albania	4
Algeria	10
Andorra	11
Antigua and Bermuda	0
Argentina	1
Armenia	4
Australia	45
Austria	1
Austria	2
Azerbaijan	4
Bangladesh	3
Barbados	1
Belarus	5
Belgium	1
Belize	1
Benin	3
Bhutan	0
Bolivia	18
Bosnia	1
Bosnia-Herzegovina	1
Botswana	5
Brazil	2
Bulgaria	2
Burkina Faso	4
Burundi	4
Cameroon	2
CAR	4
Chad	3
Chile	8
China	0

(continued)

Appendix A   (continued)

Country	Number of referendums
China PR	0
Colombia	18
Columbia (1958–1974)	0
Comoros	6
Congo B	5
Costa Rica	2
Croatia	4
Cuba	1
Cyprus	1
Czech Republic	1
Denmark	22
Djibouti	3
Dominican Republic	2
DR Congo	4
Ecuador	49
Egypt	30
Equatorial Guinea	6
Eritrea	1
Estonia	4
Ethiopia	1
Finland	2
France	22
Gambia	3
Georgia	4
Germany	3
Ghana	4
Granada	0
Greece	10
Guatemala	5
Guinea	3
Haiti	2
Honduras	1
Hungary	9
Iceland	8
India	0
Iran	2
Iraq	2
Ireland	33
Italy	71
Ivory Coast	2
Jamaica	1
Japan	0
Kazakhstan	2

(*continued*)

Appendix A   (continued)

Country	Number of referendums
Kenya	2
Kyrgyzstan	6
Latvia	3
Lebanon (1975)	0
Liberia	19
Libya	1
Liechtenstein	31
Lithuania	5
Luxembourg	8
Macedonia	3
Madagascar	6
Malawi	1
Malaysia	0
Maldives	12
Mali	2
Malta	3
Mauritania	2
Mexico	3
Micronesia	57
Moldova	2
Mongolia	1
Montenegro	1
Morocco	11
Myanmar	2
Nauru	1
Nepal	2
Netherlands	2
New Zealand	16
Niger	7
North Korea	0
Northern Ireland	0
Norway	5
Pakistan	2
Panama	7
Paraguay	3
Peru	6
Philippines	19
Poland	4
Portugal	4
Qatar	1
Romania	3
Russian Republic	5
Rwanda	4

(*continued*)

Appendix A   (continued)

Country	Number of referendums
Sao Tome and Principe	1
Saudi Arabia	0
Senegal	3
Serbia	1
Seychelles	3
Sierra Leone	2
Singapore	1
Slovakia	5
Slovenia	8
Somalia	2
South Africa	4
South Korea	5
South Sudan	1
Spain	7
Sri Lanka	1
St Kitts and Nevis	1
St Lucia	0
St Vincent and the Grenadines	1
Sudan	5
Suriname	1
Sweden	5
Switzerland	611
Syria	16
Taiwan	3
Tajikistan	3
Tanzania	6
Thailand	1
Togo	5
Trinidad and Tobago	0
Tunisia	1
Turkey	5
Turkmenistan	3
Tuvalu	2
Uganda	2
Ukraine	3
Uruguay	34
Uruguay (1952–1967)	6
Uzbekistan	4
Venezuela	9
Vietnam	2
Western Samoa	4
Yemen	2
Zimbabwe	5

NOTES

1. The smaller states (*Halbkantone*) are Oberwalden, Niewalden, Basel-Stadt, Basel-Landschaft, Appenzell, Ausserrhoden and Appenzell Innerrhoden.
2. In 1684 the *Bürger* (all male citizens over the age of 16 years) were given the right to cast their votes on the policy issues that were submitted to them *ad referendum* by the elected representatives (Pieth 1958: 146).
3. The Catholic Cantons were defeated and had to accept a broadly secular constitution (Andreas et al. 1998).
4. Based on referendums held until 1 January 2014 (see Serdült 2014).

REFERENCES

Altman, D. (2011). *Direct Democracy Worldwide*. Cambridge: Cambridge University Press.

Andreas, E., et al. (1998). *Revolution und Innovation – Die konfliktreiche Entstehung des schweizerischen Bundesstats von 1848*. Zürich: Chronos.

Aubert, J.-F. (1974). *Petite histoire constitutionelle de la Suisse*. Bern: Francke.

Auer, A. (1996). *Die Ursprünge der direkten Demokratie*. Kolloquium vom 27.–29. April 1995 Forschungs- und Dokumentationszentrum Direkte Demokratie, Faculté de Droit et le Centre d'Etudes.

Bachrach, P., & Baratz, M. S. (1962). Two Faces of Power. *The American Political Science Review, 56*(4), 947–952.

Bose, S. (2002). *Bosnia After Dayton: Nationalist Partition and International Intervention*. Oxford: Oxford University Press.

Brady, H. E., & Kaplan, C. S. (1994). Eastern Europe and the Former Soviet Union. In D. Butler & A. Ranney (Eds.), *Referendums Around the World: The Growing Use of Direct Democracy* (pp. 174–217). London: The Macmillan Press Ltd.

Dekmejian, R. H. (1978). Consociational Democracy in Crisis: The Case of Lebanon. *Comparative Politics, 10*(2), 251–265.

Eberle, T. S. (2007). Der Sonderfall Schweiz aus soziologischer Perspektive. In T. Eberle & K. Imhof (Eds.), *Sonderfall Schweiz* (pp. 7–22). Zürich: Seismo.

Eckstein, H. (1975). Case Study and Theory in Political Science. In F. Greenstein & N. Polsby (Eds.), *Handbook of Political Science Vol. 7: Strategies of Inquiry* (pp. 119–164). Reading: Addison-Wesley.

Hayes, B. C., & McAllister, I. (2001). Who Voted for Peace? Public Support for the 1998 Northern Ireland Agreement. *Irish Political Studies, 16*(1), 73–93.

Hug, S., & Schulz, T. (2007). Left—Right Positions of Political Parties in Switzerland. *Party Politics, 13*(3), 305–330.

Kant, I. (2006) [1784]. Idea for a Universal History from a Cosmopolitan Perspective. In P. Kleingeld (Ed.), *Towards Perpetual Peace and Other Writings on Politics, Peace and History* (pp. 3–16). New Haven: Yale University Press.

Klein, C. (1996). *Théorie et pratique du pouvoir constituant.* Paris: Presses universitaires de France.

Lehmbruch, G. (1993). Consociational Democracy and Corporatism in Switzerland. *Publius: The Journal of Federalism, 23*(2), 43–60.

Lijphart, A. (1968a). *The Politics of Accommodation: Pluralism and Democracy in the Netherlands.* Berkeley: University of California Press.

Lijphart, A. (1968b). Typologies of Democratic Systems. *Comparative Political Studies, 1*(1), 3–44.

Lijphart, A. (1969). Consociational Democracy. *World Politics, 21*(02), 207–225.

Lijphart, A. (1977). *Democracy in Plural Societies: A Comparative Exploration.* New Haven: Yale University Press.

Lijphart, A. (1985). The Field of Electoral Systems Research. *Electoral Studies, 4*(1), 3–14.

Lijphart, A. (1996). The Puzzle of Indian Democracy: A Consociational Interpretation. *American Political Science Review, 90*(02), 258–268.

Lijphart, A. (1999). *Patterns of Democracy. Government Forms and Performance in Thirty-Six Countries.* New haven: Yale University Press.

Lijphart, A. (2008). *Thinking About Democracy: Power Sharing and Majority Rule in Theory and Practice.* London: Routledge.

Linder, W. (2008). *Swiss Democracy: Possible Solutions to Conflict in Multicultural Societies.* London: Macmillan Press; St. Martin's Press.

Luthardt, W. (1994). *Direkte Demokratie: Ein Vergleich in Westeuropa.* Baden-Baden: Nomos Verlag.

Mac Ginty, R. (2003). Constitutional Referendums and Ethnonational Conflict: The Case of Northern Ireland. *Nationalism and Ethnic Politics, 9*(2), 1–22.

Mauzy, D. (1993). Malay Political Hegemony and 'Coercive Consociationalism. In J. McGarry & B. O'Leary (Eds.), *The Politics of Ethnic Conflict Regulation: Case Studies of Protracted Ethnic Conflicts* (pp. 106–127). London: Routledge.

McGann, A., & Kitschelt, H. (2005). The Radical Right in the Alps. *Party Politics, 11*(2), 147–171.

Mill, J. S. (1991) [1861]. Considerations on Representative Government. In J. Gray (Ed.), *On Liberty and Other Essays* (pp. 204–467). Oxford: Oxford University Press.

Morel, L. (1992). Le Référendum: état de resherches. *Revue française de science politique, 42*(5), 835–864.

Nohlen, D. (Ed.). (2005). *Elections in the Americas, Vol. II, South America.* Oxford: Oxford University Press.

O'Leary, B. (2001). The Character of the 1998 Agreement: Results and Prospects. In R. Wilford (Ed.), *Aspects of the Belfast Agreement* (pp. 49–83). Oxford: Oxford University Press.

Papadopoulos, Y. (2001). How Does Direct Democracy Matter? The Impact of Referendum Votes on Politics and Policy-Making. *West European Politics, 24*(2), 35–58.

Pieth, F. (1958, May). Das altbündnerische Referendum. *Bündner Monatsblatt: Zeitschrift für Geschichte, Landes- und Volkskunde*, (5), 137–153.

Qvortrup, M. (1999). AV Dicey: the Referendum as the People's Veto. *History of Political Thought*, 20(3), 531–546.

Qvortrup, M., et al. (2014). Appendix A. In M. Qvortrup (Ed.), *Referendums Around the World. The Continued Growth of Direct Democracy*. Basingstoke: Palgrave Macmillan.

Serdült, U. (2014). Referendums in Switzerland. In M. Qvortrup (Ed.), *Referendums Around the World: The Continued Growth of Direct Democracy* (pp. 67–93). Basingstoke: Palgrave Macmillan.

Shugart, M. S., & Carey, J. M. (1992). *Presidents and Assemblies*. Cambridge: Cambridge University Press.

Smith, T. B. (1986). Referendum Politics in Asia. *Asian Survey*, 26(7), 793–814.

Wälti, S., Küjbler, D., & Papadopoulos, Y. (2004). How Democratic Is "Governance"? Lessons from Swiss Drug Policy. *Governance*, 17(1), 83–113.

CONCLUSION: CONSOCIATIONALISM AFTER FIFTY YEARS: REFLECTIONS AND PATHWAYS FORWARD

It has been almost fifty years since the publication of *Consociational Democracy* in 1969 by Arend Lijphart. The article, which became the foundational text of consociationalism, set out the early parameters for the theory. Since then, consociationalism has developed and expanded theoretically to include a wide variety of conditions and characteristics for consociational democracies.

Likewise, we have witnessed the theory move from a theoretical realm to the practical in which policy and decision-makers have translated the theory of consociationalism into an applicable mechanism for power-sharing in deeply divided societies. We have seen its implementation in places such as Cyprus, Northern Ireland and Bosnia-Herzegovina with mixed success. It is often, as this volume has attempted to illustrate, an elite-driven, top-down and imposed process which can be seen as contentious for many. This transition from theory to practice has also provided an expanding field of empirical data on this topic.

This edited volume is the product of the *Arend Lijphart Symposium on Power-Sharing and the Politics of Intercultural Dialogue* hosted by the Centre for Trust, Peace and Social Relations at Coventry University, UK in May 2016. This symposium brought Prof. Lijphart to reflect on his personal journey of developing the theory of consociationalism as well as to consider its previous application and the future of the theory. The symposium also provided a platform for leading scholars in the field of

© The Author(s) 2018 197
M. Jakala et al. (eds.), *Consociationalism and Power-Sharing in Europe*, International Political Theory,
https://doi.org/10.1007/978-3-319-67098-0

consociationalism and power-sharing to come together to discuss and unpack the evolution, application and future of the theory with Prof. Lijphart himself.

This book reflects these discussions for example, we have seen reflection and elements of looking back on the theoretical development of consociationalism (Lijphart, and White) and the engagement with referendums (Qvortrup). This has provided the reader with a greater clarification of the foundations of the theory, its evolution over the years and its move from the theoretical to practical realms. It has also provided an important space in which to re-introduce and explore overlooked elements to consociationalism. This is seen in Doorenspleet and Maleki's examination of the link between culture and politics and the importance of understanding the cultural context to provide the "most compatible model of democracy" for a deeply divided society.

Space has also been created for critical reflection on the shortcomings of the theory and of its practical implementations both in the past but also those which inform future theoretical developments and implementation. For example, Dixon has argued that the vagueness and elasticity of consociational theory provides a space for redefinition by theorists and decision-makers and allows the theory to be molded to fit the agendas (whether positive or negative) of its proponents, as in the case of Northern Ireland. This can lead to inefficiency and governmental deadlock and stalemates and leave a consociational democracy in a state of political paralysis. White has also been critical of this elite-driven process, which can allow for changing levels of commitment by political parties and can act as a hindrance in consociational power-sharing agreement. These changing commitments hinder the process and have the potential to create political deadlock. Or in Jarrett's criticism of the assumption by some that consociationalism can create a genuine-shared identity arguing that it does not do this using the cases of Northern Ireland and Brussels.

This volume has also shown the benefit (and need) of approaching and examining consociationalism from different disciplinary perspectives such as communication studies (Rice and Sommervile). We have also attempted to explore important aspects of the theory which may not come to the forefront but have important impacts on mechanisms, institutions and methods which may assist in overcoming the theoretical and practical gaps in the implementation of consociationalism. In addition, Blick brought us to a very current place and points us to the present political situation in the United Kingdom with reference to the recent referendum to leave the

European Union. He presented the devolution of Scotland, Northern Ireland and Wales and juxtaposed it to the referendum results suggesting that the lack of European Union membership has the potential to set the United Kingdom on wider path towards consociationalism.

In many ways, this book has provided various strands of engagement with consociationalist theory, which reflect the historical and the modern as well as the theoretical, and the practical. It has also illuminated the disconnects between theory, practice, implementation and to some extent, expectations which have been garnered from empirical studies. We have presented these reflections, discussions and criticisms to provoke thought and contribute to the continued development of consociationalist theory and its practical implementation.

Lijphart, A. (1969). Consociational Democracy. *World Politics, 21*(02), 207–225.

INDEX[1]

---

[1] Note: Page numbers followed by "n" refer to notes

© The Author(s) 2018
M. Jakala et al. (eds.), *Consociationalism and Power-Sharing in
Europe*, International Political Theory,
https://doi.org/10.1007/978-3-319-67098-0